SWARAJ PARTY AND GANDHI

SWARAJ PARTY AND GANDHI

S.R. BAKSHI

ATLANTIC PUBLISHERS & DISTRIBUTORS
4215/1, Ansari Road, Darya Ganj
New Delhi-110002

Published by :
Atlantic Publishers & Distributors
4215/1, Ansari Road, Darya Ganj,
New Delhi-110002

Head Office :
B-2, Vishal Enclave, Najafgarh Road,
New Delhi-110027
Phone : 5413460

Printed at : Devendra Printers through Chawla Composers,
Hari Nagar, New Delhi

PREFACE

The suspension of the Non-Cooperation Movement led to the political differences between Mahatma Gandhi and the *Swarajists* led by C.R. Das and Motilal Nehru. The programme of Council-entry was the main issue which Gandhi opposed and the 'Changers' supported. Their contention was to contest elections in a constitutional way, seek the membership of the Central Assembly and the provincial councils and oppose the measures of the government with cogent arguments. They did well in the legislatures for a few years and obstructed several bills of the government which could not be passed on account of severe opposition by members of the Swaraj Party.

The theme contains varied aspects of the Swaraj Party, *viz.* its aims and objects, the programme for Council-entry, ideology of Mahatma Gandhi having linkage with non-entry into councils, role of C.R. Das and Motilal Nehru in strengthening the roots of the party and their active participation in public work and the Councils and the agreement between the leadership for working a joint political stage for the achievement of *Swaraj*.

I have collected material from the National Archives of India, Nehru Memorial Museum and Library, Sapru House Library, Indian Council of Historical Research Library and Delhi University Library. I feel beholden to the authorities of these institutions for extending their academic support to me during my researches.

S.R. Bakshi

PREFACE

The suspension of the Non-cooperation Movement led to serious political differences between Mahatma Gandhi and the swarajists led by C.R. Das and Motilal Nehru. The programme of Council-entry was the main issue which Gandhi opposed and the Swarajists supported. Their contention was to contest elections in a constitutional way, seek the membership of the Central Assembly and the provincial councils and oppose the measures of the government with cogent arguments. They did well in the legislatures for a few years and obstructed several bills of the government which could not be passed on account of severe opposition by members of the Swaraj Party.

This book deals with the varied aspects of the Swaraj Party, viz. its aims and objects, the programme for Council-entry, ideology of Mahatma Gandhi having linkage with non-entry into councils, role of C.R. Das and Motilal Nehru in strengthening the roots of the party and their active participation in public work and the councils and the agreement between the leaders since it was an important political stage for the achievement of swaraj.

I have collected material from the National Archives of India, Nehru Memorial Museum and Library, Sapru House Library, Indian Council of Historical Research Library and Delhi University Library. I feel beholden to the authorities of these institutions for extending their academic support to me during my research.

S.R. Bakshi

CONTENTS

INTRODUCTION

The sudden suspension of the Non-Cooperation Movement after the violent incident at Chauri Chaura raised apprehensions in the minds of prominent Congress leaders regarding the efficacy of Gandhi's political programme which did not sponsor the ideology of council-entry. Motilal Nehru, C.R. Das and others who wished a change in the Congress manifesto became emphatic votaries of the council-entry programme. Their idea was to contest the elections and opposed the official measures of the government in the Central Assembly as well as in the provincial councils. They, however, did not leave the Congress party, but founded a new party, known as the Swaraj Party.

The Congress-Khilafat Swarajya Party formed at Gaya was duly organized under the name and style of the Swarajya Party at a general meeting of the party held at Anand Bhawan, Allahabad, on 20-22 February 1923.[1] In the next meeting held on 28 February the following provincial organizers were appointed.[2] B.N. Sasmal for Bengal, T.R. Phookan for Assam, Rai Hari Prasad, Chandrabansi Sahay and Maulana Abdul Bari for Bihar, Pandit Kapildev Malaviya and Pandit Harkaran Nath Misra for United Provinces, Prof. Ruchi Ram Sahni, Maulana Abdul Quadir and Sardar Jagjit Singh for Punjab and N.W.F.P., A.S. Morwani and Sukhram Das for Sind, Seth Govind Das, E. Raghvendra Rao, B.S. Moonje, M.V. Abhyankar and M.S. Aney for C.P. and Berar, M.R. Jayakar and Jamnadas M. Mehta for Bombay, N.C. Kelkar and D.V. Gokhale for Maharashtra, Hakim Ajmal Khan, Inder Vidyavachaspati, and Pandit Radha Krishna Bhargava for Delhi and Ajmer, D.V. Brelvi for Karnataka, A.K. Pillai for Kerala, A. Rangaswamy Ayyangar and S. Satyamurti for Tamil Nadu, and

V. Ramadas, V. Lakshminarayana, and K.V.K.P. Swami for Karnataka.[3]

Soon after the Allahabad conference, Das set out on a tour of the southern regions of India. His tour proved successful as he impressed upon the people that the end should be kept in view and that the frustration, dissatisfaction and depression provided by the suspension of Non-cooperation Movement after the tragic incident and Chauri Chaura should be removed.

In February 1923, when C.R. Das was in Bombay, Maulana Azad had a long discussion with him and proposed "that both parties should suspend council propaganda for the months and work whole-heartedly to collet men and money according to the Gaya resolution of the Congress; that, if by that time the country became prepared for Civil Disobedience, the All India Congress Committee would so declare, in which case both parties should join in such Civil Disobedience; that, if on the contrary the All-India Congress Committee fail to make such declaration, each party would be at liberty to continue the council propaganda and accept the verdict of a special session of the Congress to be held in the month of June." Das, when consulted the prominent members of his party, did not receive a favourable response to the proposition put forward by Maulana Azad. He however, placed a counter proposal before Azad : " . . . that we should allow each other to work out separate programmes without interference and unitedly work out the programme in which we all agreed, that in the event of the Working Commitee not accepting our proposal, he would agree to suspend council propaganda for two months to enable the majority party to work out their scheme of Civil Disobedience unhampered in any way." The first proposal was rejected by the Working Committee and the second was never placed before it.

Maulana Azad, however, did not give up the idea of rapprochement between the two parties. In a meeting at Allahabad, where Azad played a significant role, the following terms were settled between the two parties : the suspension of the council propaganda on both sides till the 30th April, both the parties to be at liberty to work the remaining items of their respective programmes in the interval without interfering with each other: the majority party will be at liberty to carry on their propaganda in accordance with the Gaya programme about money and volunteers the minority party will cooperate with the majority party in appealing for and raising such funds and enlisting such workers as may be necessary for the constructive programme in common matters; each party to adopt such course after the 30th April as it may be advised; and this arrangement subject to the condition that there is no dissolution of the existing councils in any province before the expiry of the full term for which they have been constituted.

This kind of compromise raised numerous doubts in the minds of leaders of both the parties. The extreme element on both sides condemned it as a useless agreement. The terms agreed upon were not carried out as each desired the other to do. C. Rajagopalachari issued a statement recognizing the failure of both the parties to carry out the terms of the agreement and stated that the programme before the Congressmen was the one adopted at the Gaya session of the Congress, though the other party could pursue their own plans. This statement evoked much anger and criticism. At this point of time, there was no well-organized political programme before the country and even the constructive programme was not carried out in a systematic way.

For some time confusion prevailed in the minds of the people about the programme of the two parties. The pro-changers were speaking with hundred voices; some were for responsive cooperation, or cooperation when possible and non-cooperation when necessary, and others for wholesale continuous and unfaltering obstruction in the councils. Even those who were opposed to council-entry programme were equally divided, some of them aimed at mass civil disobedience through constructive programme. while others wanted to concentrate on the *khadi* and national education programme.

In a meeting of the General Council of the Swaraj Party held at Cocanada on 30 December 1923 and attended by prominent leaders of the party like Motilal Nehru, C.R. Das, E. Raghvendra Rao, Rafi Ahmad Kidwai, Y.M. Kale,

Mohammad Shafi, T.A.K. Sherwani, V.J. Patel, M.R. Jayakar, R.K. Sidhwa, Govind Das, M.S. Aney, A. Rangaswamy Iyengar, M.K. Acharya, T.A. Chetiar, S. Satyamurti, V. Ramdas, N.S. Pranjpye, C.V. Naidu, Satyendra Chandra Mitra, Abdur Rashid Khan and S.A.K. Jeelani, the following resolutions were passed :[4]

Resolution I

That the following resolution be provisionally adopted subject to consideration at a meeting of the elected members of the Legislatures to be held at Lucknow on the 9th January 1924 :

Whereas the reforms introduced by the Government of India Act of 1919 have repeatedly been pronounced by the Indian National Congress and all shades of Indian opinion to be inadequate and unsatifactory;

And whereas the events of the last three years and the working of the Legislatures inaugurated under the said Act during that period have amply justified Indian public opinions and shown beyond all doubt that the said Legislatures are not utterly powerless to protect true interests of the Indian people and secure to them the most elementary rights of citizenship but are entirely unable to defend them from national humiliation at home nnd abroad;

And whereas the Swarajya Party of the Indian National Congress, by its programme adopted in February 1923 at Allahabad laid down certain lines of political work including entry into the said Legislatures, having for its immediate objective the securing of the right to frame a constitution adopting such system and machinery as are most suited to the conditions of the country and the genius of the people;

And whereas in pursuance of the said programme the Swarajya Party has succeeded in winning a substantial number of seats in the said Legislatures at the General Election just concluded;

This meeting of the General Council of the Swarajya Party held at Cocanada this 30th day of December 1923 express its full agreement with the resolutions passed at several sessions of the Indian National Congress to the effect that India is fully fit for *Swarajya* and that there is no justification for withholding it from the Indian people any longer.

This meeting therefore demands that steps be forthwith taken to establish full responsible Government of India and is of opinion that with a view to ensure a proper atmosphere for the said purpose, the following preliminary measures should be immediately adopted :

(i) That the elected members of the Council and the Provincial legislatures do immediately present a demand to the Government, asking for :

(a) the immediate and unconditional release of Mahatma Gandhi;
(b) the immediate and unconditional release of all other political prisoners, convicted or under trial in India or detained in India or foreign countries on political grounds;
(c) the immediate suspension of the operation of all repressive laws and of the orders passed thereunder;
(d) the immediate summoning of Round Table Conference of Representatives of whom 1/3 shall be elected by the elected members of the Indian Legislative Assembly, 1/3 by the Indian National Congress, and 1/3 shall be nominated by Government or elected by such other bodies or communities as Government may desire.

(ii) This conference will negotiate with the Government with a view to determine the principles of a constitution for India, which shall provide *inter alia* :

(a) For a Declaration of Rights on the lines of the resolution adopted by the Indian National Congress at Amritsar in 1919.
(b) For the full control of the Legislatures, Central and Provincial, in their respective jurisdictions over all matters of Legislation, administration (Civil & Military) and finance and over the services, Imperial or Provincial.

(iii) The decisions of the said Conference, arrived at as a result of the said negotiations, will then be said before a new Legislature, elected on a wider franchise that at present to be determined by the said Round Table Conferenae and the said Legislature shall have the power to frame a constitution for India on the basis of the said decisions and the constitution so framed shall then be presented to the British Parliament to be accepted and embodied in a Statute.

Resolution II

That the Executive Committee of the General Council of the Party with the addition of Messers M.R. Jayakar, V. Ram Dass and Dr. Moonje be empowered to adopt such amendments to the provisional demand contained in resolution No. I as are not inconsistent with the principles and policy of the Party. The said Committee is requested to attend the meeting of the elected members of Legislatures at Lucknow on the 9th January 1924 and to carry out the amendments aforesaid without any further reference to the General Council.

Resolution III

That the demand as finally settled at Lucknow after being signed by as many elected members of the Legislative Assembly and the various Provincial Legislative Councils, both present at and absent from the Lucknow meeting as are willing to join in it be presented to the British Cabinet and the Government of India by registered post.

Resolution IV

That the Leader of the Party in the Assembly to be elected at the meeting in Lucknow will put a question at an early meeting of the Assembly asking the Government what steps it proposes to take on the said demand. The future action of the members of the Party in the Assembly and the Provincial Council will be regulated according to the following instructions :

I. In the event of the Government accepting the principle of the demand or taking time to consider it, the Leader of the Party in consultation with such other members of the Assembly as may be elected for the purpose, shall put himself in communication with the Government and arrange all preliminaries in regard to the various items constituting the said demand, provided that no modification in any of the sub-clauses of clause I shall be accepted without the sanction of the Executive Committee of the General Council of the Party.

II. In the event of the Government refusing to entertain the said demand or after agreeing to do so offering terms which are not acceptable, it shall be the duty of the members of the Party to resort to a policy of uniform, continuous and consistent obstruction with a view to make Government through the Council impossible. Such obstruction should be offered on all occasions when the members of the party by themselves or by joining any other party or group of members of the Assembly or a Provincial Council are in a position to defeat the Government. On other occasions the members of the party in the Assembly and the Legislative Councils of Bengal, United Provinces, Central Provinces and Bombay will take no part in the proceedings and the following instructions will be followed :

1. The members of the party will accept no office in the gift of the Government with or without salary or other remuneration.
2. No member of the party shall agree to be on the panel of chairmen nominated by the President or to serve on any select or standing committee or commission except when the formation of such Committee or Commission can be made impossible by a majority voting against every person proposed for election.
3. Members are at liberty to exercise the right of interpellation with a view to elicit information. It is expected that questions will be so framed as not to contain or imply a request for the redress of any grievance.

4. No member of the party shall move any resolution or introduce a bill. Provided that it shall always be open to members of the party to accept on such terms and conditions as are likely to promote the general policy of the party an invitation from any other party or group of members to join the latter for the purpose of defeating the Government on any non-official motion or measure opposed by the inviting party or group of members. Such invitation shall only be accepted when the members of the party by themselves or with the inviting party or group of members form a majority of Legislature concerned.
5. When members of the party are voting on any motion, all members of the party shall be bound to go into the same lobby.
6. All demands for grants in the Legislative Assembly shall be wholly opposed, thus ensuring the total rejection of the budget.
7. All demands for grants in the Provincial Council also be opposed. Provided that it shall be open to members of the party with the previous sanction of the Executive Committee of the General Council to abstain from voting on any demand for a grant if there are special reasons in any Province for such abstention.
8. All questions of doubt or difficulty not covered by these instructions or regarding the interpretation of these instructions may, if necessary, be referred to the Excutive Committee of the General Council and the decision of that Committee on such questions shall be final.
9. The members of the party in the Provincial Legislative Council will elect a leader and such other office bearers as may be necessary at an early date.
10. As very few members of the Party have been elected to the Legislative Councils of Madras and the Punjab and no combination with other parties

or groups of members is likely to be effective, the *Swarajist* members of the said Legislative Council will not take part in the proceedings and attend from time to time only with the object of preventing vacancies.

11. These instructions do not apply to the Legislative Council of Bihar and Orissa as no members of the Party as such were set up for election to that Council. It is expected however that the nationalist members of the said council will frame their own rules on the lines of these instructions as far as possible.

12. It is recommended that all *Swarajists* and other Nationalist members shall attend the meetings of the Assembly and the Provincial Council dressed pure *khadar*.[5]

Gandhi opined, "So far as I am concerned, being an out-and-out believer in non-violence, my position remains the same as at Amritsar in 1919. It do not believe in obstruction in any shape or form within the Councils. It appears to me to be an utter waste of time. I would enter the Councils only if I believed that I could make use of them for the advancement of the country. I must, therefore, have faith in the machinery and those in-charge of it. I cannot be part of the machinery and still want to destroy it.[6]

"I am therefore engaged in surrendering to the utmost of my capacity to the Swarajists. . . . We must not hinder the Swarajists in their very difficult task. Wherever No-changers cannot have a majority without a bitter struggle, they must gladly and willingly and gracefully yield to the Swarajists. . . I would like No-changers so to behave as to be wanted by Swarajists, Liberals and all others."[7]

The election manifesto issued by the Swaraj Party clearly indicated the line of action it would follow in the time to come. The principles and policy to be followed by Swarajya Party on its entry into the Legislative Assembly and the Provincial Councils have been sufficiently indicated in the programme of the Party published in February last. The relevant part of that programme is given below and it is only neceasary to explain certain points and deal with certain aspects which the events of the last eight months had brought into prominence.

"It will be convenient at the outset to make the position of the Swarajya Party in relation to the Indian National Congress perfectly clear. It was declared at the earliest possible opportunity that it was a party within the Congress and as such an integral part of the Congress. It is not and was never intended to be a rival organisation, and its promoters have always kept in view the essential principles of Non-violent Non-cooperation as they understand them. This position has now been made clear by the resolution of the recent Special Session of the Congress which while affirming those essential principles affords full opportunity of service to Congressmen who believe in carrying the good fight into the enemy's camp by entering the Councils. It was our earnest desire to arrive at a settlement. . . There are certain other points which have formed the subject of enquiry but it is obviously impossible to go into further details in this manifesto. Much will depend upon the circumstances which will arise after the elections are over. It will then be for the elected members to decide what course to adopt keeping in view the principles of non-violent non-cooperation. The Party hopes and trusts that its members will be resourceful enough to meet all eventualities.

"These are the broad lines of work which the Party has laid out for itself. How far it will meet with success depends on the support it receives from the public in general and the electorates in particular. As is well-known it starts on the campaign with a heavy handicap. Many of its best men have been disqualified by the Government from voting or standing for election for no other crime than the love of their country. Crippled as it has thus become it has only had a free hand in the matter of the forthcoming elections since the last Special Session of the Congress. Many other influences have been at work against it which it is needless to enter into as the Party knows not going back when it has once entered the field, and will fight to the last man if the country will accept its services. It does not admit that any of its members has really lost the privilege of seeking the suffrage of his countrymen and will set up some of them as its candidates in spite of the disqualification unjustly imposed upon them. By doing so the Party offers the Government an opportunity to remove those disqualifications and make the elections a fair test of the real feeling in the country. But if the Government which boasts of having conceded a substantial measure of responsible Government to the people of India cannot have the courage to admit men of tried merit and undoubted patriotism into the Legislatures of the country it stands self-condemned. The Party fully trusts that the people will stand by it in electing its candidates and thereby helping to expose the fraud practised during the last three years in their names. Detailed instructions in this behalf will follow."[8]

The constitution of the Swaraj Party was adopted at its general meeting held in Calcutta on 16-17 August 1924.[9] A few amendments were, however, agreed upon in another meeting held at Belgaum after four months on 27 December. In a comprehensive draft containing as many as twenty-six articles, its objectives, and ideology were enumerated.

The main item in the constitution of the party was the attainment of *swarajya* by the people of India by applying all kinds of legitimate and peaceful means.[10] It was thus made clear that the desired objective was to be achieved through non-violent means. The membership was open to those who were members of the Congress, and others who were not members of the Congress, were to be enrolled as 'associates' of the party.[11] The 'associates' could attend the meetings but were not authorised to vote.[12]

The membership fee was nominal : it was four *annas* for member and eight *annas* for associate members annually.[13] A central organization with branches in every province was formed.[14] There were to be a General Council, the Executive Council and special committees to be appointed from time to time by the General Council or the Executive Council.[15] The president, the general secretary and the treasurer of the party were to be elected by the General Council and were to hold office till the General Council would hold the office.[16] The Executive Council consisted of the president and the general secretary and nine members : four to be nominated by the president from among members of the General Council and five members elected by the General Council from among its members. The Executive Council enjoyed financial, general and special powers. Similarly, the Executive Committee of the Provincial Swaraj Council consisted of a president, the secretary and a treasurer and seven members. Besides, the District Swaraj Sabhas were constituted which were also responsible for work at *tahsil* or *taluka* level.[17]

Thus the goal of the Party was the attainment of *Swaraj*. Its immediate objective was the speedy attainment of full Dominion Status, that is, the securing of the right to frame a Constitution adopting such machinery and system as were most suited to the conditions of the country and to genius of the people. The Party was to set up nationalist candidates throughout the country to contest and secure the seats in the Legislative Councils and Assembly at the forthcoming general elections on the following basis :

(a) They will, when they are elected, present on behalf of the country its legitimate demands, as formulated by the Party as soon as the elections are over, and ask for their acceptance and fulfilment, within a reasonable time, by the Government.

(b) If the demands are not granted to the satisfaction of the Party, occasion will then arise for the elected members belonging to the Party to adopt a policy of uniform, continuous and consistent obstruction within the council with a view to making Government through the Councils impossible but before adopting such a policy the representatives of the Party in the Councils will, if necessary, strengthen themselves by obtaining an express mandate of the electorates in this behalf.

(c) Detailed instructions in this behalf will be given by the Party after the elections are over.

(d) In no case will any member of the Party accept office.

The following are the extracts from the speech delivered by C.R. Das at the All-India Swarajya Party Conference held at Calcutta in August 1924.

"If I rise it is not to make a long speech, I want to introduce the programme of this party to you at this gathering of the members of the Swarajya Party. I will not go into the details of that programme either, but will deal only with the salient features and certain principles upon which the whole of that programme is based. I need hardly tell you at this hour that the object of the Swarajya Party is to secure *Swaraj*. Directly I say that, all kinds of questions are raised up on that. It is asked : 'What is the kind of *Swaraj* that you are striving for ?' and some friends of mine are so anxious to have the details of the *Swaraj* that in their attempt to define they lose sight of the real principle upon which the whole fight for *Swaraj* is based, and that is that we do not want any particular system of government ; we want the right to establish our own system of government. That is the central idea of *Swaraj*. I have said elsewhere and repeat it today, that *Swaraj*—the right *Swaraj*—is not to be confused with any particular system of government. Systems of government come and go. Systems of government are established in one day, only to be broken the other day, and another system is established upon the ashes of the old system. What I want today is a clear declaration by the people of this country that we have got the right to establish our own system of government according to the temper and genius of our people. And we want that right to be recognised by our alien rulers.

"One thing is certain. We often hear of questions as to the kind of *Swaraj*, whether it will be within the Empire or outside the Empire, and questions are put with regard to that I have often been interviewed by representatives of English newspapers upon that question. When they put that question to me, I always thought they had doubts in their minds that we were creating difficulties. But my ways are perfectly clear. I want my liberty. I want my freedom. I want my right to establish our own system of government. If that is consistent with our being within the Empire, I have no objection to being within the Empire, my love for my freedom is greater than my love for the Empire. Therefore let us not try to fathom what is going to happen in future. Let us rest content with the struggle of today and let that struggle be conducted on the right to govern ourselves. We must be the judges of what system of government is good for us and what system of government will not suit us. It is not for other people to constitute themselves as our judges.

"That being the kind of *Swaraj*, the next question is : How can it be secured ? I have put forward from different platforms my view of Non-cooperation. I am told that is not the correct view. Well, let us not fight about words.

"Whatever other people may mean by Non-cooperation, I do not know. But I know what it means to me. And in the light of what I understand is to be, I maintained and still maintain that the only method of fighting this Government and winning *Swaraj* is by applying Non-cooperation everywhere. When we started this party, we defined it—not that we defined, but we described it, I am afraid of definitions. There is such a thing as Deductive Logic. I am always afraid of this. When you start a definition, critics are not wanting in this country who will ask you to define the definition and so on. This is how we put our case before the public.

"Now this party declared that the policy of no-violent non-cooperation was to create an atmosphere of resistance and include all such activities which stand to create an atmosphere of making government by the bureaucracy impossible.

"I stop here for one moment. Critics have pounced upon this and said : 'what, you destroyers, you want to make government impossible !' We have never said anything of kind. We have said that we want to make the government by the bureaucracy impossible. How does one thing follow from the other ? We have nowhere stated that we do not want any Government. We have nowhere stated that we stand for disorder and that we want to put an end to all systems of government. All that we have said, and I shall say, all that we maintained and I still maintain, is that we will not have this government by the bureaucracy. We have said that all such activities shall include on the one hand such activities that stand to create an atmosphere of resistance, making government by the bureaucracy impossible with a view to enforce our national claim and vindicate our national honour, and on the other hand it shall include for the said purpose all steps necessary for the gradual withdrawal of that cooperation of the people of this country without which it is impossible for the bureaucracy to maintain itself. These are the twofold aspects of the ideal of non-cooperation. I still maintain that, whatever details of the programme we may arrange, the central idea must be that we must try to create an atmosphere of resistance to what ? Resistance to the bureaucratic system of the government. After all, how does the bureaucracy carry on its government ? Can it be doubted for one moment that even today the bureauracy carries on its government, with the consent of the people no such government is possible. Therefore if we desire to put an end to this system of bureaucratic government we must create spirit of resistance. That is not wrong. That is not an artificial thing. That is the natural outcome of healthy life. We stand on our ownselves. And if we do stand for the destruction—I use the word advisedly—of the bureaucratic institution.[18]

In a speech at the session of the AICC held in Bombay on 23 November 1924, Gandhi clarified certain doubts lurking in the minds of no-changers. He stated that he could not afford to neglect the *Swarajists*.[19] He admitted that they represented a very strong body of public opinion in favour of council-entry. They also possessed the best intellect in the country.[20] He had the apprehension that without the cooperation of such a body, he would not be able to make any headway. "The *Swarajists*, in their own way, are an advanced party. They have evidently influenced the atmosphere of Councils and of the Legislative Assembly. I could not—nobody can—defy their political sentiment . . . I practically confess that I consider it impossible to lead the battle of non-cooperation or of civil disobedience, unless we have by us the intellect of the country. . . .That we cannot expect unless we yield to them in some respects. In making this concession about Council-entry, we find that we have got with us the Council programme workers, who are wise men, men whom I claim to be practical men,.... I believe that spinning should be a part of the Swarajists' programme like the Council programme that we should introduce *khaddar* or spinning-wheel into the franchise. . . . I do not believe that the spinning-wheel will give anything substantial to India. But is it a sin to spin? . . . . I have affection for the spinning-wheel, but there are other countrymen of ours who have real disinclination to spin; for them I have given way in regard to the spinning franchise. Therefore I had no hesitation in subscribing to the spinning franchise in the way I did to meet some of the unwilling Swarajists. I went to make this franchise a living thing in the Congress. I want to make it successful with the help of the Swaraj Party....My appeal is to the No-changers. It is equally to the Swarajists. . . . Accept it even for the sake of discipline. Accept it as an article of faith.

"The Swarjists are not idiotic, the Swarajists are not unpatriotic. They have got their own duty to perform according to the best of their ability. If they consider that it is necessary to give battle to Government by going to the Councils, let them go and make the Councils workable. They do not go to Councils to spite the No-changers. They do not go there to make harangues. They have a purpose in view. Suppose you do not allow them to go to the Councils, what are they going to do ? Are they to rot ? The No-changers should believe that the proper place for the *Swarajists* is inside the Councils and not outside."[21]

On 20 January 1925, Motilal Nehru issued a circular for the guidance of the leaders of Swaraj Party in U.P. to enrol new members and propagate the ideology of the party amongst the people. 'In my opinion it is not necessary in the U.P. to carry on an active campaign to enlist members of the Swaraj Party. All that is necessary is to consolidate the results obtained at the last elections to the Congress Committee. I have not yet had a report giving the necessary particulars as to the strength of the Swaraj Party in the *Tahsil*, District and the Provincial Committees. My instructions were that a register be opened immediately after each election showing the names of the Swarajist and non-Swarajist members of that Committee. So far as I know these instructions have not been complied with. No formal report has yet been made even of the names of the Swarajists and other members elected to the All India Congress Committee from the province. I think that the time, labour and money already spent should be turned to some good purpose. With this object I now give the following instructions :

1. That *Tahshil*, District, Provincial and All India registers of *Swarajist* and non-*Swarajist* members be forthwith completed and submitted to Headquarters.
2. That full accounts of all remittances made to workers to the end of December last be at once rendered.
3. That instructions be issued to the *Swarajists* in each *Tahsil*, District, and Provincial Congress Committee:
   (a) to resolve themselves into *Tahsil*, District and Provincial Swaraj Committees,
   (b) to carry on propaganda work among the non-*Swarajist* members of the said Committees,
   (c) to secure election of *Swarajist* members to the said Committee at bye-elections.

All this work should be honorary and can be done by the office bearers and the other prominent *Swarajists* in the various Committees. The small expenses for stationary etc. can be met by subscriptions paid by members and small donations collected from the public.

4. Registers of members should be kept up-to-date with such changes as may be made being noted from time to time and information given to the Head Office.

This is all that is necessary to maintain the integrity of the Swaraj Party in the various committees during the present years.

This will be done by newspapers and lecturing propaganda. Arrangements are being made to start a Hindu Daily at an early date. This will be followed by a Urdu Daily in due course. Lecturing propaganda will take the form of :

(a) village organisation by establishing Hindu-Muslim Unions or *Sangathans* and taking the necessary steps to raise the untouchables,

(b) taking direct charge of *Kisan Sanghs* and have their grievances ventilated in the Councils through *Swarajist* members.

(c) organising public meetings to support important measures of *Swarajist* members of the Assembly and the Local Council.

It will be seen that item (a) is the concern of the Congress as a whole including the Swaraj Party while items (b) and (c) have exclusive reference to the Swaraj Party.

"The work detailed above required an army of workers but no specific detatils can be laid down before we know that assistance is to be expected from the Congress funds for (a). The work indicated in (b) and (c) will be complimentary to the work mentioned in (a). It is therefore not possible to lay down the details of (b) and (c) in anticipation of the decision of the Working Committee of the Congress. I shall take the earliest opportunity after the next meeting of the Committee to frame a scheme. Meanwhile it is requested that the work indicated in the first part of this note be completed without delay. It must be understood that all paid workers engaged for that work will cease to draw their allowances from the end of January. Strictly speaking that work should have been finished by the end of December and the extension of allowances to January is a concession. It should however be borne in mind that paid workers will again be mobilized as soon as the new scheme is ready.[22]

Jawaharlal Nehru has given a comprehensive survey of events having a deep linkage with the problems of council-entry.[23] "My own inclination was wholly against council-entry, because this seemed to lead inevitable to compromising tactics and to a continuous watering down of our objective. But there really was no other political programme before the country. The no-changers laid stress on a 'constructive programme', which in effects was a programme of social reform, and its chief merit was that it brought our workers in touch with the masses. This was not likely to satisfy those who believed in political action, and it was inevitable that after a wave of direct action, which had not succeeded, there should be a phase of parliamentary activity. Even this activity was envisaged by Deshbandhu Das and my father, the leaders of the new movement, as one of obstruction and defiance and not of cooperation and construction.'

In September 1923, a special Session of the Congress met in Delhi under the presidentship of Maulana Mohamed Ali, the president elect of the Cocanada Congress to discuss what attitude the Congress should take regarding the new dogma of entering the councils. Mohamed Ali was easily won over by C.R. Das to give his qualified support to the Swaraj scheme and to get for it from the Poona Jail the assent of Mahatma Gandhi.[24] Indeed the whole of educated India was surprised to find the special session of the Congress in Delhi giving Das's scheme its tacit acquiescence, and allowing him and his friends to go into the council if they liked. The Delhi resolution ran as follows :

'While reaffirming its adherence to the principle of non-cooperation this Congress declares that such Congressmen as have no religious or other conscientious objection against entering the legislatures are at liberty to stand as candidates and to exercise the right of voting at the forthcoming elections, and this Congress therefore suspends all propaganda against entering councils. The Congress at the same time calls upon all Congressmen to double their efforts to carry out the constructive programme of their great leader, Mahatma Gandhi, and united endeavour to achieve *Swaraj* at the earliest possible moment."[25]

Having received permission from the Delhi Special Congress to contest the seats for the councils, the Swaraj Party now emerged into the public eye as a major party in the country. In fact it had lost much time in the squabbles in the Congress and thus found little opportunity of organising its fund or workers or propaganda efficiently. Still their appeal found a ready response from the people. The two major groups which came out in the poliltical arena seeking elections to the reformed councils were the *Swarjists* on one side and the position was a logical development from the principles of Gandhi's original campaign. The only distinction they argued, was that instead of attempting to destroy the councils by boycott and from outside which had proved impracticable, they had set themselves to wreek the machinery of the constitution from within. The *Swarajists* also stated that the reforms were unsatisfactory; that immediate advance was essential; that utmost pressure must be brought to bear upon the Executive and that the Kenya decision was monstrous. To all these statements, the Liberals could but register their agreement, but they could not confront the Swarajists with any heroic programme of their own. Such was the position of the parties at the time of the general elections in November 1923.[26]

The Swaraj Party formulated its political programme in its well-chalked out dimensions, *i.e.* (a) programme in the councils and (b) programme amongst the masses of India. The former was carried out in a systematic way by prominent *Swarajists* as individuals, with the help of their associates as well as like-minded members of other political groups in the councils. It planned to refuse supplies and reject bugdets proposed by the government; to fight against proposals for legislative enactments; to move resolutions for healthy national life and take measures for displacement of the bureaucracy; to follow a definite economic policy by preventing the drain of public wealth from the country; to safeguard commercial and industrial interests of the nation; to protect the genuine right of industrial and agricultural labour and adjust better relationship between landlords and tenants.

Besides it was enjoined upon the party workers not to accept any office as a gift of the government with or without salary or any kind of remuneration. The members were required to seek election to various councils in conformity with the strict discipline as enshrined in the party mandate.

The programme amongst the masses included political, social, economic and constructive work. The party members were required to work for the constructive programme as per the rules given in the manifesto ; to work for inter-communal unity amongst all the communities of India, more specially the removal of differences between Hindus and Muslims, and Brahmans and non-Brahamans; to remove untouchability by alleviating the social status of the depressed classes; to plan village welfare schemes ; to organise labour and peasantry to enable them to participate in the national reconstruction to devise measures for the development of commerce and industry ; to contest municipal elections and improve its administrative set up by planning new schemes; to promote *Swadeshi khadi*, national education and arbitration courts ; to boycott British goods ; to promote solidarity of Asiatic nations and promote Asiatic culture and mutual trade and commerce.

The second elections for the Legislative Assembly and the provincial councils were held in the months of November and December 1923. Besides a number of independent candidates, the two major political parties in the contest were the *Swarajists* and the Liberals. The Swaraj Party was represented by Motilal Nehru and C.R. Das, and the Liberal or Moderate party by Surendranath Banerjea and V.S. Srinivasa Sastri. In the central assembly the total membership was 145. There were 40 nominated members, 45 *Swarajists* and 60 Independents and Liberals. Through the efforts of Motilal Nehru a coalition was formed between the *Swarajists* and a considerable number of Independents, which came to be called the Nationalist Party. This was done through his efforts which were shown by consistent touch and calling occasional meetings of leaders representing these groups. Such political manoeuvres worked well and at crucial junctures the *Swarajists* became an enlarged group with the support of others outside the party.

In the elections, in Bombay, out of 40 non-Muslim seats, Swaraj Party won 23 and non-Brahmans 11, the Liberals fared badly.[27] In U.P., 40 seats went to *Swarajists* who won every seat wherever they opposed a Liberal candidate ; only 8 Liberals, 6 Independents and 43 Land-holders were returned.[28] In Bengal, of 114 seats open to general and special constituencies, 45 were captured by *Swarajists* and 20 by Independents. In the Central Provinces, the *Swarajists* enjoyed a clear majority. In Bombay and U.P., although they were returned in considerable number, they did not constitute the largest group. In Madras, they were but a handful as compared with the ministerialists of the non-Brahman party which formed the strongest single party in the council.[29] In the Punjab, Bihar and Orissa, they were extremely weak. Of the 71 seats in the Punjab, only 9 were captured by *Swarajists*.

Some of the Liberal defeats were astounding. In Calcutta, Surendranath Benerjea was defeated by a *Swarajist*, Dr. B.C. Roy; the Advocate-General S.R. Das was defeated by S.P. Roy, C.R. Das was returned uncontested from Midnapore. In Bombay Jayakar defeated Paranjype. In the Punjab, Dr. Nand Lal was defeated, by Dewan Chaman Lall. In Madras, Seshagiri Aiyar was unseated by a *Swarajist*.[30]

On January 1924, the Second Assembly under the Reform Act met for the swearing-in of the members. Next day, the Viceroy, Lord Reading opined about various issues of national and international importance. He stated, ". . . We have now entered a second stage by the election of the new Assembly. . . Differences have occurred, but I am convinced that these have left no bitterness in their work. . . I am well aware that words are often used in the heat of political conflict which perhaps convey more than is really intended . . . I cannot foretell the future ; I do not know what it holds ; but I cannot conceal from you that the political situation in India in its constitutional aspects causes me some anxiety for the future of the Reforms. I should be doing a disservice to India if I failed at this moment to give expression to my views formed not upon hasty or cursory survey ; but as the result of as profound study and reflection as I can bring to bear upon a subject of supreme interest to me. . . . It may appear easy to impair and even to destroy and to recreate. Doubtless, destruction is always easier than construction. Violent revolutions have destroyed the institutions of nations. Neglect and apathy in other cases have induced their decay and extinction ; but I beg you to remember that when influences of this nature have been set in motion, restoration and recreation become infinitely more difficult and sometimes impossible. These influences make no appeal to the British people and the British Parliament would emphatically repudiate and reject them. . .'[32]

Undoubtedly Motilal Nehru prepared the details of the agenda to be discussed in the Assembly like a serious and conscientious student doing his home-work to be shown the next day. His superb intellect, masterly adroitness and resonant voice put forward forceful arguments which put new life even in the dull and drab discussion on various issues. Jawaharlal Nehru mentioned in his *Autobiography* thus about Motilal Nehru's deep interest in the deliberations of the Central Assembly. "Father had taken to the work in the Assembly like a duck to water. It suited his legal and constitutional training and, unlike *Satyagraha* and its offshoots, he knew the rules of this game."[33] George Rainy, Leader of the House, later on, paid glowing tributes to the memory of

Motilal Nehru. He said, "The quickness of his intellect, his skill in debate, his adroitness as a tactician and his strength of purpose rendered him a formidable adversary in controversy."[34]

During the years 1924-26, the *Swarajists* successfully opposed all proposals for additional taxation and "unpopular legislation". They successfully fought for reduction of taxation and had reduced the tax on salt, abolished the cotton excise duty and the import duty on sulphur. They passed satisfactory resolutions on questions of national importance ; improvement to the condition of labour; protection to native industries ; removal of racial distinction; railway grievances of Indians abroad; economic conditions and subordinate services. They successfully fought for the repeal of repressive laws *i.e.* Bengal Regulation III of 1818; Criminal Law Amendment Act of 1908; Bengal Ordinance I of 1924; Bengal and Madras State Prisoners Act of 1850 and Prevention of Seditious Meeting Act of 1921 . They also passed various resolutions for the release of political prisoners. They had effectively carried out retrenchments, had always voted against all undue rise of expenditure ; had thrown out the Lee Commission's recommendations and many items of expenditure which government wanted to load on the heads of the Indian tax-payer. They reiterated the National Demand on the floor of the House and had thrown out the budget on a policy of refusal of supply before redress of grievances. They by their "incessant patriotic activities and by the courageous stand they took on all the national questions, effectively prevented the Indian Legislature from being used as a weapon by the bureaucracy against Indian interests. Thus they offered an effective opposition to the bureaucracy in all their attempts to strengthen their hold on India.

On the issue of Dominion Status for India, Motilal Nehru opined, ". . . There may be anarchy, if the present system of administration is continued and if our voice is not heard, or if the remedies—supposed remedies—which are not being adopted are continued to be adopted. You may talk of revolutionary crime. But what is that, Sir, except an outward symptom of the real disease. Treat the disease and not the symptom. . . . We have tried to obtain justice by means of so-called constitutional and proper ways, but we have miserably failed. The one lesson that we have learnt is that we have to depend upon ourselves."[35]

On 18 February, the Assembly by 76 votes against 48 adopted Motilal Nehru's amendment which ran as follows : "This Assembly recommends to the Governor-General-in-Council to take steps to take full Responsible Government in India and for the said purpose : (a) to summon at an early date a representative Round Table Conference to recommend with due regard to the protection of the rights and interests of important minorities the scheme of a constitution for India, and (b) after dissolving the Central Legislature to place the said scheme for approval and submit the same to the British Parliament to be embodied in a statute."[36]

On 17 March 1924, on a motion by Madan Mohan Malaviya, the Central Legislative Assembly had withheld leave to introduce the Finance Bill by 60 votes against 57. Motilal Nehru's telegram, dated 18 March said, "Finance Bill again introduced today with Viceroy's recommendation. Assembly refused leave without division." On this Gandhi wrote to Motilal Nehru, "I have your telegram about rejection of the Finance Bill. I rejoice because the victory gives you joy, but I cannot enthuse over it, nor am I amazed at the victory. With proper discipline and tact it was not an impossible fact, and I never doubted your very great tactfulness and persuasive eloquence, and your patience with threats, and I entirely agree with you that, if you had more time for organization and a larger backing from the country, you would have carried everything before in the Provincial as well as the Central Legislature."[37]

Besides the demands for grants put forward by the government were greatly discussed and opposed by the *Swarajists*. At this point of time, the government adopted the policy of caution and in a mild tone tried to gear its machinery towards persuasion, of course with some arguments of fundamental nature. In his inaugural speech during the first session of the second Legislative Assembly, the Viceroy stated thus : "I still wonder—as I wondered in the October—what purpose beneficial to India will be served by any course destined to destroy the continuity of progress in the Reform movement. . . . The

British Parliament has alredy set up the machinery now in operation for some time past."

The Viceroy also warned the *Swarajists* to desist from measures which might prompt the government to resort to a course of action not suited to its 'temper and inclination'. He observed, "These influences make no appeal to the British people and the British Parliament would emphatically repudiate and reject them."[38] But this kind of advice had no effect on the *Swarajists* who, as a matter of policy, were to act in accordance with the manifesto of their party.

Speaking on the recommendations of the Lee Commission, Motilal Nehru observed forcefully in the Legislative Assembly, "The selfish motives with which we charge the British Government be elsewhere—not in the motion of the services but in the motives which be behind the maintenance of the services. The selfish reason, however, is the maintenance of the grip over India for all time to come. That is the selfish reason. It is not that ten, twenty or a hundred young men from England should come out here every year and be provided for. No, certainly not. What we mean by selfish motives is that you are entering into our daily life day by day to such an extent that it will take—I do not know how long it will be—hundreds of years for us to shake ourselves free of you. What we want is that you should give us the right to walk erect in our streets and then you can come in any numbers you like. Come as our friends, come as our neighbours, not as our rulers."[39]

In the Legislative Council of the United Provinces, Pandit Govind Ballabh Pant, the Swaraj Party leader, was critical of the performance of local bodies in respect of the functioning of the department of health, sanitation, roads and means of communications.[40] He suggested, 'We must delegate all the powers, so far as possible, to the Indian administrator at the top so that he may not require so many checks and counter-checks above himself. . . . Nothing short of autonomy can be of any avail."[41]

Besides Nemi Saran strongly pleaded for the improvement of cottage industries in the United Provinces, and Mukandilal insisted upon the separation of judiciary—from the executive. Mohan Lal Saksena criticised the inadequate measures on the part of the government in respect of the consumption of liquor.

He stated : "Did the Government issue any hand bills, leaflets or placards to demonstrate to the people the evil consequences of this habit ?"[42]

In U.P. when the Legislative Council reassembled on 11 March 1926 to have discussion on the budget, Pandit Govind Ballabh Pant, leader of the Swaraj Party in the Council said that, "in accordance with the resolution adopted by the All India Congress Committee, the *Swarajist* members of the Council would cease to function as members of the Council, except on very special occasions."[43]

He explained that the events of the last five years had established the fact about the 'mentality of the government'. "Cooperation has only added to the intoxication and infatuation of the bureaucracy, and the more it fed on it the greater grew its craving for it." The government, he opined, was growing more and more unresponsive to public opinion. Soon after this, the *Swarajist* members withdrew and the budget discussion proceeded.[44]

In the Bombay Council when the budget of 1924-25 was discussed, a prominent member of the Swaraj Party, J.K. Mehta remarked that his party could cooperate with the government on the basis of reciprocity. Other members who brought out their indictment against the government, were M.R. Jayakar, G.R. Pradhan, K.F. Nariman, Haji Abdul Haroon, V.R. Kothari, S.S. Devi, I.B. Bhopatkar, J.G. Swaminarayan and H.B. Shivdasani. In fact, M.R. Jayakar urged upon the government to make it a humane budget so that an average toiling person in the fields might get exemption from taxation on income from land below the minimum of Rs. 2,000 per annum. In the budget debate of the next year, *i.e.* 1925-26 the critical remarks were advanced by D.B. Desai, R.G.Pradhan, Lalji Narainji, M.R. Jayakar and I.B. Bhopatkar. Lalji Narainji summed up the government point of view in a sarcastic way : "Give up the money that we want according to our own ideas and help us in taxing this Presidency as we like, and trust us and we will do everything for the nation-building departments and for all the need of the Presidency."[45]

The *Swarajists*' walk out from the provincial council on party's directive or on other issues was a glaring phenomenon during 1926-27. In the Bombay Legislative Council such a step was initiated by its leader Bhopatkar who gave a call for walk out on 10 March 1926. The idea of participation in the debates on the Development Department, the Reclamation Scheme and the Taxation Bill was given up. Before the walk out, the leader of the party explained thus : "In view of the fact that the Government of India have given no response to the demand for further advance towards *Swaraj*, made by the nation, through its elected representatives in the Legislative Assembly, the General Council of the All India Swarajya Party, with the approval and concurrence of the All India Congress Committee, has issued a mandate, to the *Swarajist* members of the legislatures in the country, to withdraw from them. We, as members of that august body, are bound to obey the same. Though some of us may have our differences of opinion with regard to the actual working of the policy and programme of the Swaraj Party, we feel that this is neither the time nor the occasion to evince or to act upon such differences.

In the Punjab Legislative Council, where the membership of the Swaraj Party was very small, it could not function well. Its resolution in respect of withdrawal of orders of the Director of Public Instructions, for the enforcement of Vernacular Final Examination for students from unrecognised schools and seeking admission into Class IX of the recognised ones, was lost by 29 votes for and 36 against it.[46]

In the Punjab, the *Swarajists* staged a walk out on 8 March 1926, when the Council reassembled and Fazl-i-Hussain moved for the grant of the first demand for Rs. 42,86,000 to the Governor-in-Council to defray charges that would come in course of payment for the year ending 31 March 1927 in respect of land revenue. Pandit Nanak Chand moved an amendment that the grant be reduced by rupee one with respect to an item of Rs. 7160. After the Financial Commissioner had spoken on the amendment, Dr. Gokul Chand Narang stood up in the opposition benches and made a statement explaining why *Swarajists* walked out of the Council. The speech of Dr. Narang created a sensation in the House and the members of the Swaraj Party who were eight in number, left the council chamber one after the other.[47]

Similarly, the members of the party were critical of the budgets presented in 1924-25-26 in the Madras Legislative Council. The prominent speakers like U. Rama Rao, M. Krishnan Nayar, C. Ramalinga Reddi, L.C. Gurusuami and G. Rameshwara Rao mounted criticism on police and jail departments, and less expenditure on nation-building projects including promotion of education in the presidency.[48]

In the Madras Legislative Council when the voting on budget grants was to take place in March 1926, twenty-three members, *Swarajists* and United Nationalists, walked out of the Council. Narasimha Raja, the leader of the opposition made the the following statement explaining the object of the walk out by the members of his party.[49] After expressing dissatisfaction with the policy of the local Government in regard to various matters, vitally effecting the interests of the people, he said that the Madras government claimed that dyarchy worked successfully in this province but even this Lord Birkenhead was not prepared to accept at its face value because, in his oft quoted statement in the House of Lords in 1925, he used cautious words. "Indeed, he said that the Madras Government say that they have worked dyarchy successfully. It is for the Madras Government to judge how far this left-handed compliment will hold them as to the position of those who are not *Swarajists* and who have now decided to abide by the Congress mandate and programme. We are convinced and we sincerely believe that the Indian National Congress represents the national will, and it is the truest representative of our national demands and our aspirations. It has been said, Sir, that in taking this step we are about to take today, we are acting against the wishes or the interests of the constituencies that have sent us here. We feel, Sir on the other hand, that far from acting against the wishes or instruction of our constituencies, if we did not on their behalf carry out in this House the mandate of the Congress. Even since the Congress took upon itself last year to guide and direct work in connection with the central and provincial legislatures, there has been abundant evidence in this province in particular that the electorates stand firmly and loyally by the Congress. We demand, Sir, in the circumstances that the verdict of the country should be obtained in this province at as early a date as possible, and we have therefore decided that until such a general election takes place, we shall not be justified in being here and carrying on any work contrary to the instructions of the Congress. We are convinced that in this we represent and carry out the wishes of our constituencies in every respect. We do not vacate our seats, but if any unforeseen circumstances arise, we will take permission from the special committee and come back. With these words, I desire to state that I propose to withdraw from the House and call upon my friends on this side of the House to follow."

In the Assam Legislative Council, the *Swarajists* staged a walkout on March 1926 on the eve of voting on budget grants.[50] In the absence of the leader of the Swaraj Party, the Deputy Leader Brajendra Narain Chowdhury, made a statement declaring that they had decided to follow the direction of the All India Congress Committee to leave their seats in this Council as a protest against the refusal by Government of their national demands put forward in the Assembly and in this Council so far as this province was concerned. They were happy in the thought that considering the determined attitude of Government to make no advance, political or administrative, their action would not be detrimental to the best interests of the country. They would respectfully request the other non-official members of this House, who joined hands with them in making a demand for provincial autonomy to do the same. As regards the future attendance in this Council, they would abide by the directions of the All India Congress Committee which must be given from time to time in the interest of the country. Sadananda Dowerah, leader of the Independent Party, announced his party's refusal to accede to the request of the Swaraj Party to walk out of the Council. He opined that a Royal Commission would be appointed soon and stated that the present action of the *Swarajists* would not accelerate their goal in any way.[51]

In the third council the political atmosphere in C.P. took a turn with the change of political ideology by two prominent leaders like S.B. Tambe and Raghvendra Rao who were converted by the government to its side to the allurement of accepting official positions.

After an exasperatingly long period of controversy and conflict the two sections of the Swaraj Party managed to come to an agreement between them. The conference was convened at the initiative of Motilal Nehru on 20 and 21 April 1924 at the Sabarmati Ashram, Ahmedabad. Attended by prominent leaders like Gandhi, Motilal Nehru, Mrs. Sarojini Naidu, Lajpai Rai, M.R. Jayakar, M.S. Aney, B.S. Moonje, D.V. Gokhale and G.A. Ogale, the discussion lasted for two days in which both the parties entered in a frank and friendly spirit.[52] The conference adopted the following agreement :

"It is hereby agreed between the undersigned, subject to the confirmation of the All-India Congress Committee that the response made by the Government shall, for purpose of Clauses (a) and (b) of the resolution 11-B (4) of the All India Congress Committee, dated 6th and 7th March 1926, be considered satisfactory in the provinces if the power, responsibility and initiative necessary for the effective discharge of their duties are secured to Ministers. A sufficiency of such power, responsibility and initiative in each province shall be decided, in the first instance, by the Congress members of the Legislative Council of that province, subject to confirmation by a Committee consisting of Pandit Motilal Nehru and Mr. M.R. Jayakar.

It is further agreed that the said Committee will decide all disputes about selection of candidates in the Congress Provinces of Bombay, Maharashtra, Berar and C.P. Marathi.

The *Swarajists* sought support of press and platform in propagation of their ideology. In Calcutta, they published a daily paper of four pages, called *Benglar Katha* and Subhas Chandra Bose became its editor. C.R. Das launched his daily paper *Forward*. In Poona, *Kesari* became the champion of their cause. In Madras, A. Rangaswami Iyengar started a Tamil daily, *Swadeshamitran*. The *Independent* functioned as mouthpiece of the party in U.P.

The Swaraj Party declared that it would not be concerned with the trivial reforms in various departments to be obtained by the grace of the government. On the other hand it would fight for the transference of power to effect necessary reforms from bureaucracy to the people themselves. It openly recognised the agricultural community of India as the backbone of the country and gave its clear verdict to safeguard its varied economic interests. "It is all the more interesting to know that while the *Swarajists* greatly cared for the interest of the masses, the interest of the classes were also not ignored at their hands. The *Swarajists*' contribution to all classes of people was really quite substantial.

On the socio-economic front the Swaraj Party carried on the programme which was tinged with Gandhian stance. It preached and promoted the manufactured and use of khadi and indigenous goods; application of *charkha* at a mass scale, upliftment of the labour and the peasants through their well-organised and disciplined organisations, removal of untouchability and promotion of their varied causes having linkage with their social, economic and educational life; propagation against intoxicants by organising a programme of prohibition at all-India level; and last but not the least, the propagation of the programme of universal education.

A serious controversy arose between changers and no-changers when a resolution regarding membership of the Congress *versus* spinning of *khadi* was presented at the A.I.C.C. meeting held at Ahmedabad on 27-29 June 1924. This resolution was as follows : "In view of the fact that the members of Congress organisation throughout the country have themselves hitherto neglected hand-spinning, in spite of the fact that the spinning wheel and its product, hand-spun *khaddar* have been regarded as indispensable for the establishment of *Swarajya* and although their acceptance has been regarded by the Congress as a necessary preliminary to Civil Disobedience, the All-India Congress Committee resolves that members of all elected Congress organisations shall, except when disabled by sickness or prevented by continuous travelling or other similar causes, regularly spin for at least half an hour every day and shall each send to the Secretary of the All-India Khadi Board, or to any person appointed by him in this behalf, at least 2,000 yards of even and well twisted yarn of their own sppining, so as to reach him not later than the 15th of August, 1924, and thereafter in regular monthly succession. Any member failing to send the prescribed quantity by the prescribed date shall, unless unavoidably prevented, be deemed to have vacated his office and such vacancy shall be filled in the usual manner, provided that the member vacating in the manner of aforesaid shall not be eligible for re-election before the next general election for the members of the several organisations.

In various Congress sessions of the time the programme of *swadeshi* had a most significant place. Not only did presidential speeches support its propagation, but it was significantly emphasised by the prominent leaders. The *Swarajists* too propagated *swadeshi*, *charkha* and *khadi*. Pandit Motilal Nehru and C.R. Das had given up wearing foreign clothes earlier and used *khadi* along with members of their family. But some *Swarajists* still had the old habit of not using *khadi* as a part of their dress. Gandhi was critical of such persons and stated in *Young India*, "*Khaddar* with them still remains a ceremonial dress, but for household wear they do not hesitate to wear *videshi* (foreign) or mill cloth."

The *Swarajists*, however, had some difference of opinion with the ideology of no-changers so far as the programme of *khadi* was concerned. Whereas they supported the programme of *khadi*, but did not think that the *swadeshi* alone would prove instrumental in making India free. C.R. Das made it clear at Gaya, when he stated, "It is stated that *khaddar* alone will bring *Swaraj*. I ask my country-men in what way it is possible for *khaddar* to lead us to *Swaraj*." He in fact recognised *khaddar* as a symbol, but not the only symbol which might foster the cause of *Swaraj*.

In the same session, he emphatically declared, "Our reason in asking the people to take to the *charkha* was not based upon any desire to enter into any competition with foreign capitalist production either from without or from within. Our idea is to enable the people to understand and fashion for themselves their economic life and utilize the spare time of their families and opportunities with a view to create more economic goods for themselves and improve their own condition. The idea is to make the people of this country self-reliant and self-contained."

The problem of untouchables was taken up from its all angles. In the Belgaum Congress in 1924, the prominent members emphatically declared for more efforts in connection with the amelioration of the condition of the untouchables and viewed the injustice done to them at various levels. The *Swarajists*, on their part, greatly appreciated and supported this kind of programme at an all-India level. On 17 August 1924, in a meeting convened in Calcutta, the *Swarajists* listed their sympathies with the satyagrahis engaged in the Vaikom campaign in the State of Travancore which was launched for the welfare of the untouchables.

The sudden death of C.R. Das in 1925 was a serious setback to the functioning of the party. Motilal Nehru rightly considered it an irreparable loss to him personally as well as to the party. Jawaharlal Nehru wrote, "For a long time, father sat still without a word, bowed down with grief. It was a cruel blow to him and had seldom seen him so effected."[53] Motilal Nehru was left alone to bear the whole burden of guiding the programme of the party.

With C.R. Das no more on the political stage on account of his untimely death, Swaraj Party received a serious jolt and the opposition which it professed and commanded greatly weakened. The government, however, was in a position to form a separate ministry. In fact, the *Swarajists* had withdrawn altogetter from the Legislature during the year 1926, as they had discredited Dyarchy and also wrecked it. During the years under review, their opposition to Dyarchy in the form of their numerous obstructive tactics, scored a brilliant success in Bengal, where in the third term of the Legislature, the then Governor felt obliged to dissolve it.

Jawaharlal Nehru commented on the politics of some of the *Swarajists* thus : "The general tone of the *Swarajists* went down. Individuals here and there began to slip away to the other side. My father shouted and thundered and talked about cutting, 'the diseased limb'. But this threat has no effect when the limb is eager to walk away by itself. Some *Swarajists* become ministers, some became Executive Councillors in the provinces later. Some of them formed a separate group calling themselves 'Responsivists' or 'Responsive Cooperators', a name originally used by Lokamanya Tilak. . . . The

Swaraj Party carried on in spite of these defections, but father and Mr. Das became a little disgusted with the turn of events and somewhat weary of what seemed to be their profitless work in the legislatures. To add to this weariness of spirit was the growing Hindu-Muslim tension in North India, leading occasionally to riots."[54]

The rise and development of the Responsivist Party gave a setback to the Swaraj Party. For a number of years, the political opinion in Maharashtra had deep linkage with Tilakites and they, therefore, did not see eye with the programme of obstruction inside the legislatures sponsored by the Swaraj Party. Often when attempts were made to bring the two groups nearer to each other, no suceess was visible. Consequently the results of elections held in 1926 were not favourable to the Swaraj Party. With the diminished strength the Responsivists could have merger of Swaraj Party with the Congress.

The merger of nationalist groups became a glaring phenomenon on account of the Nehru Report drafted and submitted in 1928, the programme of political agitation decided upon at the historic Lahore Congress, the launching of the Civil Disobedience Movement soon after the Dandi March, and last but not the least, the political atmosphere engendered by convening the Round Table Conference. In fact after the Calcutta Congress, it was not feasible for the Swaraj Party to maintain its separate identity and carry on its independent political programme which was now converted into the attainment of *Purna Swaraj* for India.

REFERENCES

1. *AICC Papers*, File 13, 1923.
2. *Ibid.*
3. *Ibid.*
4. *Ibid.*, File 7, 1923.
5. Also see Motilal Nehru Papers.
6. *The Collected Works of Mahatma Gandhi*, Vol. 25.
7. *Young India*, 23 October 1924.
8. The manifesto was issued from Allahabad on 14 October 1923. See *Motilal Nehru Papers*.

9. In fact the Swaraj Party framed its constitution at Allahabad in February 1923.
10. *The Constitution of the Swaraj Party*, 1924, Article II.
11. Article III.
12. Article III (a).
13. Article IV (a).
14. Article V.
15. Article VII.
16. Article IX.
17. Article XV and XVI.
18. *Deshbandhu Chitta Ranjan* : *Brief Survey of Life and Works* : *Provincial Conference Speeches, Congress Speeches,* Calcutta, 1927, pp. 273-82.
19. *The Collected Works of Mahatma Gandhi,* Vol. 25. pp. 349 ff.
20. *Ibid.*
21. *Ibid.*
22. *Motilal Nehru Papers.*
23. Jawaharlal Nehru, *An Autobiography*, Delhi, 1962, pp. 98-99.
24. In his address to the Congress, Maulana Mohamed Ali informed his audience that though he had no opportunity of consulting Gandhi personally in this matter. he had received a 'psychic message' from the Poona jail intimating to him Gandhi's assent to Das's proposals.
25. See the proceedings of the Delhi Congress Session, 1923.
26. The number of voters appearing at the polls was everywhere much greater than had been the case in the first election. Proportions of forty and fifty per cent were quite common in some hotly contested constituencies.
27. H.N. Mitra, *The Indian Annual Register, 1923*, Calcutta, 1925, pp. 229-30.
28. *Ibid.*
29. *Ibid.*
30. *Ibid.*
31. The complete list of the members of the Swaraj Party in the Central Assembly has been given in H.N. Mitra, *The Indian Quarterly Register*, Vol. I, January-March, 1924, Calcutta, n.d., p. 114 (b). Besides, there is a list of the Independents and others whose consent the Swarajists were able to obtain to the proposed programme. (*Ibid.*)
32. *Ibid.*, pp. 115 ff.
33. Jawaharlal Nehru, *An Autobiography*, p. 131.
34. See *Debates, Legislative Assembly*, February 1931.
35. *Debates, The Legislative Assembly*, Vol. IV, Part I, 1924, p. 542.
36. *Debates, The Legislative Assembly*, 8 February 1924. See the text on the demand for responsible government.
37. *Debates, The Legislative Assembly*, 1924, Vol. IV, Part I, p. 13,
38. *Ibid.*

39. *Debates. The Legislative Assembly*, Vol. IV, Part V, 3-16 September 1924, Simla, 1924, pp. 3160-61.
40. *Proceedings of the Legislative Council of the United Provincese*, Vol. XVII, p. 290.
41. *Ibid.*, pp. 273 ff.
42. *Ibid.*, p. 456.
43. *Debates, U.P. Legislative Council*, 11 March 1926.
44. *Ibid.*
45. *Debates, Bombay Legislative Council*, Vol. XI, February-March 1924, pp. 103 ff.
46. *Debates, Punjab Legislative Council*, January-March 1924, Vol. VI, p. 153.
47. *Debates, Punjab Legislative Council*, 8 March 1926.
48. *Ibid.*
49. *Debates, Madras Legislative Council*, 16 March 1926.
50. *Debates, Assam Legislative Council*, 8 March 1926.
51. *Ibid.*
52. *The Bombay Chronicle*, 22—24 April 1924.
53. Jawaharlal Nehru, *An Autobiography*, p. 133.
54. *Ibid.*, pp. 131-32.

CHAPTER I

THE ORGANIZATION

PRESS STATEMENTS AND INTERVIEWS

Views on the Congress Split, 15 January 1923

Q. What is your view, Sir, of the differences which have arisen in the Congress camp?

A. I think the inevitable has happened. The two schools of thought which you now see sharply divided on certain points, have existed from the very commencement of the N.C.O. movement. The unifying presence of Mahatma Gandhi which held them together having been withdrawn for the time being the only possible result has followed. Had Mahatmaji been present he would either have been convinced of the desirability of the change we advocate or would have succeeded in convincing us that it was not desirable. We would in any case have had the satisfaction that our arguments had been considered on the merit and in the light of experience instead of having back numbers of *Young India*, flung in our face in and out of season. Had no agreement been possible he would in all probability have hit upon a more effective substitute for our suggestions that the milk and water to which the Gaya Congress has treated us.

Q. Is not this division likely to lead to mutual recriminations and bad feelings?

A. If the two parties work their respective programmes without interfering with one another, as I hope and trust they will, there should be no room for mutual recrimination and bad feeling. Each party has full and free scope to develop on its own lines by following the particular method of work which appeals to it. Both have a common goal and both have to fight thir way to it with the weapon of non-violent non-cooperation. The difference lies in the three essentials : time, place and manner of using the same weapon. The programme approved by the Gaya Congress leaves these essentials undetermined and is to my mind nothing more than a hotchpotch of pious wishes with a few vague threats of terrible things to follow thrown into season the dish for the acceptance of the more impatient non-cooperator. When, where and how these terrible things will happen no one knows. We, on the other hand, mean to take practical steps and go forward with a definite objective marking each stage of the onward march. The very nature of the difference between the two programmes, wide as it is, easily admits of their being so adjusted as to avoid conflicting propaganda. If each party goes about its own business in the right spirit a time will soon come for them to join their forces. They owe it to the cause as well as to one another to see that there is no confilict of propaganda.

Q. I am afraid they have not made a good beginning that way. Are you aware that some of the accredited organs of the no-change party have already ascribed unworthy motive to you and Mr. Das and applied choice epithets such as waifs and strays of politics to members of your party?

A. Yes—but you may be sure that neither Mr. Das nor I will take any notice of personal attacks. As for the choice epithets you mention those who use them unwittingly pay the compliment to themselves as our party is mostly drawn from the present All-India Committee and the existing provincial and district committees. But I was forgetting. We are in one sense discreditable lot as I am told that political ex-convicts have swarmed into our party, and these may well be described as 'waifs and strays of politics'.

Q. But how can conflicting propaganda be avoided when there is conflict between important items of the two programmes and in some respects one is the direct negative of the other?

A. It does look like a paradox but there need be no real conflict in working the two side by side. I hope this will be made clear in the detailed programme we are about to issue. Meanwhile, I can only give you my own ideas for what they are worth. Let us take the more important items you have in mind. First, there are the Council elections. Our friends are going to tell the voter to abstain from going to the poll. They may not tell him to vote for the Moderate in preference to the non-cooperator. If we decide to stand for elections it will only be necessary to supplement this excellent advice by telling the voter that if he by any chance finds himself at the poll he is to vote for N.C.O. and not the Moderate. The worst that can happen is that he will not accept the advice of either party and if this is repeated in a large number of cases it will be evident that the N.C.O. movement has not made sufficient headway with those who enjoy the franchise. If this is the fact the sooner it is known the better.

The failure attending each vote recorded for a Moderate will have to be shared by both the Congress parties, by the one for the reason that it could not stop the voter from going to the polls and by the other for the reason that it could not get him to vote for its nominee. So that if we fail, we shall be in good company. But I have said this on the assumption that both parties will carry on an intensive propaganda among the voters and will actually come in touch with a great majority of them. This however will not happen in practice. Judging from past experience and the general nature of their propaganda our friends will hold mass meetings and return home thoroughly satisfied by a show of some thousands of hands ninety per cent of the owners of which will be neither voters nor taxpayers. We shall, however, confine ourselves as much as possible to the voters and the chances are that we shall succeed in inducing a very large number of them to accept our nominees. Next take the boycott of British goods against which so many pious reasons have been urged. Is it conceivable that our friends will carry on an active propaganda in favour of British goods? If not, there is no fear of conflict. Lastly, take the municipal and district boards. Dr. Ansari and Mr. Rajagopalachari, after agreeing to the unanimous recommendation of the C.D. Committee favouring entry into these bodies, thought it fit to oppose a resolution framed in identical terms and referred to the Gaya Congress by the All-India Committee. It is said that the opposition was merely a device for catching votes against Council elections by getting rid of the inconsistency of exhibiting holy horror at the cooperation involved in standing for the latter when precisely the same kind of cooperation was commended in the matter of municipal and district board elections. We know that many a stout N.C.O. of the purely spiritual cast has entered these bodies and many another of the same type is striving to do so. We know also that Mahatma Gandhi so far from being opposed to the capture of these bodies has written and spoken approvingly of the doings of the N.C.O. members in them. In these circumstances it is not easy to imagine how any conflict can arise on this head.

Q. But what about the civil disobedience resolution by which the Congress has undertaken to raise 25 lakhs of rupees and 50,000 volunteers? Are the two parties going to work it together?

A. I hope not. Speaking for myself and without meaning any offence the resolution is suggestive of the exploits of the immortal kinght of windmill fame. It lacks the three essentials (definiteness of time, place and manner) I have just mentioned. We are not told how this one army of 50,000 volunteers is going to be trained in the art of civil disobedience and what it is expected to do when the training is completed. That it will have an adventurous career is likely enough but more than this it is impossible to guess at the present moment. I do not believe in a course of schooling to prepare people for civil disobedience. It can only come when the general atmosphere is sufficiently charged for a spontaneous combustion. *Khaddar* alone will not guarantee strong enough current for this and there is little else in the Gaya programme calculated to do so. You cannot prepare martyrs in cold blood by making average citizens sign a pledge of martyrdom and spending lakhs of rupees on them. The idea is too ridiculous to be seriously considered and is obviously a clumsy compromise between the patient worshippers of *khaddar* as a panacea and the impatient votaries of civil disobedience. The latter seemed to have a hazy notion of following on the lines of the Ahmedabad resolution, forgetting that the organisation of volunteers under that resolution was by itself an act of civil disobedience intended to be the nation's answer to the attack made by the Government on the primary right of association. Pointed attention was drawn to this fact by the U.P. delegates who brought in an amendment at the open session of the Congress inviting other provinces to send their quota of volunteers to the U.P. and Assam where the Criminal Law Amendment Act was then in force. The Congress however refused to come up to the scratch and the Working Committee has now specially exempted the provinces in which the Act is still in force from contributing their quota of volunteers. So the 50,000 volunteers are simply meant to prepare themselves to respond to some future call on their patriotism which the Working Committee may make. I for one will not move my little finger enlist to single volunteer or to collect a single rupee for preparing for C.D. until I know what is the nature of the civil disobedience contemplatea and how it is expected to force the hands of the Government. If my party adopts this view no action will be taken by it on this resolution and there will be no conflict.

Q. Will it be open to your party to refuse to carry out the Congress resolution while it remains within the Congress?

A. There is no duty laid on Congressmen to carry out every resolution of the Congress whether they believe in it or not. This is admitted on all hands.

Q. I suppose your party also has some sort of civil disobedience in view?

A. Here again I can only give you my own view. I look upon civil disobedience as the last weapon of the N.C.O., but in the first place, it is a two-edged weapon to be used very carefully and only as a last resort and secondly, it cannot be made to order. To be perfectly frank I have no faith in general mass civil disobedience of the type Mahatmaji wanted to bring about in Bardoli and Mahatmaji knows it. The only possible kind I can conceive of is what is known as collective individual C.D. on a large scale and the only way to bring it about is to raise definite issues between the people and the Government time after time and to put the Government in the wrong every time. The every increasing volume of right on one side and of wrong on the other will sooner or later automatically create the requisite atmosphere and when the psychological moment arrives you will find yourself in the thick of C.D. withont any previous notice. This of course presupposes that your people have meanwhile developed enough power of resistance against the physical might of the Government on the one hand and the temptation to violence on the other. The unanimous report of the C.D. Committee adpoted by the All-India Committee and allowed to pass unchallenged by the Gaya Congress shows that the people have not yet acquired the power of resistance. It is idle to think of C.D. without it or to create it by simply enlisting volunteers and collecting money.

Q. Will not the kind of C.D. you contemplate take a long time to materialize? Mr. C.R. Das seems to think that an immediate occasion for it might arise out of the Near-East complications and that the Congress Resolution is too weak to provide for it?

A. You are referring to what Mr. Das said in his resignation. He explained what he meant by it at Benares the other day and his explanation fully supports my view. I have fixed no time limit for the actual starting of C.D. I say that the determining factors are (1) the nature and gravity of the issues raised between the people and the Government; (2) the public feeling behind the issue which is the chief source of the power of resistance I have spoken of and (3) the fact that the Government has put itself in the wrong. A combination of these may occur within a few weeks or it may take years to come about. The Khilafat raises very big and grave issues directly affecting millions of Indians, there is wrong public feeling behind it, and the British Cabinet has repeatedly put itself in the wrong on these issues. You thus have the volumes of right and wrong growing day by day. But I am not so sure of the adequate conservation of the two-fold power of resistance I have mentioned. The Congress and the Khilafat Working Committees will have a serious situation to face if war breaks out.

Q. What will be the attitude of your party in case war breaks out?

A. It is very difficult to say at the present moment. Much will depend on the attitude of the Khilafat Committee and the Muhammedans generally. They will have our full sympathy and cooperation in all that can be reasonably done for the protection of their religion and the freedom of common motherland.

Q. What is your opinion about the Congress resolution repudiating the public debt?

A. It is on a par with the civil disobedience resolution and merely an attempt to cover up the failure of the complete boycott of Councils by showing that the quantum of success gained by the meagre attendance at the poll has led to such practical results as the repudiation of the public debt. The learned framer of the resolution might well have spared himself the trouble to repudiate the authority of the legislatures to raise loans as they do not in fact possess any such authority. Even if they had a real control over the budget the Secretary of State or the Government of India would not be restricted in their borrowing powers by the resolutions of the Assembly. But there would be some justification for a repudiation like this if we had true representatives of the people in the Assembly and the budget had been passed by certification after being thrown out by the House. The first step to take in this direction is to create a strong feeling among our own people against investing in Government securities. As it is we find that not only the wealthy capitalist but even the poor clerk or tradesman invests his frugal savings in these securities for safety. The sufferers by the repudiation, if by any chance it turns out effective, would be our own people. I can only describe this resolution of the Gaya Congress as a colourable imitation of the declarations of the Soviet Government.

Q. Is it true that Mr. C.R. Das is conferring with Behar leaders about a compromise between the two parties in view of the Viceroy's speech in Calcutta?

A. I have no information on the point but I do not see what the Viceregal fulminations have got to do with our differences. The old threat uttered in new form shows not only the usual lack of imagination in the Government but an utter absence of the sense of humour. I do not see what there is to be afraid of in the mere fact of 50,000 volunteers being enlisted throughout India and 25 lakhs being collected. But if the Government blunders again and declares these volunteers to be unlawful assemblies it will not only justify the recruitment but precipitate C.D.

Q. Thanks for the trouble you have taken. One more question and I shall have done. The majority party in the

Gaya Congress claim to be faithful followers of Mahatma Gandhi and declare that your party has gone for western methods ignoring the spiritual basis of non-cooperation. Is this the fact?

A. The Presidential address of Mr. C.R. Das should be a sufficient answer to this. We yield to none in our respect for Mahatma Gandhi but are certainly not prepared to follow blindfold every passage of his speeches or articles in *Young India.* We do not claim to be emissaries of God sent to this world to purge it of sin but offer our services to the country as human beings to secure human rights by every legitimate and peaceful human effort at all costs and sacrifices. This is the sum total of our religion, philosophy, spirituality and politics in the Congress.

1. *The Leader*, 20 January 1923.
2. *Young India* founded as English weekly by Jamnadas Dwarkadas and others in Bombay in 1915.

CONSTITUTION OF SWARAJ PARTY

The constitution of the Swaraj Party was adopted at its general meeting held in Calcutta on 16-17 August 1924. A few amendments were, however, agreed up in another meeting held at Belgaum after four months on 27 December. In a comprehensive draft containing as many as twenty-six articles, its objectives, and ideology were enumerated.

The main item in the constitution of the party was the attainment of *Swarajya* by the people of India by applying all kinds of legitimate and peaceful means. It was thus made clear that the desired objective was to be achieved through non-violent means. The membership was open to those who were members of the Congress, and others who were not members of the Congress, were to be enrolled as 'associates' of the party. The 'associates' could attend the meetings but were not authorised to vote.

The membership fee was nominal : it was four *annas* for members and eight *annas* for associate members annually. A central organization with branches in every province was formed. There were to be a General Council, the Executive Council and special committees to be appointed from time to time by the General Council or the Executive Council. The president, the general secretary and the treasurer of the party were to be elected by the General Council and were to hold office till the General Council would hold the office. The Executive Council consisted of the president and the general secretary and nine members; four to be nominated by the president from among members of the General Council and five members elected by the General Council from among its members. The Executive Council enjoyed financial, general and special powers. Similarly, the Executive Committee of the Provincial Swaraj Council consisted of a president, the secretary and a treasurer, and seven members. Besides, the District Swaraj Sabhas were constituted which were also responsible for work at *tahsil* or *taluka* level.

Thus the goal of the Party was the attainment of *Swarajya*. Its immediate objective was the speedy attainment of full Dominion Status, that is, the securing of the right to frame a Constitution adopting such machinery and system as were most suited to the conditions of the country and to genius of the people. The Party was to set up nationalist candidates throughout the country to contest and secure the seats in the Legislative Councils and Assembly at the forthcoming general elections on the following basis :

(a) They will, when they are elected, present on behalf of the country its legitimate demands, as formulated by the Party as soon as the elections are over, and ask for their acceptance and fulfilment, within a reasonable time, by the Government.

(b) If the demands are not granted to the satisfaction of the Party, occasion will then arise for the elected members belonging to the Party to adopt a policy of uniform, continuous and consistent obstruction within the Councils with a view to make Government through the Councils impossible but before adopting such a policy the representatives of the party in the Councils will, if necessary, strengthen themselves by obtaining an express mandate of the electorates in this behalf.

(c) Detailed instructions in this behalf will be given by the Party after the elections are over.

(d) In no case will any member of the Party accept office.[1]

1. *The Constitution of the Swaraj Party*, 1924.

SWARAJ PARTY MEETING AT ALLAHABAD[1]

Proceedings of the meeting of the members of Swaraj Party held at Anand Bhawan, Allahabad on 28th February, 1923.

1. Syt. Deshbandhu Das (in the Chair)
2. ,, V.J. Patel, Bombay
3. ,, Professor Ruchi Ram Sahni, Lahore
4. ,, S. Satyamurti, Madras
5. ,, Abdur Rashid Saheb of Ambala
6. ,, Subhas Chandra Bose, Calcutta
7. ,, Sris Chandra Chatterji, Dacca
8. ,, D.V. Gokhale, Poona
9. ,, Seth Govind Das, Jubbulpore
10. ,, Lala Hansraj of Jullundur
11. ,, Lakshmidhar Sharma
12. ,, Pandit Shamlal Nehru
13. ,, Jamandas Sugnomal Khatri, Sukkur
14. ,, Pandit Motilal Nehru

RESOLUTIONS

1. Resolved that Organisers be appointed for the Provinces as follows :

Name	*Amount of Contribution*	*Organiser's name*
Bengal	Rs. 2,000	Syt. B.N. Sasmal, Calcutta, and Sris Chandra Chatterji, Dacca.
Assam	Rs. 250	Syt. T.R. Phookan.
Bihar	Rs. 2000	Syts. Rai Hari Prasad, Gaya, Chandrabansi Sahay, Patna, and Maulana Abdul Bari Patna.

United Provinces	Rs. 2,000	Pandit Kapildev Malaviya and Pandit Harkaran Nath Misra, Lucknow.
Delhi and Ajmer	Rs. 2,000	Hakim Ajmal Khan, Delhi, Professor Indra Vidyavachaspati, Delhi; Pandit Radha Krishna Bhargava, Muttra.
Punjab	Rs. 2,000	Professor Ruchi Ram Sahni and Maulana Abdul Qadir, Lahore and Sardar Jagjit Singh, Abbottabad.
Sind	Rs. 500	Syts. A.S. Motwani, Assistant Editor "New Times", Karachi, and Sukhramdas, Headmaster, National School, Sukkur.
C.P. Hindustani	Rs. 2,000	Seth Govind Das, Jubbulpore and Syt. E. Raghavendra, Bilaspur.
C.P. Marathi	Rs. 1,000	Dr. B.S. Moonje and Syt. M.V. Abhyankar, Nagpur.
Berar	Rs. 1,000	Syt. M.S. Aney, Berar.
Bombay	Rs. 5,000	Syt. M.R. Jayakar and Jamnadas M. Mehta, Bombay.
Maharashtra	Rs. 1,000	Syts. N.C. Kelkar and D.V. Gokhale, Poona.
Karnataka	Rs. 500	Syt. D.V. Brelvi, Belgaon.
Kerala	Rs. 250	Syt. A.K. Pillai, Trivandrum.
Tamil Nadu	Rs. 2,000	Syts. A. Rangaswamy Ayyangar and S. Satyamurti, Madras.
Andhra	Rs. 1,000	Syts. V. Ramadas, High Court Vakil, Mylapore, Madras and V. Lakshminarayana, Guntur, K.V.R. Swami, Rajahmundry.

Members of the Party and those intending to become members be requested to correspond with the organisers of their respective Provinces named above and to remit subscriptions to them.

II. Resolved that the amounts entered in the above list against each Province be determined to be the contribution of that Province to Central Fund for initial expenses of the General Council. These contributions to be remitted to the

General Secretary or the Provisional Treasurers before the 20th March 1923.

III. Resolved that the Organisers in each Province be requested to begin work forthwith and specially undertake the following duties :

(1) Immediate collection of Party funds out of which the contribution of each Province referred to in Resolution No. II should be remitted to the General Secretary or the Provisional Treasurers as provided for by that Resolution. And the excess over the said contribution to be retained in the Provinces subject to the payment of such part or proportion to the General Council as the Executive Council may hereafter determine.

(2) Enrolment of Congressmen in the Provinces as members of the Party and the realization of subscriptions (Rs. 3/- per annum) from them. All such subscriptions other than those received from *ex-officio* members of the General Council to be retained in the Province to be disposed of as directed by the Provincil Council when duly constituted.

(3) Organisation of Provincial Council as soon as a sufficient number of members has been enrolled to be notified to the General Secretary not later than the 20th March 1923.

IV. Resolved that the Provincial Councils when duly elected will at once proceed :

(a) To appoint the Provincial Executive Council.

(b) To elect 2 members from the Province to the General Council other than those who are members of the All India Congress Committee and are as such entitled under the Constitution to be *ex-officio* members of the General Council. The names of such elected members together with those of the members of the All India Committee in the Province who have joined the Party should be communicated to the General Secretary not later than the 20th March 1923.

(c) To constitute subordinate Party Organisations, if any, in the Province and notify the same to the General Secretary before the 15th April.

V. Resolved that Syts. Seth Govind Das and Shyam Sunder Bhargava be appointed Provisional Treasurers.

VI. Resolved that a loan of Rs. 10,000 without interest be raised within a week for a period of two months for the Central Fund to be repaid out of the contributions received from the Provinces under Resolutions II and III.

Note : Syt. Seth Govind Das present at the meeting kindly promised to raise this loan for the Party.

VII. Resolved that the actual expenses incurred since the formation of the Party at Gaya up to date according to the accounts of the General Secretary be sanctioned and a further sum of Rs. 2,000 be assigned for the office expenses of the General Secretary for the next two months.

VIII. Resolved that the President and the General Secretary be authorised to carry on all the duties of the General Executive Council till the said Council is duly organised under the Constitution.

IX. Resolved that a Sub-Committee consisting of the President, Syt. N.C. Kelkar and Professor Ruchi Ram Sahni be appointed to carry out the party programme relating to the Foreign Propaganda and Asiatic Federation.

X. Resolved that a Sub-Committee consisting of Syts. N.C. Kelkar (Convenor), Kapildev Malaviya and Jamnadas M. Mehta be appointed to take the necessary action in regard to the boycott of British goods and make their report within two months.

XI. Resolved that the question of Labour Organisation be brought up before the Executive Council when constituted.

Motilal Nehru

General Secretary

1. *M.R. Jayakar Papers.*

FOUNDATION OF SWARAJ PARTY[1]

The Congress Khilafat Swarajya Party formed at Gaya was truly organised under the name and style of the Swarajya Party at a general meeting of the Party held at Anand Bhawan, Allahabad on the 20th-22nd February, 1923. The programme and the constitution of the party as finally adopted have already been published in the press and printed copies will be sent to the members as soon as they are ready. A further meeting of the members present in Allahabad was held at Anand Bhawan, on the 28th February and the following provincial organisers were appointed. Members of the party and those intending to become members are requested to correspond with the organisers of their respective provinces and to remit the annual subscription (Rs. 3) to them.

The following are the organisers in the different provinces :

Bengal—Syt. B.N. Sasmal, 73, Harish Mukherji Road, Bhawanipur, Calcutta and Syt. Sris Chandra Chatterji, 38, Patlakhan's Lane, Dacca.

Assam—Syt. T.H. Phookan.

Behar—Syt Rai Hari Prasad, Gaya; Syt. Chandrabansi Sahay and Maulana Abdul Bari, Patna

United Provinces—Pandit Kapildev Malaviya, Allahabad and Pandit Harkaran Nath Misra, Lucknow.

Delhi and Ajmer—H.M. Hakim Ajmal (Khan) Sahib and Prof. Indira Vidyavachaspati, Delhi; and Pandit Radha Krishna Bhargava, Zemindar, Muttra.

Punjab and N.W.F. Province—Professor Ruchi Ram Sahni and Maulana Abdul Qadir, Lahore, and Sardar Jagjit Singh, Abbottabad.

Sindh—The assistant editor, *New Times*, Karachi; and Mr. Sukhramdas, Headmaster, National School, Sukkur.

C.P. Hindustani—Syt. Seth Govind Das, Jubbulpore, and Syt. E. Raghvendra Rao, Bilaspur.

C.P. Marathi—Dr. B.S. Moonje and Syt. M.V. Abhyankar, Nagpur.

Berar—Syt. M.S. Aney, Berar.

Bombay—Syt. M.R. Jayakar and Mr. Jamnadas M. Mehta, Bombay.

Maharashtra—Syts. N.C. Kelkar and D.V. Gokhale, Poona.

Kerala—Syt. A.R. Pillai, Trivandrum.

Tamil Nadu—Syt. A. Rangaswamy Ayyangar and S. Satyamurti, Madras.

Andhra—Syts. V. Ramdas, High Court Vakil, Mylapore, Madras.

1. *The Leader*, 10 March 1923.

SWARAJ PARTY LEADERS' STATEMENT[1]

We regret to say that there is little hope for a compromise now. We have for some time past been conscious of a change of opinion on the Council question in our favour in the country since the Gaya Congress, but we have always endeavoured to secure a united Congress by making all reasonable concessions to the other party. We met several times during the last few days and tried our best to arrive at a settlement which without any sacrifice of principles on either side, would secure to both an honourable place in the Congress organisation.

There is, however, a feeling in the other party that they cannot agree to any compromise which involves a departure from the Gaya programme as that would necessarily imply the giving up of some essential principle on their part. It is impossible to expect a satisfactory arrangement ; whatever when no arrangement will meet the wishes of the other party. All that we asked for was to lift the ban to enable such Congressmen as had no religious or other objections to go into the Councils and to contest elections without any opposition or hindrance from the other side.

What we want is peace with honour and on terms of perfect equality as two wings of the same Congress, who feel honestly on the Council question, but equally are pledged to the programme of non-violent non-cooperation. This, we are told, is impossible although we don't think it is because we made it perfectly clear to the other side that we put ourselves entirely in the hands of the Congress as to what is to be done when we enter into Councils. But even this was not acceptable and we are, therefore, compelled to put our views before the Subjects Committee and in the open Congress and leave the whole question in the hands of delegates who, we expect, will adopt a reasonable view.

1. *The Tribune*, 16 September 1920. Joint statement by C.R. Das, Motilal Nehru, Vithalbhai Patel, N.C. Kelkar and Hakim Ajmal Khan.

PLAN FOR UNITED PROGRAMME[1]

At an informal conference held at Delhi on the 24th April attended by Hakim Ajmal Khan, Syt. C. Rajagopalachari, Mrs. Sarojini Naidu, Dr. M.A. Ansari, Mr. T.A.K. Sherwani, Mr. Moazzam Ali and Dr. Syed Mahmud, a basis for a common understanding was arrived at with a view to all Congress leaders joining together in pressing a united programme before the people. On the 29th April Mr. C. Rajagopalachari wired to Mr. C.R. Das at Calcutta to the effect that Mr. Vallabhbhai Patel and Seth Jamnalal Bajaj did not approve the understanding arrived at in Delhi. The last attempt to secure complete unity between the two wings of the Congress has thus failed. All members of the Swarajya Party are therefore requested to begin at once an intensive Council propaganda in all Provinces and Districts. They are particularly warned against allowing themslves to be influenced by irresponsible talk of likely compromises as it has now been definitely settled that the work of organising the election campaign will not under any circumstances be interrupted.

Members of the All India Committee of the Indian National Congress are reminded that under Art. 4 of the Constitution of the Swarajya Party such of them as become members and pay the annual subscription of Rs. 3 will be *ex-officio* members of the General Swarajya Council, corresponding to the All India Committee. Under Art. 5 the President will nominate seven members of the General Swarajya Council as members of its Executive Council (corresponding to the Working Committee of the Congress) on the 10th May. It is requested that members already registered who have desire to join the Party will forthwith send their subscriptions to the General Secretary so as to allow the President as wide a field for the selection of the Executive Council as possible. Each Provincial organisation is also requested to elect two members to the General Swarajya Council and communicate their name to the General Secretary before the 15th May (Art. 4).

Provinces and Districts which have not yet appointed their General and Executive Committees are requested to do so and communicate their names to the General Secretary before the 15th May.

No more time is to be lost. An energetic propaganda must begin immediately by organising parties to collect funds and register workers and members. Public meetings should be called without unnecessary delay in towns, tehsils and other important centres to explain the programme of the party to the public. Newspapers favourably disposed towards the party are requested to take up propaganda work and give prominent insertion to party news.

Attention of Provinces which have not yet paid their initial contribution to the Central Fund is drawn to the imperative necessity of their doing so without the least delay and of continuing the collections till they have provided for all their needs. Each Province except Bombay will have to contribute 25% of its collection to the Central Fund. The Bombay contribution will be fixed later in consultation with the workers in that Province.

Anand Bhawan, Motilal Nehru
Allahabad General Secretary
May 2nd, 1923

1. *M.R. Jayakar Papers*.

ELECTION MANIFESTO OF SWARAJ PARTY

The principles and policy to be followed by the Swarajya Party on its entry into the Legislative Assembly and the Provincial Councils have been sufficiently indicated in the programme of the Party published in February last. The relevant part of that programme is given below and it is only necessary to explain certain points and deal with certain aspects which the events of the last eight months have brought into prominence.

It will be convenient at the outset to make the position of the Party in relation to the Indian National Congress perfectly clear. It was declared at the earliest possible opportunity that it was a party within the Congress and as such an integral part of the Congress. It is not and was never intended to be a rival organisation and its promoters have always kept in view the essential principles of Non-violent Non-co-operation as they understand them. This position has now been made clear by the resolution of the recent Special Session of the Congress which while affirming those essential principles affords full opportunity of service to Congressmen who believe in carrying the good fight into the enemy's camp by entering the Councils. It was our earnest desire to arrive at a settlement which would render it unnecessary to continue the separate organization of the Party by incorporating it into the Congress as one of its various departments and subjecting it to the control of the general Congress Executive. But this desire could not be fulfilled in view of the terms of the compromise finally agreed upon and confirmed by the Special Session. It is obviously impossible to carry out the object in view without an effective organization to control the proceedings of Congressmen who go into the Councils. The Swarajya Party must therefore continue to function as was clearly understood throughout the negotiations which ended so happily in the compromise adopted by the Congress. It need hardly be pointed out that the only right course open to Non-co-operators who have so far opposed Council entry and now desire to avail of the permission accorded by the Congress is to join the Swarajya Party and subject themselves to its discipline. Any other course would not only be inconsistent with the spirit of the compromise but would defeat the very object with which it was sanctioned by the Congress. It is the first and the foremost duty of the Swarajya Party to guard the honour and prestige of the Congress in and out of the Councils and it cannot approve the conduct of those non-co-operating Congressmen who did not favour Council-entry before the resolution of the Delhi Special Congress and are now setting themselves up as independent candidates without agreeing to submit to any discipline. Such conduct can only bring discredit on the Congress and the so-called independents cannot but be treated by the Party as outsiders. What they are doing is in effect counter propaganda against the Party which is the very thing the Congress resolution was intended to avoid. It is hoped that they will receive no countenance from the Working Committee of the Congress.

The Swarajya Party believes that the guiding motive of the British in governing India is to serve the selfish interests of their own country and that the so-called Reforms are a mere blind to further the said interests under the pretence of granting responsible government to India, the real object being to continue the exploitation of the unlimited resources of the country by keeping Indians permanently in a subservient position to Britain and denying them at home and abroad the most elementary rights of citizenship. It is daily becoming abundantly clear that the British while professing equality of treatment are in practice subjecting the whole Indian Nation to humiliation and insult in all parts of the world where British influence is supreme. The Party notes with pride and satisfaction that the people of India are resolved to submit no longer to the national humiliation imposed upon them by the autocratic will of their British rulers and in full concurrence with the Congress expresses its emphatic opinion that Indians have no option but to carry on a policy of progressive non-violent non-co-operation with the present system of Government until it is radically changed in accordance with the will of the people expressed through their chosen representatives.

Whilst the Swarajya Party is convinced that it is absolutely necessary to keep in view the various stages of non-co-operation and believes that by entering into the Legislative bodies it will materially help the general campaign of non-co-operation, it realises at the same time there are true nationalists in the country who without agreeing with the principles of Non-co-operation are in sympathy with the Party programme so far as it relates to Councils. With such nationalists the Party has no quarrel, it is open to them if they sign the Congress creed to join the Council Section of the Party without identifying themselves with the activities of Non-co-operation outside the Councils by giving the requisite undertaking required by the Party from all its members who stand for election. A country engaged in freedom's battle must mobilize all available forces and a national soldier fit to serve in the National Army need not be discarded simply because he is unfit or unwilling to serve in the National Navy and Air Force as well. He must, however, submit himself to the discipline of the particular department of the national organization which he elects to enter. It will be observed that the words used in Art. V of the Programme of the Party copied below are "Nationalist candidates" and not "Party members as candidates". Any nationalist who subscribes to the creed of the Congress and to the Council policy of the Party can therefore be set up by the Party as its candidate and will not thereby become a member of the Party for any other purpose. He will however be bound by all the rules which may be framed by the Party to regulate the conduct of Party members of the Councils. Some misapprehension exists in the public mind as to the exact nature of the Congress is expected to sign. It is nothing more than "the attainment of *Swarajya* by the people of India by all legitimate and peaceful means" and has no reference whatever to Non-co-operation which the Congress has adopted by resolutions passed at its periodical and special sessions, such resolutions being no part of the creed. The form of the undertaking required is given below :

In the published programme the immediate objective of the Party is stated to be "the speedy attainment of full dominion status" which is explained to mean "the right to frame a constitution adopting such machinery and system as are most suited to the conditions of the country and the genius of the people." It is essential for the self-realization of a people to be free to exercise their natural and inherent right to determine and adopt a system of government most suited to their civilization and their cherished traditions. When such a system has been fully evolved it cannot be very different from the *Swarajya* which is the ultimate goal of nationalist India. The immediate objective of the party must necessarily be something falling short of complete *Swarajya* and it is therefore referred to in the programme as the securing of the *right to frame a constitution* as distinguished from the *fully evolved constitution* itself. The words "dominion status" are used in their well-understood technical sense to convey a definite idea of the nature of the constitution to the minds of English statesmen and jurists and are not intended to mean any special form of government established in any particular dominion. It is evident that before the old order of things can give place to the new the authors of the new order must have an effective control of the old. In other words, as a necessary preliminary to the right to frame their own constitution of *Swarajya* the people of India must obtain an effective control of the existing machinery and system of Government. To remove all doubt and speculation in the matter the Swarajya Party therefore declares that it will contest the forthcoming elections on the broad basis of the incontestable right of the people to secure such effective control. It will not concern itself with trivial reforms in the various departments of the administration to be obtained by the grace of the Government but will insist on a transference of the power to effect the necessary reforms from the bureaucracy to the people themselves. Long lists of grievances have been set forth in the election manifestoes of certain parties and individuals but the means suggested for their redress have no fascination either for the Swarajya Party or, as it firmly believes, for the people of India. The Swarajya Party will not lay itself out to secure famine rations for the politically famished people of India but will devote all its energy to provide them with a feast of substantial rights of citizenship which is their due. On questions like the salt tax certification and the Kenya betrayal the Party has no faith in halting measures of the nature suggested in certain quarters but believes in the complete eradication of a system which makes such atrocities as the only remedy. Under existing conditions the party considers it an abuse of the suffrage of an Indian electorate on the part of its representatives to engage in such questions as the readjustment of the powers and duties of the Secretary of State, the Government of India, the provincial Governmets, and various other officials. The Swarajya party maintains that the powers those functionaries exercise vest in the people by right and can only be properly exercised by their representatives.

The demand to be made by the members of the Party on entering the Legislative Assembly will therefore in effect be that the right of the people of India to control the existing machinery and system of Government shall forthwith be conceded and given effect to by the British Government and the British Parliament. It is no answer to this demand to say that the Government of India has no power under the Act to entertain it. We know it has not and we do not ask it to find some power within the four corners of the Act to deal with it. It has indeed nothing whatever to do with the forms prescribed for resolutions, or other motions or with the Act itself. We take the position of the Government of India to be precisely what the late Lord Morley said it was *viz.* that of an agent of the British Cabinet. The demand will be addressed to the principal through the accredited agent as soon as practicable after the results of the elections are declared and before the Legislative session begins, in such manner and form as the elected members of the Party may determine. It will in its nature be an offer of certain terms which it will be for the agent to accept or refuse on behalf of the principal or take such other action thereon as he may be advised.

The attitude of the elected members of the Party in the Assembly and the Councils will depend on the action taken by the Government on the demand formulated by them on the lines indicated above. If the right itself is conceded it will be a matter for negotiation between the Government and the Nationalist members in the Assembly as to the manner in which the right is to be given effect to. But in the event of the Government refusing to entertain the said demand or after agreeing to do so offering terms which are not acceptable it shall be the duty of members of the Party elected to the Assembly and the Provincial Councils, if they constitute a majority, to resort, in the words of the Party programme, to a policy of "uniform continuous and consistent obstruction with a view to make government through the Assembly and the Councils impossible". The objection that the Government will not have sufficient time between the date on which the demand is made and the opening Session of the Legislature to consider it is met by the publication of this manifesto which indicates clearly the essential features of the demand and copies of which are being forwarded to the India Office and the Government of India. There is ample time between now and January 1924 for the Government to be prepared to make up its mind at least as to whether it will dismiss the demand summarily or try to arrive at a settlement. In the former case the course to be adopted by the Party members of the Assembly and the Councils has been clearly indicated above. In the latter it well be easy to arrange the terms and conditions on which the negotiations are to proceed.

The Swarajya Party desires to make it quite clear to the other political parties in the country and the people at large that it is pledged to obstruction against the Government and not against any other party in the Legislature. It will not be inconsistent with its principles to support a non-official measure introduced by any other party or group of members if such measure is opposed by the Government. It shall also be always open to members of the Party to accept on such terms and conditions as are likely to promote the general policy of the Party, *a bonafide* invitation from any other party or group of members of the Legislature to join the latter for the purpose of defeating the Government on any non-official measure opposed by the Government, or on an official measure opposed by the inviting party or group of members. In the event of the members of the Swarajya Party being in a minority they will accept such invitation only when they form a majority of the Legislature concerned along with the inviting party or group of members in the Assembly or the Councils to support it whole-heartedly in the initial demand set out above and to that end invites their assistance and co-operation in formulating and presenting it. Indeed it is impossible to conceive that there can be any serious differences between true nationalists to whichever party they may belong as to the general attitude they ought to take in the Assembly and the Councils towards a system of Government which stands wholly discredited in the eyes of all classes of Indians.

The agriculturist of India needs no assurance of the unswerving loyalty of the Swarajya Party to his cause. He is the backbone of the country and the mainstay of the whole Congress movement. It has now been fully demonstrated that he believes in the Congress and the Congress believes in him. The Swarajya Pa ty would miserably fail in its primary duty if it did not make the betterment of his deplorable condition its first and foremost concern. It is a happy sign of the times that he is fully convinced that his salvation does not lie in the temporary benefits which a "benign" Government is likely to confer or well-meaning friends are expected to gain. He believes in *Swarajya* as the only remedy for his many ills and knows that his party is the party which strives for nothing short of *Swarajya.* The case with the landowning classes is however different and it has to be noted with regret that the tongue of slander has of late been more than usually busy to estrange them from the Swarajya Party. All sorts of fanciful stories are being circulated to the prejudice of the Party. The *Swarajya* which the Party aims at is represented as something which has no place whatever for this ancient order the members of which have in the past furnished many a brilliant chapter to the history of the country and even in these degenerate days have a number of ardent nationalists among them. The Party can only appeal to these latter to set at rest the doubts and misgivings of their less enlightened brethren by explaining to them the obvious fact that those who desire to help in the building up *Swarajya* cannot possibly dream of such madness as to undermine the very foundations of society as it has existed for hundreds of years in India by trying to eliminate an important and influential class from it. True it is that the Party stands for justice to the tenant but poor indeed will be the quality of that justice if it involves any injustice to the landlord. The Party believes that it is only by serving the true interests of both that it can find a solid basis for *Swarajya* and is pledged to stand by the one as firmly as by the other in its hour of need. It welcomes nationalist zamindars who intend contesting the elections as comrades-in-arms if they will only agree to avail of the many opportunities for co-operation with the Party which they are bound to have within the limitations of their well-known disabilities. As has already been stated the *Swarajya* Section of the Party is open to all who will satisfy the very simple conditions to which no true nationalist can have any possible objection. For reactionaries whether they are zamindars or others Party has no sympathy whatsoever.

There are certain other points which have formed the subject of enquiry but it is obviously impossible to go into further details in this manifesto. Much will depend upon the circumstances which will arise after the elections are over. It will then be for the elected members to decide what course to adopt keeping in view the principles of Non-violent No-cooperation. The Party hopes and trusts that its Members will be resourceful enough to meet all eventualities.

These are the broad lines of work which the Party has laid out for itself. How far it will meet with success depends on the support it receives from the public in general and the electorates in particular. As is well-known it starts on the campaign with a heavy handicap. Many of its best men have been disqualified by the Government from voting or standing for election for no other crime than the love of their country. Crippled as it has thus become it has only had a free hand in the matter of the forthcoming elections since the last Special Session of the Congress. Many other influences have been at work against it which it is needless to enter into as the Party knows no going back when it has once entered the field and will fight to the last man if the country will accept its services. It does not admit that any of its members has really lost the privilege of seeking the suffrage of his countrymen and will set up some of them as its candidates in spite of the disqualification unjustly imposed upon them. By doing so the Party offers the Government an opportunity to remove those disqualifications and make the elections a fair test of the real feeling in the country. But if the Government which boasts of having conceded a substantial measure of responsible Government to the people of India cannot have the courage to admit men of tried merit and undoubted patriotism into the Legislatures of the country it stands self-condemned. The Party fully trusts that the people will stand by it in electing its candidates and thereby helping to expose the fraud practised during the last three years in their names. Detailed instructions in this behalf will follow.

Motilal Nehru
General Secretary
Swarajya Party

Anand Bhawan,
Allahabad
October 14, 1923

1. *A.I.C.C. Papers.*

MEETING OF THE GENERAL COUNCIL OF THE SWARAJ PARTY AT COCANADA[1]

Resolutions passed at the meeting of the General Council of the Swarajya Party held at Cocanada on the 30th December 1923.

The following gentlemen were present :

1. Syt. A. Rangaswamy Iyengar—Bombay
2. ,, M.S. Aney, Berar
3. ,, M.K. Acharya—Madras
4. ,, R.N. Mandlik—Maharashtra
5. ,, D.V. Gokhale, Maharashtra—Poona
6. ,, T. Adinarayana Chetiar, Madras—Tamil Nadu
7. ,, Govind Das, C.P. Hindustani
8. ,, R.K. Sidhwa, Sind—Karachi
9. ,, S. Satyamurti, Madras—Tamil Nadu
10. ,, M.R. Jayakar—Bombay
11. ,, V.J. Patel— ,,
12. ,, V. Ramadas—Madras
13. ,, D.S. Ramachandra Rao
14. ,, T.A.K. Sherwani—U.P.
15. ,, Nilkantha Das—Utkal
16. ,, Mohammad Shafee—Bihar
17. ,, Y.M. Kale
18. ,, R.A. Kanitkar-Berar
19. ,, N.S. Paranjpe ,,
20. ,, C. Venkatarangam Naidu, Madras—Tamil Nadu
21. ,, Satyendra Chandra Mitra—Bengal
22. ,, Abdur Rashid Khan ,,
23. ,, S.A.K. Jeelani, Madras—N.
24. ,, S. Murtuza, Madras—N.
25. ,, Rafi Ahmad Kidwai—U.P.
26. ,, E. Raghavendra Rao—C.P.
27. ,, Pandit Motilal Nehru—U.P.
28. ,, C.R. Das—Bengal

Resolution I

That the following resolution be provisionally adopted subject to consideration at a meeting of the elected members of the Legislatures to be held at Lucknow on the 9th January 1924.

Whereas the reforms introduced by the Government of India Act of 1919 have repeatedly been pronounced by the Indian National Congress and all shades of Indian opinion to be inadequate and unsatisfactory.

And whereas the events of the last three years and the working of the Legislatures inaugurated under the said Act during that period have amply justified Indian public opinion and shown beyond all doubt that the said Legislatures are not only utterly powerless to protect true interests of the Indian people and secure to them the most elementary rights of citizenship but are entirely unable to defend them from national humiliation at home and abroad.

And whereas the Swarjya Party of the Indian National Congress, by its programme adopted in February 1923 at Allahabad laid down certain lines of political work including entry into the said Legislatures, having for its immediate objective the securing of the right to frame a constitution adopting such system and machinery as are most suited to the conditions of the country and the genius of the people.

And whereas in pursuance of the said programme the Swarajya Party has succeeded in winning a substantial number of seats in the said Legislatures at the General Election just concluded.

This meeting of the General Council of the Swarajya Party held at Cocanada this 30th day of December 1923 expresses its full agreement with the resolutions passed at several sessions of the Indian National Congress to the effect that India is fully fit for *Swarajya* and that there is no justification for withholding it from the Indian people any longer.

This meeting, therefore, demands that steps be forthwith taken to establish full responsible Government in India and is of opinion that with a view to ensure a proper atmosphere for the said purpose, the following preliminary measures should be immediately adopted :

(i) That the elected members of the Council and the Provincial Legislatures do immediately present a demand to the Government, asking for

- (a) the immediate and unconditional release of Mahatma Gandhi;
- (b) the immediate and unconditional release of all other political prisoners, convicted or under trial in India or detained in India or foreign countries, on political grounds;

(c) the immediate suspension of the operations of all repressive laws and of the orders passed thereunder;

(d) the immediate summoning of a Round Table Conference of Representatives of whom 1/3 shall be elected by the elected members of the Indian Legislative Assembly, 1/3 by the Indian National Congress, and 1/3 shall be nominated by Government or elected by such other bodies or communities as Government may desire.

(ii) This Conference will negotiate with the Government with a view to determine the principles of a constitution for India, which shall provide *inter alia*

(a) for a Declaration of Rights on the lines of the resolution adopted by the Indian National Congress at Amritsar in 1919;

(b) for the full control of the Legislatures, Central and Provincial, in their respective jurisdictions over all matters of Legislation, Administration (Civil & Military) and Finance and over the Services, Imperial or Provincial.

(iii) The decisions of the said Conference, arrived at as a result of the said negotiations, will then be laid before a new Legislature, elected on a wider franchise than at present to be determined by the said Round Table Conference and the said Legislature shall have the power to frame a constitution for India on the basis of the said decisions and the constitution so framed shall then be presented to the British Parliament to be accepted and embodied in a Statute.

Resolution II

That the Executive Committee of the General Council of the Party with the addition of Messrs M.R. Jayakar, V. Ramadas and Dr. Moonje be empowered to adopt such amendments to the provisional demand contained in Resolution No. 1 as are not inconsistent with the principles and policy of the Party. The said committee is requested to attend the meeting of the elected members of Legislatures at Lucknow on the 9th January 1924 and to carry out the amendments aforesaid without any further reference to the General Council.

Resolution III

That the demand as finally settled at Lucknow after being signed by as many elected members of the Legislative Assembly and the various Provincial Legislative Councils, both present at and absent from the Lucknow meeting, as are willing to join in it presented to the British Cabinet and the Government of India by registered post.

Resolution IV

That the Leader of the Party in the Assembly to be elected at the meeting in Lucknow will put a question at an early meeting of the Assembly asking the Government what steps it proposes to take on the said demand. The future action of the members of the Party in the Assembly and the Provincial Councils will be regulated according to the following instructions :

I. In the event of the Government accepting the principle of the demand or taking time to consider it, the Leader of the Party in consultation with such other members of the Assembly as may be elected for the purpose shall put himself in communication with the Government and arrange all preliminaries in regard to the various items constituting the said demand, provided that no modification in any of the sub-clauses of clause I shall be accepted without the sanction of the Executive Committee of the General Council of the Party.

Provided further that the line of action to be adopted by the members of the party in the Assembly and the Provincial Legislative Councils before the final acceptance or rejection of the demand by the Government shall be regulated by such instructions as the Executive Committee of the General Council of the party may issue in that behalf from time to time.

II. In the event of the Government refusing to entertain the said demand or after agreeing to do so offering terms which are not acceptable, it shall be continuous and consistent obstruction with a view to make Government through the Councils impossible. Such obstruction should be offered on all occasions when the members of the party by themselves or by joining any other party or group of members of the Assembly or a Provincial Council are in a position to defeat the Government. On other occasions the members of the party in the Assembly and the Legislative Councils of Bengal, United Provinces, Centeral Provinces and Bombay will take no part in the proceedings and the following instructions will be followed :

1. The members of the party will accept no office in the gift of the Government with or without salary or other remuneration.

2. No member of the party shall agree to be no the panel of chairmen nominated by the President or to serve on any select or standing committee or commission except when the formation of such committee or commission can be made impossible by a majority voting against every person proposed for election.

3. Members are at liberty to exercise the right of interpellation with a view to elicit information. It is expected that questions will be so framed as not to contain or imply a request for the redress of any grievance.

4. No member of the party shall move any resolution or introduce a bill. Provided that it shall always be open to members of the party to accept on such terms and conditions as are likely to promote the general policy of party an invitation from any other party or group of members to join the latter for the purpose of defeating the Government on any non-official motion or measure opposed by the inviting party or group of members. Such invitation shall only be accepted when the members of the party by themselves or with the inviting party or group of members form a majority of the Legislature concerned.

5. When members of the party are voting on any motion, all members of the party shall be bound to go into the same lobby.

6. All demands for grants in the Legislative Assembly shall be wholly opposed, thus ensuring the total rejection of the budget.

7. All demands for grants in the Provincial Councils shall also be opposed. Provided that it shall be open to members of the party with the previous sanction of the Executive Committee of the General Council to abstain from voting on any demand for a grant if there are special reasons in any Province for such abstention.

8. All questions of doubt or difficulty not covered by these instructions or regarding the interpretation of these instructions may if necessary be referred to the Executive Committee of the General Council and the decision of that Committee on such questions shall be final.

9. The members of the party in the Provincial Legislative Council will elect a leader and such other office-bearers as may be necessary at an early date.

10. As very few members of the party have been elected to the Legislative Councils of Madras and the Punjab and no combination with other parties or groups of members is likely to be effective, the *Swarajist* members of the said Legislative Councils will not take part in the proceedings and attend from time to time only with the object of preventing vacancies.

11. These instructions do not apply to the Legislative Council of Bihar and Orissa as no members of the party as such were set up for election to that council. It is expected however that the Nationalist members of the said council will frame their own rules on the lines of these instructions as far as possible.

12. It is recommended that all *Swarajist* and other Nationalist members shall attend the meetings of the Assembly and the Provincial Councils dressed in pure *khaddar*.

Motilal Nehru
General Secretary
Swarajya Party

1. *AICC papers*.

ELECTION MANIFESTO OF 1923[1]

The election manifesto of 1923 was a very significant document, for it fully adumbrated the *Swarajist* programme.

It was thorough and extensive and it deals with several aspects of the country's politics to which attention should have most pointedly been drawn. In view of the fact that the Congress originally initiated the policy of the boycott of the Councils and carried on for a sufficiently long time a campaign of vilification against them after the Gaya Congress, it was necessary that the election manifesto should deal with the classification of its position in the Congress, as emerged, in consequence of the settlement arrived at the Special Session of the Congress at Delhi. It was emphasised that the Swaraj Party was a party within the Congress and, as such, it was its integral part. "It is not," stated the manifesto, "and was never intended to be a rival organisation and its promoters have always kept in view the essential principles of Non-violent Non-cooperation as they understsnd them."

As such, it was boldly affirmed that the Swaraj Party believed in carrying on a good fight into the enemy's camp by entering the Councils. The *Swarajists* wished that they should dispense with their separate organisation and subject themselves to the control of the General Congress Executive. But this desire could not be fulfilled in view of the terms of compromise at the Special Session and they continued to function almost as a separate body. They, however, took it as their foremost duty to guard the honour and prestige of the Congress in and out of the Councils and they could not approve the conduct of those non-cooperating Congressmen who did not favour Council-entry before the resolution of the Delhi Special Congress and were then setting themselves up as independent candidates without agreeing to submit to any discipline.

The Swaraj Party firmly believed that the British Government in India was guided by the interests of its own country. Thus the Reforms of 1919 were a mere bland to further the said interests under the pretence of granting responsible government to India, the real object being to continue the exploitation of the unlimited resources of this country by keeping Indians permanently in a subservient position to Britain and denying them at home and abroad the most elementary rights of citizenship. While professing equality of treatment, the Britishers were really perpetrating the worst humiliation on Indians throuhout the sphere of their influence in the world. The Indians, therefore, were left with no recourse but to resort to a policy of progressive non-violent non-cooperation with the object of getting the system of government radically changed in accordance with the will of the people expressed through their chosen representatives.

The *Swarajists* realised that there were true nationalists in the country who, without agreeing to the principles of non-cooperation, were in sympathy with their programme, so far as it related to the working of Councils. The Party, therefore, extended a welcome to them to join it. "A country," said the *Swarajists*, "engaged in freedom's battle must mobilise all available forces and a national soldier fit to serve in the national army need not be discarded simply because he is unfit or unwilling to serve in the National Navy and Air Force as well." This offer opened wide the doors to nationalists of all shades of opinions who subscribed to the Congress creed and to the council policy of the *Swarajists*, for they could be set up as the Party candidates for contesting the ensuing elections. But it was obligatory on their part to be bound by all the rules which might be framed by the Party to regulate the conduct of the Party members of the Councils.

The Party declared its immediate objective to be the speedy attainment of 'full dominion status' which included the right to frame a constitution suiting the country. It insisted on the transference of power from the bureaucracy to the people themselves. The manifesto laid down : "Long lists of grievances have been set forth in the election manifestoes of certain parties and individuals but the means suggested for their redress have no fascination either for the Swaraj Party or, as it firmly believes, for the people of India." It remained satisfied with a less ambitious immediate objective of attaining dominion status. But within its framework it maintained that the powers that the Secretary of State, the Government of India, the Provincial Governments and various other officials exercised were vested in the people by right and could only be properly wielded by their representatives.

Consequently, the *Swarajists* would demand after entering Legislative Assembly the right of the Indian people to control the existing machinery of the Government. The Government of India should not side-track the matter by saying that, under the Act of 1919, it could not entertain a demand of that character, for Lord Morley had well defined its position to be one of an agent to the British Cabinet and, as such, the demand would be addressed to the principal through the accredited agent as soon as practicable. The agent would have several courses open to him. He might accept or refuse on behalf of the principal or take such action thereon as he might be advised. Moreover, if the right was conceded, the nationalist members would negotiate with the Government as to the manner in which it was to be given effect to. If it was rejected or not entertained, then the Party would resort to uniform continuous and consistent obstruction with the object of making the operation of Government through the Central Assembly and the Provincial Councils impossible.

The Swaraj Party felt it necessary to clarify its position in relation to other political parties and declared that it was pledged to obstruction against the Government and not against any party in the legislative bodies. "It will", ran the manifesto, "not be inconsistent with its principles to support a non-official measure introduced by any other party or group of members if such a measure is opposed by the Government. The Swaraj Party expected all other parties and elected Indian members in the Assembly or the Councils to support it wholeheartedly in its national demand for Dominion Status. It was expected that all the nationalists would oppose the Government which stood wholly discredited in the eyes of all Indians.

The manifesto espoused the cause of the agriculturists and maintained that *Swaraj* was the only remedy for their many ills rather than temporary benefits which the Government was likely to confer. The agriculturists exhorted to remain uninfluenced by all base propaganda against the Party. But whereas the Party favoured the agriculturists, it did not like to ignore the landlords. The manifesto stated : "True it is that the Party stands for justice to the tenant but poor indeed will be the quality of that justice, if it involves any injustice to the landlord. The Party believes that it is only by serving the true interests of both that it can find a solid basis for *Swaraj* and is pledged to stand by the one as firmly as by the other in its hour of need."

1. Lal Bahadur, *Indian Freedom Movement and Thought*: Politics of 'Pro-Change' *Versus* 'No-Change' (1919-1929), New Delhi, 1983, pp. 137-140.
The Swaraj *Party of the Indian National Congress Election Manifesto*, October 14, 1923, p. 1-5.

PROGRAMME OF SWARAJISTS : WRECKING CONSTITUTIONAL REFORMS

The implementaion of the attainable principles of the Swaraj Party required the destruction of the existing machinery devised by the British Government to perpetuate the system of bureaucracy in this country. For bringing about its demise, the evolution of a sound programme was necessary. The Party therefore, resolved to adopt a programme consisting of two parts—activities inside and outside the Central and Provincial legislative bodies. It was decided that inside the legislative bodies, the Party, whenever possible, would :

1. (a) refuse supplies and throw out budgets unless and until the system of Government was altered in recognition of our rights, or as a matter of settlement between Parliament and the people of India;

(b) throw out all proposals for legislative enactments by which the white bureaucracy proposed to consolidate its powers;

(c) move resolutions and introduce and support measures and bills necessary for the healthy growth of national life and the consequent displacement of the bureaucracy;

(d) help the constructive programme of the Indian National Congress;

(e) follow a definite economic policy to prevent the drain of public wealth from India by checking all activities leading to exploitation and to advance national, economic, industrial and commercial interests of the country; and

(f) protect the rights of labour—agricultural and industrial—and adjust the relations between landlords and tenants, capitalists and workmen.

2. No member of the Party would accept office as a gift of the Government with or without salary or other remuneration.

3. With a view to making the work of the Party effective it was open to its members in the Central Assembly and the various Provincial Councils to seek election to every post and place in the Assembly or the Councils and on their committees which might be open to them by election. Provided that no member would seek election in contravention of any rules framed by the members of the party in the Assembly or any of the Councils, as the case might be.

4. In all other matters the members of the Party in the Assembly and the Councils were to be guided by their own rules which would be submitted for the sanction of the Executive Councils as soon, after they were framed, as convenient. Provided that any of said rules disapproved by the Executive Councils would cease to have effect from the date when such disapproval was communicated to the members concerned.

Outside the Councils, the Party would work for :

1. Inter-communal unity with a view to bringing about a complete understanding between Hindus, Mohammedans, Sikhs, Parsees, Jews, Indian Christians (including domiciled Anglo-Indians) and all other communities living in India; more specially the removal of the disputes and differences between Hindus and Mohammedans and Brahmins and Non-Brahmins.

2. Removal of untouchability and raising the status of the so-called depressed classes.

3. Village organisation.

4. Organisation of labour in the country, industrial as well as agricultural, including ryots and peasants, with a view to protecting and promoting its interests and enabling it to take its proper place in the struggle for *Swaraj.*

5. Acquisition of the economic control of the country including development of commerce and industry.

6. Acquisition of the control of nationalists over local and municipal affairs by contesting elections to level and municipal boards in several Provinces.

7. Carrying out of constructive programme of the Congress in such a manner as it thought necessary in relation to

Swadeshi, *Khaddar*, temperance, national education and arbitration courts.

8. The boycott of selected British goods manufactured outside India on the advice of a Committee with a view to using it as a political weapon in the pursuit of *Swaraj*.

9. The formation of a federation of Asiatic countries and nationalities with a view to securing the solidarity of Asiatic nations, including Egypt, to promote Asiatic culture and mutual help in the matter of trade and commerce.

10. Organisation of agencies of foreign propaganda for Indian affairs with special reference to the dissemination of accurate information and the securing of the sympathy and support of foreign countries in the country's struggle for *Swaraj*.

1. Lal Bahadur, *Indian Freedom Movement and Thought* : Politics of 'Pro-Change' *Versus* 'No-Change' (1919-1929), New Delhi, 1983, pp. 124-126.

PROGRAMME OF SWARAJ PARTY[1]

The following are the extracts from the speech delivered by C.R. Das at the All-India Swarajya Party Conference held in Calcutta in August 1924.

If I rise it is not to make a long speech, I want to introduce the programme of this party to you at this gathering of the members of the Swarajya Party. I will not go into the details of that programme either, but will deal only with the salient features and certain principles upon which the whole of the programme is based. I need hardly tell you at this hour that the object of the Swarajya Party is to secure *Swaraj*. Directly I say that, all kinds of questions are raised upon that. It is asked : 'What is the kind of *Swaraj* that you are striving for? And some friends of mine are so anxious to have the details of the *Swaraj* that in their attempt to define they lose sight of the real principle upon which the whole fight for *Swaraj* is based, and that is that we do not want any particular system of government; we want the right to establish our own system of government. That is the central idea of *Swaraj*. I have said elsewhere and repeat it, today, that *Swaraj*—the right *Swaraj*—is not to be confused with any particular system of government. Systems of governmnet come and go. Systems of government are established in one day, only to be broken the other day, and another system is established upon the ashes of the old system. What I want today is a clear declaration by the people of this country that we have got the right to establish our own system of government according to the temper and genius of our people. And we want that right to be recognised by our alien rulers.

One thing is certain. We often hear of questions as to the kind of *Swaraj*, whether it well be within the Empire or outside the Empire, and questions are put with regard to that I have often been interviewed by representatives of English newspapers upon that question. When they put that question to me, I always thought they had doubts in their minds that we were creating difficulties. But my ways are perfectly clear. I want my liberty. I want my freedom. I want my right to establish our own system of government. If that is inconsistent with our being within the Empire, my love for my freedom is greater than my love for the Empire. Therefore let us not try to fathom what is going to happen in future. Let us rest content with the struggle of today and let that struggle be conducted on the right to govern ourselves. We must be the judges of what system of goverment is good for us and what system of government will not suit us. It is not for other people to constitute themselves as our judges.

That being the kind of *Swaraj*, the next question is : How can it be secured? I have put forward from different p!atforms my view of Non-cooperation. I am told that is not the correct view. Well, let us not fight about words.

Whatever other people may mean by non-cooperation, I do not know. But I know what it means to me. And in the light of what I understand it to be, I maintained and still maintain that the only method of fighting this Government and winning *Swarraj* is by applying Non-cooperation everywhere. When we started this party, we defined it—not that we defined, but we described it, I am afraid of definitions. There is such a thing as Deductive Logic. I am always afraid of this. When you start a definition, critics are not wanting in this country who will ask you to define the definition and so on. This is how we put our case before the public.

Now this party declared that the policy of non-violent Non-Cooperation was to create an atmosphere of resistance and include all such activities which stand to create an atmosphere of making government by the bureaucracy impossible.

I stop here fore one moment. Critics have pounced upon this and said; What, you destroyers, you want to make government impossible!' We have never said anything of kind. We have said that we want to make the government by the bureaucracy impossible. How does one thing follow from the other? We have nowhere stated that we do not want any Government. We have nowhere stated that we stand for disorder and that we want to put an end to all systems of government. All that we have said, and I shall say, all that we maintained and I still maintain, is that we will not have this government by the bureaucracy. We have said that all stand to create an atmosphere of resistence, making government by the bureaucracy impossible with a view to enforce our national claim and vindicate our national honour, and on the other hand it shall include for the said purpose all steps necessary for the gradual withdrawal of that cooperation of the people of this country without which it is impossible for the bureaucracy to maintain itself. These are the two-fold aspects of the idea of Non-cooperation. I still maintain that, whatever details of the programme we may arrange, the central idea must be that we must try to create an atmosphere of resistance in the people of this country. Resistance to what ? Resistance to the bureaucratic system of the government? Can it be doubted for one moment that even today the bureaucracy carries on its government, with the consent of the people no such government is possible. Therefore if we desire to put an end to this system of bureaucratic government we must create a spirit of resistance. That is not wrong. That is not an artificial thing. That is the natural outcome of healthy life. We stand on our ownselves. And if we do stand on our ownselves, we stand for the destruction—I use the word advisedly—of the bureaucratic institution.

Now, if you develop or gather the strength of resistance, what is your next duty? You must tell the government in plain words : 'This is my demand—it is my right to live; it is my right to govern myself; it is my right to establish a system of government which is consistent with the genius of our people—and you must be prepared to recognise that right which is undoubtedly mine, whether you realise it today or tomorrow or year after'. And we tell the government that until they recognise that clear right of ours, we do not want the government to confer that right on me. You have got no power to confer that right on me. We can confer a right and seize that right and to compel the government to recognize what they have already seized and that seizure is really possible by realization. We tell the government it is our undoubted right, as we have told the government today. And that unless they recognise that right, it would be our duty to gradually withdraw all cooperation from them with a view that it may become impossible for them to carry on this system of government—not that no government should be carried on, but this particular system of government which exists not for the good of somebody else.

These are the two broad principles upon which our programme must be based. What is your method ? Is it non-cooperation ? Well, Gentlemen, I have given you the idea. Choose your phrase. It does not matter to me whether you call it non-cooperation or not. I am not used to Deductive Logic. 'O, is it responsive cooperation ?' they ask. I have seen wise people shake their hands and say : 'O, you are going back to responsive cooperation'. I say I am willing to come back to anything provided I see clearly before me my right and I see that I can seize upon that right by following a particular method. If it is responsive cooperation, let it be so. The whole idea is this that you want to bring in old phrases to suit new facts of life. You bring in a phrase 'responsive cooperation' which was used some years back with regard to the then facts. But a new situation has been brought about in the country and people are singing with another note. And if you apply the same phrase 'responsive cooperation', well, that phrase must include this. What is there in the phrase ? Call it non-cooperation, call it responsive cooperation if you want, or if you like call it responsive non-cooperation, as my friend Mr. Kelkar who is absent today would like to call it. It does not matter to me. I say, give me the thing I want, I do not care what name you give to it.

It was two years ago, I believe, when I was speaking at Buldana, Mr Kelkar advanced the idea that his programme was responsive non-cooperation. I said : 'Yes, it must be responsive cooperation because you put forward your demand. If the Government does not accept it, then they do not respond to you. Then what follows is non-cooperation.' Then Mr. Kelkar said responsive cooperation was the same thing as responsive non-cooperation. If this is so, I do not know what name you apply to it. But I want to have my programme put absolutely clearly. We will not shrink from destroying any system which stands against our system. We will not shrink from telling the government that until and unless you recognise our legitimate rights, we will try to destory your system of government, because we cannot build our system without destroying your system—not that there is a particular pleasure in destruction, but we cannot build unless we remove something which stands in our way.

I appeal to you—make no appeal to the Bureaucracy or to the Sectetary of State—I appeal to you, stand fast by the principle which the *Swarajists* have put forward before country. Let us act. Give us breathing time. Do not overwhelm us with criticisms and questions. I have thought and thought about it for the last twenty years of my life and now I have devoted the rest of my life to the cause of my country. Believe in me, and I tell you that, God willing, I shall not die before I have accomplished my object.

1. Deshbandhu Chitta Ranjan : ***Brief Survey of Life and Works* : *Provincial Conference Speeches, Congress Speeches*,** Calcultta, 1927, pp. 273-82.

MANIFESTO OF SWARAJ PARTY

The election manifesto issued by the Swaraj Party clearly indicated the line of action it would follow in the time to come. The principles and policy to be followed by the Swarajya Party on its entry into the Legislative Assembly and the Provincial Councils have been sufficiently indicated in the programme of the Party published in February last. The relevant part of that programme is given below and it is only necessary to explain certain points and deal with certain aspects which the events of the last eight months had brought into prominence.

It will be convenient at the outset to make the position of the Swarajya Party in relation to the Indian National Congress perfectly clear It was declared at the earliest possible opportunity that it was a party within the Congress and as such an integral part of the Congress. It is not and was never intended to be a rival organisation, and its promoters have always kept in view the essential principles of Non-violent Non-cooperation as they understand them. This position has now been made clear by the resolution of the recent Special Session of the Congress which while affirming those essential principles affords full opportunity of service to Congressmen who believe in carrying the good light into the enemy's camp by entering the Councils. It was our earnest desire to arrive at a settlement which would render it unnecessary to continue the separate organization of the Party by incorporating it into the Congress as one of its various departments and subjecting it to the control of the general Congress Executive. But this desire could not be fulfilled in view of the terms of the compromise finally agreed upon and confirmed by the Special Session. It is obviously impossible to carry out the object in view without an effective organization to control the proceedings of Congressmen who go into the Councils. The Swarajya Party must therefore continue to function as was clearly understood throughout the negotiations which ended so happily in the compromise adopted by the Congress. It need hardly be pointed out that the only right course open to Non-cooperators who have so far opposed Council entry and now desire to avail of the permission accorded by the Congress is to join the Swarajya Party, and subject themselves to its discipline. Any other course would not only be inconsistent with the spirit of the compromise but would defeat the very object with which it was sanctioned by the Congress. It is the first and the foremost duty of the Swarajya Party to guard the honour and prestige of the Congress in and out of the Councils, and it cannot approve the conduct of those non-cooperating Congress men who did not favour Council entry before the resolution of the Delhi Special Congress and are now setting themselves up as independent candidates without agreeing to submit to any discipline. Such conduct can only bring discredit on the Congress and the so-called independents cannot but be treated by the Party as outsiders. What they are doing is in effect counter propaganda against the party which is the very thing the Congress resolution was intended to avoid. It is hoped that they will receive no countenance from the Working Committee of the Congress.

The Swarajya Party believes that the guiding motive of the British in governing India is to serve the selfish interests of their own country and that the so-called Reforms are a mere blind to further the said interests under the pretence of granting responsible government to India, the real object being to continue the exploitation of the unlimited resources of the country by keeping Indians permanently in a subservient position to Britain, and denying them at home and abroad the most elementary rights of citizenship. It is daily becoming abundantly clear that the British while professing equality of treatment are in practice subjecting the whole Indian nation to humiliation and insult in all parts of the world where British influence is supreme. The party notes with pride and satisfaction that the people of India re-resolved to submit no longer to the national humiliation imposed upon them by the autocratic will of their British rulers, and in full concurrence with the Congress expresses its emphatic opinion that Indians have no option but to continue to carry on a policy of progressive Non-violent Non-co-operation with the present system of Government until it is redically changed in accordance with the will of the people expressed through their chosen representatives.

Whilst the Swarajya Party is convinced that it is absolutely necessary to keep in view the various stages of No-cooperation and believes that by entering into the Legislative bodies it will materially help the general campaign of Non-cooperation, it realises at the same time that there are true nationalists in the country who without agreeing with the principles of Non-cooperation are in sympathy with the Party programme so far as it relates to Councils. With such nationalists the Party has no quarrel. It is open to them if they sign the Congress creed to join the Council Section of the Party without identifying themselves with the activities of Non-cooperators outside the Councils by giving the requisite undertaking required by the party from all its members who stand for election. A country engaged in freedom's battle must mobilize all available forces and a national soldier fit to serve in the National army need not be discarded simply because he is unfit or unwilling to serve in the National Navy and Air Force as well. He must, however, submit himself to the discipline of the particular department of the national organization which he elects to enter. It will be observed that the words used in Art. V of the programme of the Party copied below are 'Nationalist candidates' and not (Party members as candidates). Any nationalist who subscribes to the creed of the Congress and to the Council policy of the Party can, therefore, be set up by the Party as its candidate and will not thereby become a member of the Party for any other purpose. He will, however, be bound by all the rules which may be framed by the Party to regulate the conduct of Party members of the Councils, some misapprehension exists in the public mind as to the exact nature of the Congress creed which an intending candidate who is not already a member of the Congress is expected to sign. It is nothing more than 'the attainment of *Swarjya* by the people of India by all legitimate and peaceful means' and has no reference whatever to Non-cooperation which the Congress has adopted by resolutions passed at its periodical and special sessions, such resolutions being no part of the creed. The form of the undertaking required is given below.

In the published programme the immediate objective of the Party is stated to be 'the speedy attainment of full dominion status which is explained to mean the right to frame a constitution adopting such machinery and system as are most suited to the conditions of the country and the genius of the people'. It is essential for the self-realization of a people to be free to exercise their natural and inherent right to determine and adopt a system of government most suited to their civilization and their cherished traditions. When such a system has been fully evolved it cannot be very different from the *Swarajya* which is the ultimate goal of nationalist India. The immediate objective of the party must necessarily be something falling short of complete *Swarajya* which is the ultimate goal of nationalist India. The immediate objective of the Party must necessarily be some thing short of complete Swarajya, and it is, therefore, referred to in the programme as the securing of the right to frame constitution as distinguished from the fully evolved constitution itself. The words 'dominion status' are used in their well understood technical sense to convey a definite idea of the nature of the constitution to the minds of English statesmen and jurists and are not intended to mean any special form of government established in any particular dominion. It is evident that before the old order of things can give place to the new, the authors of the new order must have an effective control of the old. In other words, as a necessary preliminary to the right to frame their own constitution of *Swarajya*, the people of India must obtain an effective control of the existing machinery and system of Government.

To remove all doubt and speculation in the matter, the Swarajya Party, therefore, declares that it will contest the forthcoming elections on the broad basis of the people to secure such effective control. It will not concern itself with trivial reforms in the various departments of the administration to be obtained by the grace of the government, but will insist on a transference of the power to effect the necessary reforms from the bureaucracy to the people themselves. Long lists of grievances have been set forth in the election manifestoes of certain parties and individuals but the means suggested for their redress have no fascination either for the Swarajya Party or, as it firmly believes, for the people of India. The Swarajya Party will not lay itself out to secure faminerations for the politically famished people of India, but will devote all its energy to provide them with a feast of substantial rights of citizenship which is their due. On questions like the salt tax certification and the Kenya betrayal the Party has no faith in halting measures of the nature suggested in certain quarters but believes in the complete eradication of a system which makes such atrocities possible as the only remedy. Under existing conditions the Party considers it an abuse of the suffrage of an Indian electorate on the part of its representatives to engage in such questions as the readjustment of the powers and duties of the Secretary of State, the Government of India, the Provincial Governments, and various other officials. The Swarajya Party maintains that the powers those functionaries exercise vest in the people by right and can only be properly exercised by their representatives.

The demand to be made by the members of the Party on entering the Legislative Assembly will, therefore, in effect be that the right of the people of India to control the existing machinery and system of Government shall forthwith be conceded and given effect to by the British Government and the British Parliament. It is no answer to this demand to say that the Government of India has no power under the Act to entertain it. We know it has not, and we do not ask it to find some power within the four corners of the Act to deal with it. It has indeed nothing whatever to do with the forms prescribed for resolutions, or other motions or with the Act itself. We take the position of the Government of India to be precisely what the late Lord Morley said it was, *viz.*, that on an agent of the British Cabinet. The demand will be addressed to the principal through the accredited agent as soon as practicable after the results of the elections are declared and before the Legislative Session begins, in such manner and form as the elected members of the Party may determine. It will in its nature be an offer of certain terms which it will be for the agent to accept or refuse on behalf of the principal or take such other action thereon as he may be advised.

The attitude of the elected members of the Party in the Assembly and the Councils will depend on the action taken by the Government on the demand formulated by them on the lines indicated above. If the right itself is conceded, it will be a matter for negotiation between the Government and the Nationalist members in the Assembly as to the manner in which the right is to be given effect to. But in the event of the Government refusing to entertain the said demand or after agreeing to do so offering terms which are not acceptable it shall be the duty of members of the Party elected to the Assembly and the Provincial Councils, if they constitute a majority to resort, in the words of the Party programme, to a policy of 'uniform continuous and consistent obstruction with a view to make government through the Assembly and the Councils impossible.' The objection that the government will not have sufficient time between the date on which the demand is made and the opening Session of the legislature to consider it is met by the publication of this manifesto which indicates clearly the essential features of the demand and copies of which are being forwarded to the India Office and the Government of India. There is ample time between now and January 1924 for the Government to be prepared to make up its mind at least as to whether it will dismiss the demand or try to arrive at a settlement. In the former case the course to be adopted by the Party members of the Assembly and the Councils has been clearly indicated above. In the latter, it will be easy to arrange the terms and conditions on which the negotiations are to proceed.

The Swarajya Party desires to make it quite clear to the other political parties in the country and the people at large that it is pledged to obstruction against the Government and not against any other party in the Legislature. It will not be inconsistent with its principles to support a non-official measure introduced by any other party or group or members if such measure is opposed by the Goverment. It shall also be always open to members of the Party to accept on such terms and conditions as are likely to promote the general policy of the Party, a bonafide invitation from any other party or group of members of the Legislature to join the latter for the purpose of defeating the Government on any non-official measure opposed by the inviting party or group of members. In the event of the members of the Swarajya Party being in a minority they will accept such invitation only when they form a majority of the Legislature concerned along with the inviting party or group of members. The Swarajya Party expects all other parties and elected Indian members in the Assembly or the Councils to support it whole-heartedly in the initial demand set out above, and to that end invites their assistance and cooperation in formulating and presenting it. Indeed it is impossible to conceive that there can be any serious differences between true nationalists to whichever party they may belong as to the general attitude they ought to take in the Assembly and the

Councils towards a system of Government which stands wholly discredited in the eyes of all classes of Indians.

The agriculturist of India needs no assurance of the loyalty of the Swarajya Party to his cause. He is the backbone of the country and the mainstay of the whole Congress movement. It has now been fully demonstrated that he believes in the Congress and the Congress believes in him. The Swarajya Party would miserably fail in its primary duty if it did not make the betterment of his deplorable condition its first and foremost concern. It is a happy sign of the time that he is fully convinced that his salvation does not lie in the temporary benefits which a 'benign' government is likely to confer or well meaning friends are expected to gain. He believes in *Swarajya* as the only remedy for his many ills and knows that his party is the party which strives for nothing short of *Swarajya.* The case with the landowning classes is however different, and it has to be noted with regret that the tongue of slander has of late been more than usually busy to estrange them from the Swarajya Party.

All sorts of fanciful stories are being circulated to the prejudice of the Party. The *Swarajya* which the Party aims at is represented as something which has in past furnished many a brilliant chapter to the history of the country and even in these degenerate days have a number of ardent nationalists among them. The Party can only appeal to these latter to set at rest the doubts and misgivings of their less enlightened brethren by explaining to them the obvious fact that those who desire to help in the building up of *Swarajya* cannot possibly dream of such madness as to undermine the very foundations of society as it has existed for hundreds of years in India by trying to eliminate an important and influential class from it. True it is that the Party stands for justice to the tenant but poor indeed will be the quality of that justice if it involves any injustice to the landlord. The Party believes that it is only by serving the true interests of both that it can find a solid basis for *Swarajya* and is pledged to stand by the one as firmly as by the other in its hour of need. It welcomes nationalist *zamindars* who intend contesting the elections as comrades in arms if they will only agree to avail of the many opportunities for cooperation with the Party which they are bound to have within the limitations of their well-known disabilities. As has already been stated the *Swarajya* Section of the Party is open to all who will satisfy the very simple conditions to which no true nationalist can have any possible objection. For reactionaries whether they are *zamindars* or others the Party has no sympathy whatever.

There are certain other points which have formed the subject of enquiry but it is obviously impossible to go into further details in this manifesto. Much will depend upon the circumstances which will arise after the elections are over. It will then be for the elected members to decide what course to adopt keeping in view the principles of non-violent non-cooperation. The Party hopes and trusts that its members will be resourceful enough to meet all eventualities.

These are the broad lines of work which the Party has laid out for itself. How far it will meet with success depends on the support it receives from the public in general and the electorates in particular. As is well-known it starts on the campaign with a heavy handicap. Many of its best men have been disqualified by the Government from voting or standing for election for no other crime than the love of their country. Crippled as it has thus become it has only had a free hand in the matter of the forthcoming elections since the last Special Session of the Congress. Many other influences have been at work against it which it is needless to enter into as the Party knows not going back when it has once entered the field, and will fight to the last man if the country will accept its services. It does not admit that any of its members has really lost the privilege of seeking the suffrage of his countrymen and will set up some of them as its candidates in spite of the disqualification unjustly imposed upon them. By doing so the Party offers the Government an opportunity to remove those disqualifications and make the elections a fair test of the real feeling in the country. But if the Government which boasts of having conceded a substantial measures of responsible Government to the people of India cannot have the courage to admit men of tried merit and undoubted patriotism into the Legislatures of the country it stands self-condemned. The Party fully trusts that the people will stand by it in electing it candidates and thereby helping to expose the fraud practised during the last three years in their names. Detailed instructions in this behalf will follow.

1. The manifesto was issued from Allahabad on 14 October 1923. *See Motilal Nehru Papers.*

THE IDEOLOGY OF SWARAJ PARTY[1]

The object of the Party, as laid down in its constitution, was the attainment of *Swarajya* by the people of India by all legitimate and peaceful means. It is significant that the object of attainment of independence by the country was to be fulfilled through non-violent means. The exact nature of *Swarajya* was, however, left undefined in the constitution, and, perhaps, it was undesirable to have done so, for it would have unnecssarily tied the hands of the Party, specially when our British masters' intentions were set in the opposite direction.

Orgarisation : Every person who was a member of the Congress and subscribed to the objects, constitution and programme of the party was eligible to be its member and persons who were not members of the Congress but subscribed to the objects, constitution and programme of the Swaraj Party were also eligible to be "Associates" of the Party. The "Associates" had the power to be present at all meetings of the Party and express their views but were not eligible for elections as members of the General Council of the Party and were not to enjoy the right of voting at its meetings. As the Swaraj Party was meant to be a party within the Congress, it was natural that every member of the Congress who wanted to subscribe to its creed as well should be declared eligible for its membership. But it was also necessary that others who were not for the Congress programme should be attracted to it at least in the capacity of its sympathisers and well-wishers and this accounts for the provision for 'Associates'.

The Council work of the *Swarajists* required a wide appeal to be made to all persons, irrespective of their Congress membership. Opinions may differ as to the consequences of this appeal. Though it was necessary to do so, under the prevailing circumstances, it introduced serious abuses in the Party. Pandit Jawaharlal Nehru rightly observed : "During the early days of the Party it had to contend against the 'no-changers' in the Congress and many undesirables were taken in to increase its strength within the Congress. Then came the elections and these demanded funds which had to come from the rich. So these rich folk had to be kept in good humour, and some were even asked to become *Swarajists* candidates."

The subscription for membership of the Party was almost normal. Every member was to pay four annas (25 paise) and every Associate was to subscribe eight annas (50 paise) annually. Besides, every Provincial Organisation might fix an additional annual subscription payable by its own members as well as the members of the subordinate committees within its jurisdiction. Every member of the General Council was required to pay an additional subscription of eight annas per annum.

Structure : There was to be one central organisation and as many provincial ones as there were provinces in India. The number of Provinces and the geographical limits of each were, for the purpose of this provision, to be the same as prescribed by the constitution of the Indian National Congress. The Central Organisation of the Swaraj Party consisted of the General Council, the Executive Council and such special committees as the General or Executive Council might, from time to time, appoint from among the members of the Party.

The General Council of the Swaraj Party was an appreciably large body, but all members of the Party were not its members. It consisted only of all members of the Swaraj Party in the Assembly and in the Council of State and one-fourth of the members of the Swaraj Party in each Provincial Legislative Council to be elected by the said Party, provided that in calculating the number of members allotted to each Province fractions of one half or more counted as one and those of less than half were not counted at all. The General Council also included all *Swasajist* members of the All-India Congress Committee and two members to be elected by each Provincial Organisation from among its members in such a manner as the said organisation might determine. It was to hold office for the term of the Legislative Assembly and the Provincial Council, constituted for the time being, provided that in case of a fresh General Election of the members of the All-India Congress Committee or of the Assembly or any Provincial Council or the Council of State the members of the General Council, who failed to secure re-election, would go out and those *Swarajists* who were newly elected would take their places.

The President of the Party, the General Secretary and the Treasurer were to be elected by the General Council, provided that the office-bearers so elected would hold office for the term of the General Council until a fresh election took place. This stipulation prolonging their life till a fresh election took place was necessary in the disturbed politics of the time when the repressive hand of the British Government was frequently applied leading to arrest leader and creating uncertainty in the matter even of conducting elections. Therefore, the General Council was also to continue to function notwithstanding any vacancy in it for the time being. It was to have very wide powers and it was specifically laid down that the jursdiction of the Council would extend to all matters affecting the party, its policy, programme and organisation with plenary and disciplinary power over all members of the Party and might frame rules for its own guidance and issue instructions for the guidance of *Swarajist* members of the Legislative Assembly and the Provincial Councils and for generally carrying out the policy and programme of the Party throughout India.

A meeting of the General Council could be held when summoned by the Executive Council at such time and place as it might determine. Let the Executive Council should be negligent or deliberately hostile to it in self-interest or otherwise, a check was imposed on its authority of calling the meeting of the General Council. It was, therefore, provided that a meeting of the General Council would also be held on the requisition of not less than forty members as soon as might be convenient after the said requisition was delivered to the General Secretary. Such a requisition would clearly specify the motion to be made on the subject to be discussed at such a meeting. The requisitionists also enjoyed the authority to require the meeting of the General Council to be held at a time and place named by them and the said meeting would be held at such a time and place, unless the Executive Committee was of the opinion that it should be held at different time or place. A counter-check in the matter of requisitioned meetings was, thus, provided and the machinery to resolve differences of opinion was somewhat cumbersome, for the constitution laid down that, in case of such difference of opinion, the question would be decided in accordance with the opinion of majority of Provincial Organisations.

It meant that in the event of a conflict arising between the requisitionists of the meeting and the Executive Councillors, the latter could occasion abnormal delay in conducting the meeting so that, by the time the General Council met, the need of the meeting might disappear altogether. But so long as the Swaraj Party was offering resistance to the Government, the possibility of a serious difference of opinion *inter se* was non-existent. The quorum for a meeting of the General Council was forty. The notice of meeting was valid if in the case of the General Council if (specifying time and place) was posted to each member not less than two weeks before the date of the meeting. In addition to all these provisions pertainting to the General Council, it was also provided that it would act as the subjects committee for general meetings of the Party.

The Executive Council consisted of the President and the General Secretary as its *ex-officio* members, four persons nominated by the President from among the members of the General Council and five members elected by the General Council from among its members. This very provision concerning the Executive Council recognised the principle of checks and balances and, *inter alia*, aimed at reconciling the principle of nomination with election and a happy blend of the two was effected. The Executive Council was to hold office for the term of the General Council, provided that any vacancy among the office-bearers or the elected members of the Executive Council would be filled up by the President pending due election of such office-bearers and elected members and, if the President vacated office for any cause whatsoever, the General Secretary would act in his place and perform his duties until another President was duly elected. The Executive Council enjoyed very extensive powers which could easily be classified as financial, general and special. It was to be the Chief Executive of the Swaraj Party with power to raise and disburse funds and authorise the office-bearers or anyone or more of them to draw upon the Party funds for Party purposes. It was to supervise the carrying out of all resolutions, rules and instructions issued by the General Council and take such steps as might be necessary to enforce the same.

When the General Council could not meet in time to dispose of any urgent matter requiring immediate decision, the Executive Committee could exercise all powers of the General Council and all resoultions passed and instructions issued by it were binding on all members and subordinate organisations until such resolutions and instructions were modified or superseded by the General Council, provided that all cases of the exercise of emergency powers under this provision were to be reported to the General Council without delay. In addition to this, the special powers of the Executive Council were further curtailed by giving enough discretion to the President who was empowered to decide whether any matter was sufficiently urgent to be dealt with in the aforesaid manner. In all cases of extreme urgency, he also enjoyed the power to issue such directions as he thought fit pending its disposal by the Executive Committee. In addition to all this Executive Council could be summoned by the President or the General Secretary as often as was necessary and the quorum for its meeting was five. The notice of its meeting was valid if (specifying time and place) it was either posted not less than one week or telegraphed not less than three days before the date of the meeting.

1. *The Constitution of the Swaraj Party, 1924.*

MEETING OF THE EXECUTIVE COMMITTEE OF THE SWARAJ PARTY AT NAGPUR[1]

Minutes of a meeting of the Executive Committee of the Swaraj Party held at Tulsibagh, Nagpur, on the 11th and 12th January 1925.

11th January 1925

Present:
- Pandit Motilal Nehru (in the chair)
- Syt. M.R. Jayakar.
- ,, N.C. Kelkar.
- ,, M.S. Aney.
- ,, E. Raghavendra Rao.

About 35 *Swarajist* members of the C.P. Council were present by invitation.

1. Read telegram from Mr. C.R. Das nominating Mr. M.S. Aney as a member of the Executive Committee in place of Maulana Hasarat Mohani (who) resigned. Mr. M.S. Aney accordingly took his seat in the Committee.

2. The situation in the C.P. was fully discussed with the *Swarajist* members of the Provincial Council and certain resolutions were verbally agreed upon.

3. Messrs Nehru and Jayakar were asked to draft the resolutions as agreed upon and the meeting was adjourned to the 12th January.

12th January 1925

Present as before with the exception of Mr. M.S. Aney. *Swarajist* members of the Council also present.

4. The following resolutions were unanimously passed :

(1) That the action of the Swaraj Party in the C.P. Council in throwing out the budget in the session of 1924 was both constitutional and justified by the circumstances then existing in the country arising from the stubbornly hostile attitude of the Government of India and the British Cabinet in refusing to make adequate response to the popular demand for Self-Government.

And that insofar as that attitude continues unchanged it would be the obvious duty of the Swaraj Party in the local Council even this year to oppose the Government by all legitimate means in its power.

(2) That on a careful consideration of the speech made by His Excellency the Governor of the C.P. to the Darbaris of the Nagpur Division on the 19th January 1925, this Committee records its emphatic opinion—

(a) That His Excellency the Governor has indulged in a gross perversion of the attitude and activity of the Swaraj Party in the local Council.

(b) That the unwillingness of the Swaraj Party to accept office in the Provincial Government arose not from any desire to avoid constructive responsibility which the holding of office involves but from a reasoned belief that the system of Government in which the Party was called upon to take an ineffectual part was inadequate disingenuous and to failure as it has now been clearly established to be.

(c) That in regard to the hope expressed in the following passage of His Excelleney's speech that is to say :

"We have exercised great patience before taking any retrograde step, in the hope that the members of the Legislative Council would abandon their policy of obstruction. We desire to give them a further opportunity of working the constitution in the manner in which it was primarily intended that it would be worked. A meeting of the Legislative Council will be summoned in March next, when the budget will be presented. That budget will be prepared on the assumption that the transferred departments will be carried on by Ministers, and will include provision for new and beneficent schemes of development in the transferred and nation building departments. The Legislative Council will thus be given an opportunity of ensuring that the transferred departments are administered on popular and representative lines. I earnestly hope that the Legislative Council will embrace this last opportunity of working the constitution."

This Committee declares that if it is the genuine desire of the Government to carry on the administration on popular and representative lines by bringing about suitable changes in the constitution the Swaraj Party will not be averse to shouldering responsibility provided such responsibility is real and genuine.

(3) That with a view to make the position of the Swaraj Party perfectly definite and clear this Committee appoints a Sub-Committee consisting of the gentlemen

named below to go into the whole question and report to this Committee by the 15th February after a careful investigation of the special circumstances of the C.P. and general situation in the country.

(a) The conditions upon which the lines of policy so far followed by *Swarajists* in the C.P. Council may in the circumstances be altered consistently with the general principles of the Party.

(b) The extent and particulars of such alteration.

(c) The manner in which such alterations should be given effect to.

1. Deshbandhu C.R. Das
2. Pandit Motilal Nehru
3. Syt. M.S. Aney, M.L.A.
4. ,, M.V. Abhyankar, M.L.A.
5. ,, E. Raghavendra Rao, M.L.C.
6. ,, S.B. Tambe, M.L.C.
7. ,, Ghanshyam Singh Gupta, M.L.C.
8. Dr. B.S. Moonje, M.L.C.
9. Dr. N.B. Khare, M.L.C.

Mr. M.V. Abhyankar will act as Secretary of the Committee and 5 members shall form the quorum.

Motilal Nehru
General Secretary

1. *A.I.C.C. Papers.*

IS A SWARAJIST A CONGRESSMAN ?[1]

I have before me a curious letter in which the writer says, a distinction is being made by Congressmen in Sind between *Swarajists* and Congress, and the former are obstructed by the latter. I should have hoped that such a thing would be impossible after the Belgaum Congress which recognizes the Swaraj Party as an integral party of the Congress and which suspends the non-co-operation programme. Every *Swarajist* who subscribes to the Congress creed and conforms to the new franchise is as much a Congressman as the one who is not a *Swarajist*, that is to say, who does not believe in Council-entry. Let it be also remembered that the Swaraj Party has itself altered its constitution to make it obligatory on every member of that party to accept the Congress franchise. There should therefore not only be no obstruction by one of the other but each should help the other wherever the help is not inconsistent with one's conscience. . . .

1. *Young India*, 5 February 1925.

CHAPTER 2

COUNCIL-ENTRY

'Whereas the working of the Legislative Councils during the first term has, besides proving a serious impediment to the redress of the Khilafat and Punjab wrongs and the speedy attainment of *Swaraj*, caused great misery and hardship to the people and whereas it is desirable for the furtherance of non-violent, non-cooperation to avoid a recurrence of the evil, it is resolved with reference to the report of the Civil Disobedience Enquiry Committee that this committee do recommend to the Indian National Congress that Non-cooperators should contest the ensuing elections on the issue of the redress of the Punjab and Khilafat wrongs and immediate *Swaraj* and make every endeavour to be returned in a majority. It further recommended that in view of the new Councils assembling early in January 1924 the Congress session of 1923 be held during the first instead of the last week of December and the matter be again brought up for such final mandate by the Congress as it may under the circumstances deem fit to issue.'

1. *The Leader*, 23 November 1922. Resolution moved at the AICC meeting, Calcutta, 21 November 1922.

DECISION AT THE GAYA CONGRESS 1922[1]

It is resolved with reference to the report of the Civil Disobedienee Enquiry Committee that non-cooperators should contest the elections on the issue of the redress of the Punjab and the Khilafat wrongs and immediate *Swaraj* in accordance with the principle of non-violent, non-cooperation and make every endeavour to be returned in a majority. It is further resolved that in in view of the new Councils assembling early in January 1924 the Congress session of 1923 be held during the first, instead of the last week of December and the matter be again brought up for such final mandate by the Congress as it may under the cricumstances deem fit to issue.

1. *The Leader*, January 3, 1923.

MOHAMED ALI'S COUNCIL-ENTRY PROGRAMME[1]

This was the main question to be dealt with at Delhi even though the Special Session was held in order to arrive at a settlement of the Council-entry questions. I have devoted so large a portion of my address to it not only because of its importance, but also because happily the other is no longer a live issue. At Delhi at my solicitation the Congress removed the ban and permitted those who had no religious or other conscientious objections against entering the Legislatures or voting at the then forthcoming elections to do so, and suspended the propaganda in favour of the boycott of Councils which had achieved such signal success three years previously. The elections have been held, and it can, in my humble judgment, serve no useful purpose to re-open a question which kept us occupied in much sterile activity for more than a year and sorely tried our tempers. I hold strong views on the subject of the triple boycott of Councils, law-courts and schools and colleges, and did not shrink from giving expression to them in strong, or, as my *Swarajist* friends complained, perhaps in too strong language in the course of the discussion in the Subjects Committee at Delhi. I hold the same views today and would gladly give expression to them again in equally language if I could be convinced that it was necessary in the interests of the Congress and the country. But of this I am as little convinced as of the soundness of the Swaraj Party views, and, on the contrary, I am fully convinced that no word should escape me which would estrange from the Indian National Congress a single Indian who has any national feeling. In fact, I desire to take a leaf out of the book of the late Lord Morley, whose recent death has removed from the world one who had shown both courage and recource in asking his fellow-countrymen also to do such justice to India as he himself was capable of doing. "Let us really be Moderates."

The Moderates and the Imperial Conference

I take no party view of the recent elections, and the franchise is far too restricted to read in them the judgment of the nation. But if one thing is more certain than another it is this, that India refuses to co-operate any longer with its foreign rulers or with those who co-operate with them. Many things have helped to disillusion those honest Nationalists who still held the opinions which many of us held as recently as four years go including Mahatma Gandhi. The discussions in the Imperial Council with regard to the status of Indians overseas have been so extensively advertised that it must be a very foolish fish that would still be deceived by the poor bait offered. South Africa where the Indian population still numbers 160,000 is adamant. The Imperial Government which cannot plead its impotence to interfere in the so-called "internal affaris" of the free Dominions when Kenya and other Crown Colonies are concerned, cannot hold out any hopes of reversing its palpably iniquitous decision, and has only consented to hear Indian's case once more. But the other Dominions are "sympathetic" since sympathy costs so little, and even here they are not quite optimistic where the Indians in British Columbia, of the "Komagata Maru" fame, still numbering some 1100 are concerned, though the rest of Canada, which has only a bare hundred, is disposed to be generous. I am prepared to give the fullest credit to the impassioned advocacy and highly emotional appeals of Dr. Sapru and his victory has been complete. But alas! He had aimed so low from the very outset that his victory leaves such of us as could not like him feel the heat of the encounter uncomfortably cold.

It reminds me of a friend who had left a lucrative enough post, and, making a new departure for an up-country Muslim graduate, had started business as a commission agent in Bombay. One day he met me with every show of exultation, and announced that he had closed the day with cent per cent profit in the transaction that had kept him so fully engaged.

But when I asked for more details I learnt that my friend had sold a few dozen Japanese paper several times and that the cent per cent profit would hardly pay the day's rent of his office. After long and weary years of strife the Imperial Council passed in 1921 a Resolution recognising the desirability of conceding equal status to Indian overseas, but *Hamlet* was acted with the part of the Prince of Denmark carefully cut out by General Smuts, the Imperial Dramotic Censor. And yet India was asked to rejoice over her cent-per-cent profits. However, as it happened the profits remained unrealised, and two whole years later the battle had to be fought again over the Imperial counter. There were doubts about the nature of the bargain. Such as whether payment was only desirable or necessary, and here the alim Boer General wanted to rescind the entire transactions. But luck has favoured the travelling agents of India again, even though there was much disagreement among them and one of the two has made a discovery not less remarkable than that of Columbus inasmuch as he has discovered in the Boer General a skilfuly disguised friend of India. We have secured cent-per-cent profit again, and a roving commission will go out to each of the partners in the other party's firm and by direct dealing ascertain what prospect there is of any payment. This, then, is the net gain. Dr. Sapru's travelling agents, no doubt some of the Great Unemployed, will have the great privilege of having direct dealings with the partners of John Bull Sons & Co. Lest I may be suspected of belittling the results achieved, I quote the conclusion laboriously reached by the *Times* at the fag end of its leading article on "India and the Commonwealth." "The spirit of sympathy", concludes the *Times*, "and of goodwill expressed by the representatives of the British Government and of the Dominions Overseas, the sincere appreciation of the share of India in the Commonwealth—these are hardly less important to her than the practical recognition of her right to negotiate for herself with the other partners." Yes, Dr. Sepru and his royal companion have indeed secured "the practical recognition of India's right to negotiate for herself with the other partners"; but when will the bargain be concluded and payment received, and what will be its amount?

Imperial Conferences will no doubt continue to succeed each other with great regularity, and the success of the Indian despondency at each will be advertised more and more extensively. In 1921, you know, they won something, which they said, was first-class citizenship. What are they going to win in 1923? They said : Implementation. When I was in jail, I was unable to know what this implementing was. This implementation is to try to bring into some sort of realisation the promise of 1921. But there is no chance of that yet. Perhaps we shall have to attend many more conferences for that. But it is too much for poor human nature to wait patiently and continue to hope while the Imperial stratification proceeds from the Archean or Pre-Cambrian stratum through all the Paleozoic, Mesozoic, Cainozoic strata or divisions in their true order of antiquity, and the long list of sub-divisions, such as the Eocene, Oligocene, Miocene, and Pliocene, before we come to the Pleistocene or Glacial and finally the Post-Glacial or Human period. No honest moderate would be so moderate as to be satisfied with this crawling pace of our Imperial progress and no honest Liberal could be no liberal as to give unlimited time to England to do us bare justice, especially when they recognise, as they must more and more clearly as each day passes, that a wrong system of education is fast paralysing us and robbing us of our youth and manhood.

Friends, if our fathers, and still more, if our grandfathers had realised, as we realise today, the condition of our slavery, we should have been free even within a month. They had the power to be free, but they did not know they were slaves. We, those few of us who are non-cooperators, recognise this that we are slaves. But we have not yet the power and the self-discipline that can achieve freedom.

When their disillusionment is just as complete as ours, the question still have to be answered : "How far are they prepared to go?" Non-co-operation has from the very outset required only the minimum sacrifice from the maximum number, though even the minimum in the post-Gandhi era far exceeds the maximum in most cases of the pre-Gandhi period. But Liberty can neither be won nor retained on the principle of Limited Liability. Dr. Sapru's advocacy may have been all that it could be, but what is there to follow it? Only "resolutions", petitions and protests, and at best a stilly *hartal*[2] to wind up with? If that is all, let us leave off this crazy pursuit of politics. Those whose ancestors have won freedom on the field of Runnymede or after the "crowning mercy" of Worcester or by razing the Bastile to the ground may play with politics. We have yet to win our *Magna Carta* and our Bill of Rights, and it is premature for us to treat politics as a Western pastime. For long we thought in terms of the Penal Code, and now we think we have advanced very far on the road of Reform if we think in terms of Dicey and of Erskine May. We forget that we have still to think in terms of History; I am prepared to admit that the Liberal gun is long enough. The length of the barrel, however, counts for little. It is the charge behind that matters. Once every Liberal or Moderate makes up his mind that patriotism must be to him as it was to every patriot in the world's history who won freedom for his country from a foreign yoke—a matter of unlimited liability, then—all is well. The Congress is his proper place even though he may at first proceed at a slow pace from force of habit. And it is just because I know that the leaders of the Swaraj Party are prepared to go to any length that I refused to be party to driving them out of the Congress. I will challenge any man to tell me that Deshabandhu Das and Pandit Motilal Nehru are not willing to make as many sacrifices as any of the best No-changers including myself. I hold that their principles and methods are wrong. I know that they will not co-operate with the Government, but will co-operate with us. Because, they still stick to his path and love the Mahatma as much as we do, even though we pride ourselves upon that fact that we are the only ones who love him.

Bardoli and the Swaraj Party

It is true many of the *Swarajists* have retained to this day something (not all, please don't take offence), of their laboriously acquired Western mentality and revel in parliamentary discussions and debates. Many more who have willingly relinquished all thought of the use of force even for purposes of self-defence want the spice of this wordy warfare to make the insipid fare prepared at Bardoli piquant enough for their jaded palates. Let me tell you an interesting anecdote, what a merchant told me in Calcutta. When the Mahatma and I, just before my incarceration, went to the Colootola street a merchant friend of mine came to us and told the Mahatma that he had ruined him. "Are you dealing in piece-goods?" asked the Mahatma. He replied "No, I was dealing in British scents, scented soaps, pickles and jams." These are things that we Indians are consuming in larger quantities than even the European themselves. The Mahatma remarked to him : "I never asked anybody to boycott these things, though I would be very pleased if they did." The merchant said : "All right. But do you think, Sir, that any man is going to spend Rs. 7 or Rs. 8 over a small scented bottle to put it over the dirty *khaddar* which you want all people to wear?" Another said to the Mahatma that he put on *khaddar* one day and began to eat *pullav*[3]. But he soon felt ashamed of himself and never liked to taste the dainty afterwards. That is the revolution that the *charkha* and *khaddar* have effected on human mentality. Many more still have not fully understood the almost unlimited possibilities of the *charkha* which must revolutionise Indian life while it frees us from economic slavery. Above all, the Swaraj Party is the embodiment of the depression experienced by all India when Mahatma Gandhi, after having brought the country to the very door of *Swaraj*, suddenly had to declare that it was unwise to force that door by resorting to mass Civil Disobedience, and that his plan of action must be changed from an offensive bold to the verge of audacity to a defensive which to those who did not know our generalissimo looked almost like a surrender. But, as I told the Mahatma when I was passing through Bardoli on my way from the Karachi gaol to the Bijapur gaol, his change of plan was out of his strength and not out of his weakness and had he been left free for some weeks longer he would have changed the face of the whole situation. He would have put new life into the Bardoli programme in spite of taking away all the aggressive features of the non-co-operation movement. He was, however, arrested and imprisoned before the people had recovered from the first depressing shock of Bardoli, and although there were hundreds and thousands, nay, hundreds of thousands and millions, who loved him and left the pang of separation, apparently there was none who could put a new life into the Bardoli programme and make full use of the weapons of offence which the Government had placed in Indian hands by treating the Mahatma as a felon. I have not sufficient data at my disposal to enable me to say whether the Mahatma was justified in listening to the despairing counsel of those who hastened to inform him that mass Civil Disobedience free from grave danger of violence was impossible after the Chauri-Chaura affair. But I do not think Civil Disobedience from such danger was possible immediately on the imprisonment of Mahatma Gandhi, and I would have deliberately disobeyed my chief and fought the Government with the weapon it had placed in my hand. No physician, as my brother says, is permitted to prescribe anything for himself when he is ailing, and after Mahatma Gandhi was "buried alive", it was enough if we paid due regard to his creed of Non-violence, without having to carry out his testamentary injunction with regard to the suspension of Civil Disobedience also. Had such a course been followed I doubt if the Swaraj Party would have come into being.

Future Relations of the Congress and the Swaraj Party

Be that as it may, the existence of the Swaraj Party cannot be ignored whatever view we may have formed about its genesis. I will not be free to speak to you. You may decide when the question arises. Its early beginnings were small enough, but the findings of the Civil Disobedience Committee, which occupied the time, attention and energies of some of our best workers, also succeeded in diverting the attention of all from the work of construction, and drove many of the most zealous among our younger men into the group which sought to enter the Councils. It is an idle speculation now, except to the extent that it helps us to formulate a plan for future work, to estimate how the chances of this group would have been effected if the programme of constructive work had been pushed forward and the younger men had been kept busy. On the other hand, some of my *Swarajist* friends also want me plunge into speculation and estimate how much greater would have been their success at the polls than it has already been if the Delhi self-denying ordinance suspending our boycott propaganda had been issued at Gaya. I might answer them by suggesting another line of speculation based on characteristic self-conceit, *viz.*, whether there would have been any Swaraj Party in existence at all if I had been permitted to be with them at Gaya to dissuade them from following a course of such doubtful wisdom. But all this is idle talk now. The Swaraj Party is there today, and even though it may be composed of some very dissimilar elements, it is undoubtedly strong enough in numbers today and has always been strong in the quality of its leadership. More than all else, it was permitted at Delhi to go to the polls on its own moral and religious responsibility. It has gone there, and has achieved great enough success considering what forces were arrayed against it, how short a time it had in which to organise its own forces and how greatly it was handicapped by the fact that some of its best members were disqualified from contesting the elections owing to their having undergone longer terms of imprisonment than those which do not affect eligibility. Then, too, electoral rolls were most defective, mainly perhaps because three years ago notably but the Liberals cared for such things and until very recently even those who ultimately joined the Swaraj Party had not finally made up their minds to contest the elections or to go to the polls. It is true a very large number of votes have been given not to the individuals that sought them, but to the Congress, and,—"tell it not in Gath; whisper it not in the streets of Ascalon"—to Mahatma Gandhi himself! There are friends of mine whose distress at such things is very deep, and who consider it a sacrilege thus to take the name of the Mahatma in vain. I greatly sympathise with them, and certainly cannot say that I approve of such political methods. But it must be remembered that those to whom the people offered such votes were immeasurably nearer to Mahatma Gandhi than those who are opposed to them. Moreover, there were some among them who were inclined to sneer in a superior sort of way at a Mahatma so little versed in the affairs of this world as to pin his faith to the silly *charkha* which even our womenfolk had discarded in these advanced days. I must here mention that my friend Deshabandhu Das has told me that he had never meant that the Mahatma had blundered. They thought that he was something of a bungler and a blunderer where finesse was required in dealing with the bureaucrats and with a Viceroy who was supposed to have out-Yankeed the Yankees during the War. Their election experiences must have convinced not a few of these men that the Mahatma's name is still one to conjure with, and that whatever skill is finessing they may possess, their strength even in the Councils lies in the backing which the people who loved and revered the Mahatma were prepared to give to them as his followers and associates. This experience is a valuable asset to them, and the good sense, restraint and dignity which their leaders have shown in the hour of their victory in full conformity with our expectations from them, make them a valuable element in the Congress. It is true we have no such expectations from their programme as they have themselves; but, while removing, where really necessary, any idea that may be lurking in the people's mind that it is not the constructive programme but the Councils that bring in *Swaraj*, we must give to the *Swarajists* a perfectly free hand, and add to that our heartiest good wishes that they may succeed. We suspended at Delhi the exercise of our right to carry on a propaganda of Council-boycott; but we surrendered no principle. Only the other day, while coming from Bombay, I had the privilege of being with my old friend, Mr. Vithalbhai Patel who wanted to talk to me about the Council-entry question. I told him that I was not prepared to listen to anything that he might say in the Council nor agree to what he proposed to do. I plainly told him that I was not prepared to adopt the Swaraj Party programme. Nor are we prepared to do that today, as we shall no doubt be doing if we agree to accept any responsibility of guiding the *Swarajists* in the Councils. This we cannot do. Obviously, the *Swarajists* will not be able to spare as much time for the constructive work as those of us who have not to attend to Council duties: but I have satisfied myself that their responsible leaders intend to assist us to the best of their power and ability, and in this way strengthen their own hand also in the Councils. If they have to leave the Councils at any later stage, the work that will have by then been done outside in their constituencies through our joint efforts will ensure this much, that no bureaucratic Cromwell could say of their exit that not a dog barked when they took their departure. And if as a result of their labours in the Councils, *swaraj* is achieved, I for one would certainly not refuse to accept it. If peace, harmony and goodwill were needed at Delhi to preserve the great reputation of the Congress, they are still needed today and needed in a greater measure today to enhance that reputation and to help us to carry out the constructive programme. Friends, I have reason to believe that the biggest shock of surprise that I ever gave to my enemies was, when I, the fighter, came out as a peace-maker at Delhi. They still very much wish to divide us on this Council-entry question. They want you to war.

The Constructive Programme

It was in the interest of this programme that I interested myself in the settlement at which we arrived at Delhi, for a whole year had been all but wasted by the major portion of the provinces in mutual recriminations, and if Mahatma Gandhi's release was to be obtained by appeals *ad misericordiam* but through our own efforts, it was necessary to resume the work to which the Mahatma had rightly pinned his faith. I did not at the time itself realise the full extent of the havoc wrought since his removal; but the replies that I have received to my enquiries about the details of the work done are sufficient indication that through one cause or another little work has been done. It is true there are provinces like Gujarat the work of which does credit to my friend Sriyut Vallabhbhai Patel and to the bond of devoted workers that Mahatma Gandhi left to work under him. Few provinces could show anything like as good a record of educational work, and but for Gujarat, the *Khadi* produced in other provinces would have remained unsold too long. Remember this. The great glory of the Mahatma, however, was not that he changed the face of Gujarat, I know that it is difficult to change, but that he has also changed the face of the whole of India. No province did he leave exactly where he had found it. Gujarat is even now preparing a surprise for those who think that no area could be fit for Civil Disobedience if the Mahatma's characteristically high standard of preparation was to be retained. We have to hear of Borsad yet. But the example of Gujarat has not proved infectious enough, and we cannot afford to wrap ourselves up in self-sufficiency. The speed of the fleet is the speed of the slowest boat, and there are alas; too many slow boats in our fleet, though, thank God, all are still sea-worth. I could not place before my No-Change friends sounder canons of criticism than "A No-Changer" writing in *Young India* from Delhi has done:

There is a limit (he writes) beyond which reason and agrument cannot go. Some conclusions are in the nature of action, and they go beyond the pale of pure rationality. Where reason fails to persuade, experience becomes the hard task-master. We realised that we had arrived at such a crisis. One year of argument and paralysis, mind, they are their own words, was tending to harden men in their Pharisaism and self-complacency. The testing time had come not only on the *Swarajists*, not only on the Centrists, not only on Mohamed Ali, but on us also, the No-Changers. (I hope I am also a No-Changer.) We have to submit ourselves to the discipline of tacts. Since the days of the Calcutta Special Congress, Gandhism had won all along the line : and we, Gandhites, have been in continuous peril of loose thinking and draggled effort. It is good for everybody to be beaten. If there is truth in us the very castigation of defeat will lead us to examine ourselves anew and find strength. If, on the contrary, Gandhism has become in our hands a plea for lethargy and refusal to re-think the implications of fast-developing reality, we are not the true followers of our Chief, we are not worthy to be the custodians of his message to the world. Reality that is the ultimate touchstone.

Yet, Reality is the ultimate touchstone, the truest and the surest that ever existed and *Swarajists* and No-Changers, and you and I, all us, friends shall be tested and measured by Reality. That is why I preach to you the gospel of work. It is not as easy a gospel to practise as it is easy to preach, and that is why we have more critics than workers. But work well done furnishes an exhilarating experience which the sterile pleasures of criticism even in victories can never equal. As the

Sanskrit poet, referring to the creative efforts of poetry, says: "Little does the barren women know of the pain and anguish of a mother's labours and less still of the indescribable joy of motherhood at the sight and touch of the new-born babe." Through labour alone shall a free India be re-born.

The Bardoli Programme to be Carried Out

You will no doubt ask me what should be our work; and my reply after the most careful consideration is that we cannot better the much-maligned Bardoli programme. If we continue to give up each item of work on finding difficulties and obstacles in our way, we shall never accomplish anything. Many people tell you Non-Co-operation has failed when they only mean that they, or we, both, have failed to rise to the height of our ideal. And yet, as I have already told you the steps proposed by the Mahatma are easy. Remember what the commonest of common soldiers is prepared to sacrifice when you feel that you must re-start your practice as a lawyer, or file your law-suit, or send your boy to a a better-equipped but co-operating school. . .

1. Presidential addres at Cocanada.
2. Strike.
3. Sweet-dish.

RESOLUTIONS AT COCANADA[1]

In a meeting of General Council of the Swaraj Party held at Cocanada on 30 December 1923 and attended by prominent leaders of the party like Motitlal Nehru, C.R. Das, E. Raghavendra Rao. Rafi Ahmad Kidwai, Y.M. Kale, Mohammad Shafee, T.A.K. Sherwani, V.J. Patel, M.R. Jayakar, R.K. Sidhwa, Govind Das, M.S. Aney, A. Rangaswamy Iyengar, M.K. Acharya, T.A. Chetiar, S. Satyamurti, V. Ramadas, N.S. Pranjpye, C.V. Naidu, Satyendra Chandra Mitra, Abdur Rashid Khan and S.A.K. Jeelani, the following resolutions were passed.

Resolution I

That the following resolution be provisionally adopted subject to consideration at a meeting of the elected members of the Legislatures to be held at Lucknow on the 9th January 1924.

Whereas the reforms introduced by the Government of India Act of 1919 have repeatedly been pronounced by the Indian National Congress and all shades of Indian openion to be inadequate and unsatisfactory;

And whereas the events of the last three years and the working of the Legislatures inaugurated under the said Act during that period have amply justified Indian public opinions and shown beyond all doubt that the said Legislaures are not only utterly powerless to protect true interests of the Indian people and secure to them the most elementary rights of citizenship but are entirely unable to defend them from national humiliation at home and abroad;

And whereas the Swarajya Party of the Indian National Congress, by its programme adopted in February 1923 at Allahabad laid down certain lines of political work including entry into the said Legislatures, having for its immediate objective the securing of the right to frame a constitution adopting such system and machinery as are most suited to the conditions of the country and the genius of the people;

And whreas in pursuance of the said programme the Swarajya Party has succeeded in winning a substantial number of seats in the said Legislatures at the Central Election just concluded;

This meeting of the General Council of the Swarajya Party held at Cocanada this 30th day of December 1923 expresses its full agreement with the resolutions passed at several sessions of the Indian National Congress to the effect that India is fully fit for *Swarajya* and that there is no justification for withholding it from the Indian people any longer.

This meeting therefore demands that steps be forthwith taken to establish full responsible Government of India and is of opinion that with a view to ensure a proper atmosphere for the said purpose, the following preliminary measures should be immediately adopted :

(i) That the elected members of the Council and the Provincial Legislatures do immediately present a demand to the Government, asking for :

(a) the immediate and unconditional release of Mahatma Gandhi,

(b) the immediate and unconditional release of all other political prisoners, convicted or under trial in India or detained in India or foreign countries on political grounds,

(c) the immediate suspension of the operation of all repressive laws and of the orders passed thereunder,

(d) the immediate summoning of a Round Table Conference of Representatives of whom 1/3 shall be elected members of the Indian Legislative Assembly, 1/3 by the Indian National Congress, and 1/3 shall be nominated by Government or elected by such other bodies or communities as Government may desire.

(ii) This conference will negotiate with the Government with a view to determine the principles of a constitution for India, which shall provide *inter alia* :

(a) for a Declaration of Right on the lines of the resolution adopted by the Indian National Congress at Amritsar in 1919,

(b) for the full control of the Legislatures, Central and Provincial in their respective jurisdictions over all matters of legislation, administration (Civil & Military) and finance and over the services, Imperial or Provincial.

(iii) The decisions of the said Conference, arrived at as a result of the said negotiations, will then be laid before a new Legislature, elected on a wider franchise than at present to be determined by the said Round Table Conference and the said Legislature shall have the power to frame a constitution for India on the basis of the said decisions and the constitution so framed shall then be presented to the British Parliament to be accepted and embodied in a Statute.

Resolution II

That the Executive Committee of the General Council of the Party with the addition of Messrs M.R. Jayakar, V. Ram Dass and Dr. Moonje be empowered to adopt such amendments of the provisional demand contained in Resolution No. I as are not inconsistent with the principles and policy of the Party. The siad Committee is requested to attend the meeting of the elected members of Legislatures at Lucknow on the 9th January 1924 and to carry out the amendments aforesaid without any further reference to the General Council.

Resolution III

That the demand as finally settled at Lucknow after being signed by as many elected members of the Legislative Assembly and the various Provincial Legislative Councils, both present at and absent from the Lucknow meeting as are willing to join in it be presented to the British Cabinet and the Government of India by registered post.

Resolution IV

That the Leader of the Party in the Assembly to be elected at the meeting in Lucknow will put a question at an early meeting of the Assembly asking the Government what steps it proposes to take on the said demand. The future action of the members of the Party in the Assembly and the Provincial Council will be regulated according to following instructions :

I. In the event of the Government accepting the principle of the demand or taking time to consider it, the Leader of the Party in consultation with such other members of the Assembly as may be elected for the purpose, shall put himself in communication with the Government and arrange all preliminaries in regard to the various items constituting the said demand, provided that no modification in any of the sub-clauses of clause I shall be accepted without the sanction of the Executive Committee of the General Council of the Party.

II. In the event of the Government refusing to entertain the said demand or after agreeing to do so offering terms which are not acceptable it shall be the duty of the members of the Party to resort to a policy of uniform, continuous and consistent obstruction with a view to make Government through the Council impossible. Such obstruction should be offered on all occasions when the members of the party by themselves or by joining any other party or group of members of the Assembly or a Provincial Council are in a position to defeat the Government. On other occasions the members of the party in the Assembly and the Legislative Councils of Bengal, United Provinces, Central Provinces and Bombay will take no part in the proceedings and the following instructions will be followed :

1. The members of the party will accept no office in the gift of the Government with or without salary or other remuneration.
2. No members of the party shall agree to be on the panel of chairmen nominated by the President or to serve on any select or standing committee or commission except when the formation of such Committee or Commission can be made impossible by a majority voting against every person proposed for election.
3. Members are at liberty to exercise the right of interpellation with a view to elicit information. It is expected that questions will be so framed as not to contain or imply a request for the redress of any grievance.
4. No member of the party shall move any resolution or introduce a bill. Provided that it shall always be open to members of the party to accept on such terms and conditions as are likely to promote the general policy of the party an invitation from any other party or group of members to join the latter for the purpose of defeating the Government on any non-official motion or measure opposed by the inviting party or group o f members. Such invitation shall only be accepted when the members of the party by themselves or with the inviting party or group of members form a majority of Legislature concerned.
5. When members of the party are voting on any motion, all members of the party shall be bound to go into the same lobby.
6. All demands for grants in the Legislative Assembly shall be wholly opposed, thus ensuring the total rejection of the budget.

7. All demands for grants in the Provincial Council shall also be opposed. Provided that it shall be open to members of the party with the previous sanction of the Executive Coommittee of the General Council to abstain from voting on any demand for a grant if there are special reasons in any Province for such abstention.
8. All questions of doubt or difficutly not covered by these instructions or regarding the interpretation of these instructions may, if necessary, be referred to the Executive Committee of the General Council and the decision of that Committee on such questions shall be final.
9. The members of the party in the Provincial Legislative Council will elect a leader and such other office bearers as may be necessary at an early date.
10. As very few members of the Party have been elected to the Legislative Councils of Madras and the Punjab and no combination with other parties or groups of members is likely to be effective, the *Swarajist* members of the said Legislative Council will not take part in the proceedings and attend from time to time only with the object of preventing vacancies.
11. These instructions do not apply to the Legislative Council of Bihar and Orissa as no members of the Party as such were set up for election to that Council. It is expected however that the nationalist members of the said council will frame their own rules on the lines of these instructions as far as possible.
12. It is recommended that all *Swarajists* and other Nationalist members shall attend the meetings of the Assembly and the Provincial Councils dressed in pure *khaddar*.

1. *A.I.C.C. Papers* : File 7, 1923.

STATEMENT ON COUNCIL-ENTRY BY C.R. DAS AND MOTILAL NEHRU[1]

We are obliged to Mahatma Gandhi for the trouble he has taken to discuss with us the various points involved in the question of Council-entry and are indebted to his courtesy for the opportunity we have had of seeing an advance copy of the statement he has issued to the press. The views expressed by him in the course of the conversations and those embodied in the press statement have all been considered by us with care and attention due to his great personality, but with all the reverence we entertain for him and his opinions we remain unconvinced by his reasoning.

Soundness of the Swarajist Position

We regret we have not been able to convince Mahatma Gandhi of the soundness of the *Swarajists* position regarding Council-entry. We fail to understand how such entry can be regarded as inconsistent with the doctrine of non-cooperation resolution of the Nagpur Congress. But if non-cooperation is more a matter of mental attitude than of the application of a living principle to the existing facts of our national life, we conceive it to be our duty to sacrifice even non-cooperation to serve the real interest of the country. In our view this includes self-reliance in all activities which makes healthy growth of the nation and resistance to the bureaucracy as it impedes our progress towards *Swaraj*. We are, threfore, anxious to end this fruitless verbal discussion making it clear, however, that Council-entry is, and can be, thoroughly consistent with the principle of non-cooperation as we understand that principle to be.

Obstruction not in Parliamentary Sense

We desire further to make it clear that we have not used in our programme the word obstruction in the technical sense of English parliamentary history. Obstruction in that sense is impossible in subordinates and limited legislative bodies such as the Legislative Assembly and the Provincial Legislatures under the Reforms Act undoubtedly are. Possibly another word should have been found to convey our meaning. We may state, however, that our position is really not so much of obstruction in the parliamentary sense as that of resistance to the obstruction placed in our path to *Swaraj* by the bureaucratic Government. It is this resistance which we meant to imply when we used the word obstruction. This was clearly indicated in the way we defined and described non-cooperation in the preamble to the constitution of the Swaraj Party. It is the spirit of such resistance which we desire to strengthen and it is the removal of such bureaucratic obstruction which we feel we must emphasise. This is the policy which we have hitherto followed in the legislative bodies and it is this policy which must in future be more effectively directed to the varying needs and problems of our national life.

Here again we are anxious to end all verbal discussion as to whether this can be aptly described as a policy of uniform continuous and consistent obstruction. We are content to detail our policy and then leave it to our friends to give it a more appropriate name should they so desire.

Future Programme

In the light of this principle and policy we would here state [our] future programme of action within and outside the legislative bodies.

Within the legislative bodies we must continue :

(1) To throw out budgets unless and until the system of government is altered in recognition of our rights or as a matter of settlement between parliament and the people of this country. In justification of this step all that we need point out are a few salient facts connected with the budget in the central government which are more or less true of provincial budgets also. Out of a total of Rs. 131/- crores (excluding railways) only Rs. 26 crores are votable. Further, out of the non-votable amount as much as Rs. 67 crores *i.e.* more than half the amount of the budget, are for military expenditure. It is thus clear that the people of this country have a right to vote only on less than 1/7 of the total amount of the budget and even the exercise of this limited right is subject to the power of restoration in the Governor-General. It is, therefore, clear that the people neither any voice in the framing of the budget nor any control over those who frame it. They have no power either over the raising of revenue or its expenditure. On what principle then, may we ask, is it our duty to pass such a budget and take the responsibility of being a party to it. We have no doubt of the support of many self-respecting men in the country in holding, as we do, that it is our clear

duty to throw out such budgets in all legislative bodies unless and until this vicious system is changed.

(2) To throw out all proposals for legislative enactments by which the bureaucracy proposes to consolidate its power. It is conceivable that some good may identically result from a few of such measures, but, we are clearly of opinion that in the larger interests of the country it is better to temporarily sacrifice such little benefits rather than add an iota to the powers of the bureaucracy which are already irresistible.

(3) To introduce all resolutions, measures and Bills which are necessary for the health growth of our national life and the consequent displacement of the bureaucracy. We gratefully accept the suggestion made by Mahatma Gandhi in his statement and we think that the resolutions mentioned by him in support of the constructive programme of the Congress should certainly be accepted by the Swaraj Party. The principle of self-reliance to the bureaucratic obstruction upon which we have hitherto acted calls for their adoption and if the constructive work of the Congress comes within the principles of non-cooperation no less do these resolutions although they represent the constructive activity within the legislative bodies.

(4) To follow a definite economic policy based on the same principle to prevent the drain of public wealth from India by checking all activities leading to exploitation.

(5) To make this policy effective we should take and occupy every place which is open to the members of the central and provincial legislatures by election. In our opinion we should not only fill elective posts but serve on every committee when it is possible. We invite the attention of the members of our party to this important question and we call upon them to decide this matter as soon as possible.

(6) Our policy outside the legislative bodies should be as follows :

In the first place we should give our whole-hearted support to the constructive programme of Mahatma Gandhi and work that programme unitedly through the Congress organisation. We are decidedly of opinion that our Council work must necessarily lose much of its strength without the backing of the outside constructive work, for it is not inside and outside the legislatures that we must look for that sanction without which the effective carrying out of our Council policy is impossible. Indeed, in the matter of the constructive work the mutual support of inside and outside activity must, in our opinion, give strength to the very sanction upon which we rely. In this connection we unhesitatingly accept the suggestion of Mahatma Gandhi regarding civil disobedience. We can assure him that the moment we find that it is impossible to meet the selfish obstinacy of the bureaucracy without civil disobedience we will retire from the legislative bodies and help him to prepare the country for such civil disobedience if by that time the country has not already become prepared and we will then unreservedly place ourselves under his guidance and work through the Congress organisation under his banner in order that we may unitedly work out a systematic programme of civil disobedience.

In the second place we must supplement the work of the Congress by helping labour and peasant organisations throughout the county. The problem of labour is always a difficult problem to solve in every country but in India the difficulties are greater. On the one hand we must find out a way of organisation by which we can prevent exploitation of labour by capitalists or by landlords but on the other hand we must be on our guard to see that these very organisations may not themselves be the source of oppression by nursing extravagant and unreasonable demands. Labour undoubtedly requires protection, but so [do] industrial enterprises. Our organisation must protect both from exploitation and the Trade Union Congress must be so organised as to be able to serve this useful purpose. We hold that in the long run the real interests of both and the country at large are identical.

We feel happy that we have had this opportunity of putting our views before the country side by side with Mahatma Gandhi's opinion for we feel certain that the perusal will make it obvious that notwithstanding some differences of view there is an abiding and fundamental unity amongst both parties of the Indian National Congress. Both parties feel the necessity of working the constructive programme whether within or outside the legislative bodies. In this direction, we feel confident, lies the germ of fruitful alliance between Mahatma Gandhi and the Swaraj Party. Our joint effort in the same or different directions will furnish a fitting answer to the bureaucracy unwilling to recognise the rights and liberty of the Indian people and we emphatically assert that in our determination to work with the same object in the same or different spheres is expressed the determination of the Indian Nation the struggle for *Swaraj* to a successful issue.

1. *A.I.C.C. Papers.*

PROGRAMME OF THE SWARAJISTS : WRECKING CONSTITUTIONAL REFORMS

The implementation of the attainable principles of the Swaraj Party required the destruction of the existing machinery devised by the British Government to perpetuate the system of bureaucracy in this country. For bringing about its demise, the evolution of a sound programme was necessary. The Party, thererore, resolved to adopt a programme consisting of two parts—activities inside and outside the Central and Provincial legislative bodies. It was decided that inside the legislative bodies, the Party, whenever possible, would :

1. (a) refuse supplies and throw out budgets unless and until the system of Government was altered in recognition of our rights, or as a matter of settlement between Parliament and the people of India;

(b) throw out all proposals for legislative enactments by which the white bureaucracy proposed to consolidate its powers;

(c) move resolutions and introduce and support measures and bills necessary for the healthy growth of national life and the consequent displacement of the bureaucracy;

(d) help the constructive programme of the Indian National Congress;

(e) follow a definite economic policy to prevent the drain of public wealth from India by checking all activities leading to exploitation and to advance national, economic, industrial and commercial interests of the country; and

(f) protect the rights of labour—agricultural and industrial—and adjust the relations between landlords and tenants, capitalists and workmen.

2. No member of the Party would accept office as a gift of the Government with or without salary or other remuneration.

3. With a view to making the work of the Party effective, it was open to its members in the Central Assembly and the various Provincial Councils to seek election to every post and place in the Assembly or the Councils and on their committee which might be open to them by election. Provided that no member would seek election in contravention of any rules framed by the members of the party in the Assembly or any of the Councils, as the case might be.

4. In all other matters the members of the Party in the Assembly and the Councils were to be guided by their own rules which would be submitted for the sanction of the Executive Council as soon, after they are framed, as convenient. Provided that any of the said rules disapproved by the Executive Council would cease to have effect from the date when such disapproval was communicated to the members concerned.

Outside the Councils, the Party would work for :

1. Inter-communal unity with a view to bringing about a complete understanding between Hindus, Mohammedans, Sikhs, Parsees, Jews, Indian Christians (including domiciled Anglo-Indians) and all other communities living in India; more specially the removal of the disputes and differences between Hindus and Mohammedans and Brahmins and Non-Brahmins.

2. Removal of untouchability and raising the status of the so-called depressed classes.

3. Village organisation.

4. Organisation of labour in the country, industrial as well as agricultural, including ryots and peasants, with a view to protecting and promoting its interests and enabling it to take its proper place in the struggle for *Swaraj*.

5. Acquisition of the economic control of the country including development of commerce and industry.

6. Acquisition of the control of nationalists over local and municipal affairs by contesting elections to local and municipal boards in several Provinces.

7. Carrying out of constructive programme of the Congress in such a manner as it thought necessary in relation to

Swadeshi, Khaddar, temperance, national education and arbitration courts.

8. The boycott of selected British goods manufactured outside India on the advice of a Committee with a view to using it as a political weapon in the pursuit of *Swaraj.*

9. The formation of a federation of Asiatic countries and nationalities with a view to securing the solidarity of Asiatic nations, including Egypt, to promote Asiatic culture and mutual help in the matter of trade and commerce.

10. Organisation of the agencies of foreign propaganda for Indian affairs with special reference to the dissemination of accurate information and the securing of the sympathy and support of foreign countries in the country's struggle for *Swaraj.*

OPPOSITION OF SWARAJ PARTY[1]

After the elections, the Governor of C.P., Frank Sly was faced with a difficult situation as no member of the Swaraj Party showed his willingness to accept office in consideration of the manifesto of his organization. The Governor sent for the leader, B.S. Moonje and offered him one of the two ministerships. The leader of the Swaraj Party refused to accept any office in the government. At this the Governor adopted an unconstitutional method and appointed S. M. Chitnavis and Syed Hifazat Ali as ministers. These appointments were, however, met with critical remarks by some members of the council.

In the Central Provinces the opposition of the members of the Swaraj Party attained its intensity at numerous occasions. Early in the session when a vote of no-confidence in the ministry was adopted by the Council by a majority, the entire budget was thrown out. The emergency thus created implied the Governor to authorize expenditure on the reserved subjects and on the transferred subjects at the minimum required for the carrying on of each department. But as he had no authority to raise such funds, he had to transfer the administration of the department from the ministers to the Executive Councillors.

The resolution for the dismissal of ministers was moved by no less a prominent leader like E. Raghavendra Rao. Other members like Ravi Shanker Shukla, B.S. Moonje, B.G. Khaparde, D.K. Kane and M.K. Golwalkar levelled trenchant criticism against this measure of the government. The resolution was carried by 44 members voting in favour and 24 against it.

The resolution for the abolition of the posts of Divisional Commissioners was moved, put to vote and carried. Besides N.B. Khare moved a resolution to the fact that articles manufactured in any part of the British empire should not be used in government departments of the Central Provinces. In support of his argument, he gave examples of Dyer and Dyarchy. "...And Dyer was not only given a pension for his crime, but long after the event money was quietly collected and a purse was presented to him privately by the commercial community of his race. After all this, how can anyone feel like buying goods from the Empire?" G.V. Deshmukh and others supported this resolution with their arguments and votes, and 40 members voted for it and 22 against it.

The Swarajists assailed the policy of education followed by the C.P. Government. A prominent member of the Party, Chandra Gopal Misra opined, "One item alone will suffice to expose the policy of this Department . . . A provision of Rs. 4,800 has been made for European Lady Lecturer in Kindergarten. Could an Indian . . . not qualify himself got the post after a few months training either in India or in England ?" Another member, Y.M. Kale criticised the government for showing lack of interest in technical and industrial education in the province. S.B. Tambe stated, "how government was wasting huge amounts of money for construction of government buildings."

As the Swarajists commanded a sizeable majority in the council, it became an easy task for them to reject demands for grants. Practically, all demands for grants were systematically negatived. In fact, "...the Government fared better in the matter of demands for grant it did in 1924. For example, Y.M. Kale's motion for the reduction of Rs. 24,794 under outlay on improvement under the head Land Revenue (Reserved) and B.G. Khaparde's proposal for reduction of Rs.

76,321 for Survey and Settlements under the head Land Revenue (Reserved) could not succeed in the House."

"In spite of a perceptible change in the attitude of the Swarajists, overtaking them in the course of time, the year 1925 also did not turn out to be wholly favourable to the rulers and no Bill promoted by the Government could be proceeded with. The only exception was the President's Salary Bill which was passed into law. In the Third Legislative Council, the position of the Government was, however, strengthened due to important Swarajist defections and the Government was fairly more successful in the Third than in the Second Council."

1. C. P. Council Proceedings, Vol. I, Jan. 1924, pp. 4, 71, 76 ff.

VICEROY'S ANXIETY FOR REFORMS[1]

On 30 January 1924, the Second Assembly under the Reform Act met for the swearing-in of the members. Next day, the Viceroy, Lord Reading opined about various issues of national and international importance. He stated, '...We have now entered a second stage by the election of the new Assembly... Differences have occurred, but I am convinced that these have left no bitterness in their work .. I am well-aware that words are often used in the heat of political conflict which perhaps convey more than if really intended... I cannot foretell the future; I do not know what it holds; but I cannot conceal from you that the politcal situation in India in its constitutional aspects causes me some anxiety for the future of the Reforms. I should be doing a disservice to India if not I failed at this moment to give expression to my views formed upon a hasty or cursory survey; but as the result of as profound study and reflection as I can bring to bear upon a subject of supreme interest to me ... It may appear easy to impair and even to destroy and recreate. Doubtless, destruction is always easier than construction. Violent revolutions have destroyed the institutions of nations. Neglect and apathy in other cases have induced their decay and extinction; but I beg you to remember that influences of this nature have been set in motion, restoration and recreation become infinity more difficult and sometimes impossible. These influences make no appeal to the British people and the British Parliament would emphatically repudiate and reject them..."[2]

1. The complete list of members of the Swaraj Party in the Central Assembly has been given in H.N. Mitra, *The Indian Quarterly Register*, Vol. I, January-March 1924, Calcutta, n d., p. 114 (b) Besides, there is a list of the Independents and others whose consent the *Swarajists* were able to obtain to the proposed programme. *Ibid.*
2. *Ibid*., p. 115 ff.

DEMANDS FOR GRANTS[1]

Besides the demands for grants put forward by the government was greatly discussed and opposed by the Swarajists. At this point of time, the government adopted the policy of caution and in a mild tone tried to gear its machinery towards persuasion, of course with some arguments of fundamental nature. In his inaugural speech during the first session of the second Legislative Assembly, the Viceroy stated thus : "I still wonder—as I wondered in the October—what purpose beneficial to India will be served by any course destined to destroy the continuity of progress in the Reform movement . . . The British Parliament has already set up the machinery now in operation for some time past."

The Viceroy also warned the Swarajists to desist from measures which might prompt the government to resort to a course of action not suited to its 'temper and inclination'. He observed, "These influences make no appeal to the British people and the British Parliament would emphatically repudiate and reject them."[2] But this kind of advice had no effect on the Swarajists who, as a matter of policy, were to act in accordance with the manifesto of their party.

1. *Debates, The Legislative Assembly*, 1924, Vol. IV, Part I, p. 13.
2. *Ibid.*

BUDGET-DEBATE[1]

In the Bombay Council when the budget of 1924-25 was discussed, a prominent member of the Swaraj Party, J.K. Mehta, remarked that his party could cooperate with the government on the basis of reciprocity. Other members who brought out their indictment against the government, were M.R. Jayakar, G.R. Pradhan, K.F. Nariman, Haji Abdul Haroon, V.R. Kothari, S.S. Devi, L.B. Bhoptkar, J.K. Swaminarayan and H.B. Shivdasani. In fact, M.R. Jayakar urged upon the government to make it a human budget so that an average toiling person in the fields might get exemption from taxation on income from land below the minimum of Rs. 2,000 per annum. In the budget debate of the next year, *i.e.* 1925-26 the critical remarks were advanced by D.P. Desai, G.R. Pradhan, Lalji Narainji, M.R Jayakar and L.B. Bhoptkar. Lalji Narainji summed up the government point of view in a sarcastic way : "Give up the money that we want according to our own ideas and help us in taxing this Presidency as we like, and trust us and we will do everything for the nation-building departments and for all the need of the Presidency."

The Swarajists' walk out from the provincial council on party's directive or on other issues was a glaring phenomenon during 1926-27. In the Bombay Legislative Council such a step was initiated by its leader Bhoptkar who gave a call for walk out on 10 March 1926. The idea of participation in the debates on the Department, the Reclamation Scheme and the Taxation Bill was given up. Before the walk out, the leader of the party explained thus : "In view of the fact that the Government of India have given no response to the demand for further advance towards Swaraj, made by the nation, through its elected representatives in the Legislative Assembly, the General Council of the All India Swarajya Party, with the approval and concurrence of the All India Congress Committee, has issued a mandate, to the Swarajist members of the legislatures in the country, to withdraw from them. We, as members of that august body, are bound to obey the same. Though some of us may have our differences of opinion with regard to the actual working of the policy and programme of the Swaraj Party, we feel that this is neither the time nor the occasion to evince or to act upon such differences.

'I wish to say on behalf of my Swarajist colleagues here, that notwithstanding our feelings of utter dissatisfaction and condemnation of the most callous indifference exhibited by the powers that be towards the National Demand for further advance upon the present system of Government my experience tell me that the policy pursued by this Government also has been most retrograde in character and on lines calculated to negative whatever little good the Reforms Act is capable of yielding.

'I therefore hereby call upon all my Swarajist colleagues in this Council to walk out of this House as desired by the General Council of the All India Swaraj Party and the All India Congress Committee of the Indian National Congress.'

1. *Debates, Bombay Legislative Coucil*, Vol. XI, February-March 1924, pp. 103 ff.

GANDHI'S VIEWS ON COUNCIL-ENTRY[1]

After week-long discussions, from 29 March to 5 April 1924 in Bombay with Motilal Nehru, Lajpat Rai and other Swarajist leaders, Gandhi formulated his stand on the question. And in a document entitled 'Thoughts On Council-Entry', he stated thus :[2] ". . . .I retain the opinion that Council-entry" is inconsistent with non-cooperation. There is an honest and fundamental difference between the Swarajists and myself. I have failed to convince them that to be out of the Legislative bodies is, to say the least, far more advantageous to the country than to be in them. But I recognize that so long as they think otherwise, their place is undoubtedly in the Coucils. It is the best for us all. If their work prospers and the country benefits, such an ocular demonstration cannot but convince honest sceptics like me of our error and I know the *Swarajists* to be patriotic enough to retrace their steps when experience disillusioned them. I would therefore be no party to putting any obstacle in their way. I cannot actively help in a project in which I do not believe.

I differ too as to the method of work in the Councils. I do not believe in obstruction within the Councils. I should only enter a Legislative body, if I found I could at all use it to advantage. If, therefore, I entered the Councils I should endeavour to give strength to the constructive programme of the Congress. I should, therefore, move resolutions requiring the Central and the Provincial Governments : (1) to make all their cloth purchase in hand-spun and hand-woven *kaddar* (2) to impose a prohibitive duty on foreign cloth, (3) abolish the drink and drug reserve and correspondingly reduce the army expenditure. If the government refuse to enforce resolutions carried in the Legislatures, I should invite them to dissolve them and take the vote of the electors on the specific points. If the Government will not dissolve, I should resign and prepare the country for civil disobedience. When that stage is reached, the Swarajists willl find me ready to work with and under them. My test of fitness for civil disobedience remains the same as before."

1. *C.W.M.G.* Vol. XXIII, pp. 413-14.

DICUSSION BETWEEN GANDHI, MOTILAL NEHRU AND C. R. DAS[1]

Bombay
22 May 1924

After having discussed with the Swarajist friends the vexed question of entry into the Legislative Assembly and the Councils by the Congressmen, I am sorry to have to say that I have not been able to see eye to eye with the *Swarajists.* I assure the public that there has been no lack of willingness or effort on my part to accept the Swarajist position. My task would be much simpler if I could identify myself with it. It can be no pleasure to me to oppose even in thought the most valued and respected leaders, some of whom have made great sacrifices in the cause of the country and who yield to no one in their love of freedom of the motherland, but, in spite of my effort and willingness I have failed to be convinced by their argument.

Nor is the difference between them and myself one of mere detail. There is an honest and fundamental difference. I retain the opinion that Council-entry is inconsistent with non-co-operation as I conceive it. Nor is this difference a mere matter of interpretation of the word "non-co-operation", but relates to the essential mental attitude resulting in different treatment of vital problems. It is with reference to such mental attitude that the success or the failure of the triple boycott is to be judged and not merely by a reference to the actual results attained. It is from that point of view that I say that to be out of the legislative bodies is far more advantageous to the country than to be in them.

I have, however, failed to convince my Swarajist friends. But I recognize that, so long as they think otherwise, their place is undoubtedy in the Councils. It is the best for us all. It was hardly to be expected that the Swarajists could be convinced by the arguments I advanced in the course of the conversations. They are many of them amongst the ablest, most experienced and honest patriots. They have not entered the legislative bodies without full deliberation and they must not be expected to retire from the position until experience has convinced them of the futility of their methods.

The question, therefore, before the country is not an examination and determination of the merits of the Swarajist view and mine. The question is: what is to be done now regarding Council-entry as a settled fact? Are the Non-cooperators to keep up their hostility against the Swarajists' method or are they to remain neutral and even help, whenever it is possible or consistent with their principles ?

The Delhi and Cocanada resolutions have permitted those Congressmen who have no conscientious scruples to enter the Councils and the Assembly, if they want to do so. In my opinion, the Swarajists are therefore justified in entering the legislative bodies and expecting perfect neutrality on the part of the No-changers". They are also justified in resorting to obstruction, because such was their policy and the Congress laid down no conditions as to their entry. If the work of the Swarajists prospers and the country benefits, such an ocular demonstration cannot but convince honest sceptics like me of our error, and I know the Swarajists to be patriotic enough to retrace their steps when experience has disillusioned them.

I would, therefore, be no party to putting any obstacles in their way or so carrying on any propaganda against the Swarajists' entry into the Legislatures, though I cannot actively help them in a project in which I do not believe. The purpose of the Delhi and Cocanada resolutions was to allow the Swarajists a chance of trying the method of Council-entry and that purpose can be served only if the "No-changers", with scrupulous honesty, allow the Swarajists full liberty to pursue their programme in the Councils, unfettered by any obstruction from them.

With regard to the method of work in the Councils, I will say that I would enter a legislative body if only I found that I could at all use it to advantage. If, therefore, I enter the Councils, I should, without following a general policy of obstruction, endeavour to give strength to the Constructive programme of the Congress. I should, therefore, move resolutions requiring the Central or the Provincial Government, as the case may be,

(1) to make all their cloth purchases in hand-spun and hand-woven *khaddar*;

(2) to impose a prohibitive duty on foreign cloth;

(3) to abolish the drink and drug revenue; and

(4) at least correspondingly reduce the army expenditure.

If the Government refuses to enforce such resolutions when carried in the Legislature, I should invite them to dissolve them and take the vote of the electors on the specific points. If the Government would not dissolve, I should resign my seat and prepare the country for civil disobedience. When that stage is reached, the Swarajists will find me ready to work with and under them.

My test of fitness for civil disobedience remains the same as before. During the state of probation, I should advise the "No-changers" not to worry about what the *Swarajists* are doing or saying and to prove their own faith by prosecuting the Constructive Programme with undivided energy and concentration. The *khaddar* and the national schools are enough to occupy every available worker who believes in quiet, honest and undemonstrative work. The Hindu-Muslim problem too will tax the best energy and faith of the workers. The "No-changers" can justify their application through the Constructive Programme even as the "Pro-Changers" must justify their entry by results.

The "No-changers" are in one respect in an advantageous position; for they can secure the co-operation of the "Pro-changers". The latter have declared their faith in the Constructive

Programme, but their contention is that by itself, the Constructive Programme cannot enable the country to reach the goal. In the prosecution, however, of the Constructive Programme outside the Legislatures, all "No-changers", "Pro-changers" and others can, if they will, work in unison through their respective organizations, if necessary.

The statement is incomplete without an examination of the working of the Congress organization. I hold drastic expression for a future, though early, occasion.

1. *The Hindu*, 23 May, 1924.

C.R. DAS AND MOTILAL NEHRU ON COUNCIL-ENTRY[1]

22 May 1924

We are obliged to Mahatma Gandhi for the trouble he has taken to discuss with us the various points in the question of Council-entry and are indebted to his courtesy for the opportunity we have had of seeing an advance copy of the statement he has issued to the Press. The views expressed by him in the course of conversation and those embodied in the Press statement have all been considered by us with care and attention due to his great personality, but with all the reverence we entertain for him and his opinions, we remain unconvinced by his reasoning.

We regret we have not been able to convince Mahatma Gandhi of the soundness of the Swarajists position regarding Council-entry. We fail to understand how such entry can be regarded as inconsistent with the doctrine of the Non-co-operation resolution of the Nagpur Congress.

But if non-co-operation is more a matter of mental attitude than of the application of a living principle to the existing facts of our national life with special reference to the varying attitudes of the bureaucratic Government which rules that life, we conceive it to be our duty to sacrifice even non-co-operation to serve the real interests of the country.

In our view this principle includes self-reliance in all activities which make for the healthy growth of the nation and resistance to the bureaucracy as it impedes our progress towards Swaraj. We are, however, anxious to end this fruitless verbal discussion making it clear, however, that Council-entry is and can be thoroughly consistent with the principle of non-cooperation as we understand that principle to be.

We desire further to make it clear that we have not used in our programme the word 'obstruction' in the technical sense of English Parliamentary history. Obsruction in that sense is impossible in subordinate and limited Legislative bodies, such as the Legislative Assembly and Provincial Legislatures under the Reforms Act undoubtedly are. Possibly another word should have been found to convey our meaning. We may state, however, that our position is really not so much of obstruction in the Parliamentary sense as that of resistance to the obstruction placed in our path to Swaraj by the bureaucratic Government. It is this resistance which we meant to imply when we used the word obstruction. This was clearly indicated in the way we defined and described non-co-operation in the preamble to the constitution of the Swaraj Party. It is the removal of such bureaucratic obstruction which we feel we must emphasize. This is the policy which we have hitherto followed in the Legislative bodies and it is this policy which must in future be more and more effectively directed to the varying needs and problems of our national life.

Here again we are anxious to end all verbal discussion as to whether this can be aptly described as a policy of "unifrom, continuous and consistent". We are content to detail our policy and then leave it to our friends to give it a more appropriate name, should they so desire.

In the light of this principle and policy, we would here state our future programme of action within and outside the Legislative bodies.

Within the Legislative bodies we must continue :

(1) To throw out budgets unless and until the system of Government is altered in recognition of our rights or as a matter of settlement between the Parliament and the people of this country. In justification of this step, all that we need point out are a few salient facts connected with the budget in the Central Government, which are more or less true of Provincial budgets also. Out of a total of 131 crores (excluding Railways), only 16 crores are votable. Further, out of the non-votable amount, as much as 67 crores, *i.e.*, more than half the amount of budget, is for military expenditure. It is thus clear

that the people of this country have a right to vote only on less than one-eighth of the total amount of the budget, and even the exercise of this limited right is subject to the power of the restoration in the Governor-General. It is, therefore, clear that the people have neither any voice in the framing of the budget nor any control over those who frame it. They have no power either over the raising of the revenue or its expenditure. On what principle then, nay we ask, is it our duty to pass such a budget and take the responsibility of being a party to it ? We have no doubt the support of many self-respecting men in the country in holding, as we do, that it is our clear duty to throw out such budget in all Legislative bodies, unless and until this vicious system is changed.

(2) To throw out all proposals for legislative enactments by which the bureaucracy proposes to consolidate its power. It is conceivable that some good may incidentally result from a few of such measures but we are clearly of opinion that in the larger interests of the country, it is better to temporarily sacrifice such little benefits rather than add an iota to the powers of the bureaucracy which are already irresistible.

(3) To introduce all resolutions, measures and bills which are necessary for the healthy growth of our national life and the consequent displacement of the bureaucracy. We heartily accept the suggestion made by Mahatma Gandhi in his statement and we think that the resolutions mentioned by him in support of the constructive programme of Congress should certainly be accepted by the Swaraj Party. The principle of self-reliance and resistance to the bureaucratic obstruction, upon which we have hitherto acted, calls for their adoption, and if the constructive work of the Congress comes within principle of non-co-operation, no less do these resolutions although they represent constructive activity within the Legislative bodies.

(4) To follow a definite economic policy based on the same principle to prevent the drain of public wealth from India by checking all activities leading to exploitation.

To make this policy effective we should take and occupy every place which is open to the members of the Central and Provincial Legislatures by election. In our opinion, we should not only fill elective posts, but serve on every committee when it is possible to invite the attention of the members of our party to this important question and we call upon them to decide this matter as soon as possible.

Our policy outside the Legislative bodies should be as follows :

In the first place, we should give our whole-hearted support to the constructive programme of Mahatma Gandhi and work that programme unitedly through the Congress organizations. We are decidedly of opinion that our Council work must necessarily lose much of its strength without the backing of the outside constructive work; for it is not inside but outside the legislatures that we must look for the sanction without which the effective carrying out of our Council policy is impossible. Indeed, in the matter of constructive work, the mutual support of both inside and outside activity must, in our opinion, give strength to the very sanction upon which we rely. In this connection, we unhesitatingly accept the suggestion of Mahatma Gandhi regarding civil disobedience. We can assure him that the moment we find that it is impossible to meet the selfish obstinacy of the bureaucracy without civil disobedience, we will retire from the Legislative bodies and help him to prepare the country for such civil disobedience, if by that time the country has not already become prepared, and we will then universally place ourselves under his guidance and work through the Congress organization under his banner in order that we may unitedly work on a substantial programme of civil disobedience.

In the second place, we must supplement the work of the Congress by helping labour and peasant organizations throghout the country. The problem of labour is always a difficult problem to solve in every country, but in India the difficulties are greater. On the one hand we must find out a way of orgnization by which we can prevent exploitation of labour by capitalists or by landlords, but on the other hand we must be on our guard to see that those very organization may not themselves be the source of oppression by nursing extravagant and unreasonable demands. Labour undoubtedly requires protection, but so do industrial enterprises. Our organization must protect both from exploitation and the Trade Union Congress must be so organized as to be able to serve this useful purpose. We hold that in the long run the real interests of both and the country at large are identical.

We feel happy that we have had this opportunity of putting our views before the country side by side with Mahatma Gandhi's opinion, for we feel certain that the perusal will make it obvious that, notwithstanding some differences of view, there is an abiding and fundamental unity amongst both parties of the Indian National Congress. Both parties feel the necessity of working the constructive programme whether within or outside the Legislative bodies. In this direction, we feel confident, lies the germ of a fruitful alliance between Mahatma Gandhi and the Swaraj Party. Our joint effort in the same or different directions will furnish a fitting answer to the bureaucracy unwilling to recognize the rights and liberty of the Indian people, and we emphatically assert that, in our determination to work with the same object in the same or different spheres is expressed the determination of the Indian nation to bring the struggle for Swaraj to a successful issue.

1. *The Voice of Freedom*, pp. 519-23.

THE COUNCIL-ENTRY PROGRAMME[1]

After the closing of the AICC, Pandit Motilalji went to Rajkot for a domestic visit and halted at Ahmedabad on his way to Bombay. We met during the halt. In the course of our discussion, I happened to say that it would be disastrous if the *Swarajists* retired from the Councils at this stage. He immediately reminded me of any previous writing that if I could convince the *Swarajists*, I would ask them to withdraw. I said I saw no contradiction between the two : The one statement is permanent and based upon principle, the other is applicable to the immediate present only and is based on expedience. There is no doubt that the *Swarajists* have created a stir in the Government circles. There is no doubt, too, that any withdrawal at the present moment will be misunderstood as a rout and weakness. As a matter of fact, so far as the AICC is concerned, the *Swarajist* position has been never so strong as it is now. They are entitled to claim a moral victory. Believing as they do in giving battle to the Government in the Assembly and the Councils, they have no reason whatsoever for withdrawing from the Legislative bodies at the present moment. Their withdrawal at this juncture can only add to the present depression in the country and strengthen the hands of a Government which wants to give nothing to justice and which yields gracelessly and reluctantly to pressure.

The only opportune time for the *Swarajists* to come out will be when we the whole-hoggers have become active workers of our own programme, which we consider to be the only one that can bring us *swaraj*, and shown progressive success, or when the *Swarajists* are by bitter experience convinced that the Councils can only give condiments but no bread, and that, therefore, they should give their whole time and attention to the constructive programme.

The key to the situation lies in the hands of us whole-hoggers. We claim that the masses are behind us. I at least feel so. If they are, we must show it by results—not by merely securing a majority at the Congress, but by showing substantial work. All the No-changers in all the provinces cannot show adequate results. The fault is probably not theirs. We like the programme, but we have not evolved the capacity for working it. But if that be the true diagnosis, we must now work, for work—not words—will give us the capacity. Then and not till then, when we have shown substantial results, will the *Swarajists* of their own accord come away from the Councils.

There is, in my opinion, no room for a centre party. A centre party is a party of vacillation. It floats with the tide, whereas the time has come for us all to decide one way or the other. Those who believe in the Councils must remain in or, being out, enter them or organize work for them. It will be disastrous for them and for the country if, in spite of their belief in the Councils, they retired from them for fear of public opinion. No one who wants swaraj can dare idle away his or her time.

My Position

I would like to retain my hold on the Congress not by a fictitious or manufactured majority—not merely because my withdrawal is likely to create disorgnization and depression. Even that must be faced if I cannot make my programme acceptable. Enervation is bound to be followed by rejuvenation. The Congress had become a reality in 1920-21. There is fear of its becoming an unreality worse than before 1920. In 1920 there was no organized dishonesty. Then there was no limitation of delegates, no obligation upon Congressmen to do any continuous work and no purse. Now we have a limitation to the number of delegates, resolutions are almost all addressed to them and we have even now a purse such as the Congress never possessed at any time before 1920.

The natural result must, therefore, be dishonesty if we are not incessantly watchful. *Swarajists* tell me that the No-changers have dishonestly worked the constitution and the latter pay the same compliment to the former. I do not know the truth. But I do know that it bodes ill for *Swaraj* if we cannot or do not work the Congress constitution with the utmost honesty.

I would like the Congress to become progressively popular. I would, therefore, man it with mercantile, artisan and agricultural class. I would, therefore, also keep all the boycotts intact and have on the executive only those who fully carry them out in their own persons. Those who cannot but still believe in them can help those who do carry them out, but who are inexperienced in the management of institutions or who are not known to the public as workers. It should be the privilege of educated classes to be behind and push into public life those who have hitherto kept aloof.

In an organization thus conceived, privileged classes have no place on the executive. They can all be in the annual deliberative assembly. Pandit Motilalji suggests a small standing deliberative assembly. I should not mind it. It would perhaps be an advantage to have such a body with all the powers of the Congress. There is no doubt that the constitution requires some drastic changes. We must secure efficiency and swiftness. And these cannot be secured even under a perfect constitution, if we who have to work it are not honest or do not want efficiency and swiftness.

1. *Young India*, 10 July 1924 (Gandhi's meeting with Motilal Nehru).

CONTRIBUTION OF GOVIND BALLABH PANT

In the Legislative Council of the United Provinces, Pandit Govind Ballabh Pant, the Swaraj Party leader, was critical of the performance of the local bodies in respect of the functioning of the department of health, sanitation, roads and means of communications.[1] He suggested, "We must delegate all the powers, so far as possible, to the Indian administrator at the top so that he may not require so many checks and counterchecks above himself. . . . Nothing short of autonomy can be of any avail."[2]

Besides Nemi Saran strongly pleaded for the improvement of cottage industries[3] in the United Provinces, and Mukandilal insisted upon the separation of judiciary—from the executive.[4] Mohan Lal Saxena criticised the inadequate measures on the part of the government in respect of the consumption of liquor. He stated : "Did the Government issue any hand bills, leaflets or placards to demonstrate to the people the evil consequences of this habit ?"[5]

In U.P. when the Legislative Council reassembled on 11 March 1926 to have discussion on the budget, Pandit Govind Ballabh Pant, leader of the Swaraj Party in the Council said that, "in accordance with the resolution adopted by the All India Congress Committee, the *Swarajist* members of the Council would cease to function as members of the Council, except on very special occasions."[6]

He explained that the events of the last five years had established the fact about the 'mentality of the government'. "Cooperation has only added to the intoxication of the bureaucracy, and the more it fed on it the more grew its craving for it."[7] The government he opined was growing more unresponsive to public opinions.[8] Soon after this, the *Swarajist* members withdrew and the budget discussion proceeded.[9]

1. *Proceedings of the Legislative Council of the United Provinces*, Vol. XVII, 290.
2. *Ibid.*, p. 273 ff.
3. *Ibid.*, p. 329.
4. *Ibid.*, p. 326.
5. *Ibid.*, p. 456.

6. *Dabates, U.P. Legislative Council*, 11 March 1926.
7. *Ibid.*
8. *Ibid.*
9. *Ibid.*

VIEWS OF RAJENDRA PRASAD

Dr. Rajendra Prasad opined, "The work of the Swaraj Party led as they were with tact and firmness, was creditable and they achieved whatever could be achieved by their tactics under the Constitution."[1] T. Prakasam called it a mass-based political party, having linkages even at *taluka* level. "The village was connected with the *taluq*, the *taluq* was connected with the district, the district was connected with the province and the province to the Indian Congress Committee—a constitution had been given to the nation and a parallel Government was established in every village ; revenue was collected, money was spent, institutions maintained and contributions were given to the superior committees.[2]

The element of constructive work was greatly fostered by the efforts of the members of the Swaraj Party. It directed its attention towards Hindu-Muslim unity in various regions of the country. In spite of vehement criticism by numerous Bengal Hindus, C.R. Das was instrumental in signing the Bengal Pact which forged strong bonds of unity amongst the two communities.

1. *Young India, 1924-26*, p. XXVI.
2. *Report of the Indian National Congress, Forty-First Session, Gauhati*, 1926.

VIEWS ON STATE PRISONERS[1]

The most annoying topic for questions was pertaining to state prisoners and the Swarajists exhibited added zeal in the matter, as it was vital to the national interest. Therefore, the year 1926 also witnessed a number of enquiries on the subiect in the Bengal Legislative Council. Manmath Nath Roy's questions pertaining to detenus were answered by the Government by a statement that it was not prepared to publish any information regarding the places of their detention, the number of places where each one of them was removed, the weight of each one of them and the names of such of the political prisoners as had been ill since they were taken into custody.[1] The Government was also not prepared to publish the information sought by J.M. Sen-Gupta concerning the internment of Amarendra Nath Basu.[2] The same reply was given when Harendra Nath Chaudhuri made inquiries about state prisoners and detenus.[3] As to his enquiries about the steps taken to provide the detenus with food to which they were accustomed and with attendants who could understand the language spoken by them, the reply given was : Government have addressed the Government of Bombay with a view to obtaining for the detenus, comforts and privileges similar to those which detenus enjoy in Bengal jails, but they have left the details of those arrangements to the discretion of the Government of Bombay."[4]

1. *The Bengal Legislative Council Proceedings* (*Official Report*), Twentieth Session, 1926, (1st and 2nd March 1926), Vol. XX—No. 2, p. 19.
2. *Ibid.*, 15th to 19th and 22nd March 1926), Vol. XX—No. 3, pp. 12 and 13.
3. *Ibid.*, Twenty-sixth Session, 1927 (23rd to 26th August 1927), Vol. XXVI, p. 108.
4. *Ibid.*, p. 123.

RELEASE OF POLITICAL PRISONERS

In 1926, a resolution for the unconditional release of political prisoners was brought by the *Swarajists.* They put forward the plea that such prisoners were not to be guilty of or charged with any act of violence. It also requested the government to show consideration towards the Indian exiles in foreign countries and they might be permitted to come back to India and settle here on reasonable and honourable terms. Lala Lajpat Rai forcefully supported the resolution by stating that, "So long as our people are treated practically like dogs, because they have had no trial, so long as important men, men of education and culture like Subhas Chandra Bose are being treated in that way, the government cannot expect the Nationalist Party in this country to cooperate with them unreservedly."[1] But in spite of support from prominent member like Maulvi Mohammad Shafee, M. K. Acharya and Kumar Sankar Ray, this resolution could not succeed.

1. *Debates, The Legislative Assembly*, September 1925, Vol. IV, Part II, pp. 1005-1006.

DIFFERENCES IN CONGRESS PARTY[1]

By the end of July 1926 serious differences among the Congressmen that had been brewing in the Central Provinces for some time past culminated in the secession of the prominent members of the Legislative Council. The following statement was issued under the signature of E. Raghvendra Rao, leader of the Swaraj Party in the Central Provinces Legislative Council and several other associated with him both inside and outside the Council :

"We the undersigned Congressmen in the Hindi districts of the Central Provinces, being of the opinion that the prssent political situation in the country warrants a modification of the programme chalked out by the Congress at Kanpur within the Legislative Councils with a view to secure more effective coordination between the different shades of opinion in this province and secure the largest representation of Congressmen in the local Legislative Council, do hereby declare as under :

1. That the policy of obstruction in the Provincial Councils should be pursued having regard to the verdict of the electorate throughout the country and not as a result of the return of a majority of Congressmen in this province alone. We are of opinion that unless and until Congressmen are returned in a majority in at least two of the major provinces, Bengal, Madras, Bombay and United Provinces, the Central Provinces alone should not be harnessed to an obstruction programme, as we consider that any isolated pursuit of that policy in a minor province is

not likaly to advance the objective of the Indian National Congress.

2. We do not agree ourselves to accept offices as part of our political creed. If, after election, should the response made by the Government be satisfactory, and if power or responsibility and initiative necessary for the effective discharge of their duties are secured to Ministers, we shall consider the response on its own merits. The decision in our opinion should be left to a majority of the Congressmen in the country's Councils. It shall be our endeavour to convert the next Congress to this view. In pursuance of this declaration, we solemnly promise to stand independent Congressmen in the forthcoming election to the local Legislative Council and will honestly carry out the objects, stated above, in letter and spirit.

Thus the cessation of the prominent members of the C.P. Hindustani Party completed the split in the C.P Swaraj Party and all attempts to bring about a compromise failed. E. Raghvendra Rao formed his own party of Independent Congressmen on the line of Responsivists taking his stand on the broken Sabarmati Pact. He set up candidates of his own party in opposition to Congress candidates. The Responsivists counted upon the support of Rao and his new party, for the programmes of both the parties were similar in many respects and the points of differences were almost negligible.

N.B. Khare made an assessment of the prevailing political situation in C.P. and commented thus: "The British people ......are past masters in the art of diplomacy. We cannot match them; we admit our inefficiency in this respect. They began by hypontising, then they made suggestions and they found that the suggestions they made failed to fructify, then they offered baits and the administration of Sir Montagu Butler very cleverly attempted two of our stalwart fighters and made them eat the humble pie by offering them custard and plum-cakes."

1. *Proceedings of the Legislative Council of the Governor of the Central Provinces*, Vol. II, March 1927, p. 232.

NEHRU'S VIEWS ON COUNCIL-ENTRY

Jawaharlal Nehru has given a comphensive survey of events having a deep linkage with the problems of Council-entry. "My own inclination was wholly against Council-entry, because this seemed to lead inevitably to compromising tactics and to a continuous watering down of our objective. But there really was no other political programme before the country. The no-changers laid stress on a 'constructive progromme', which in effects was a programme of social reform, and its chief merit was that it brought our workers in touch with the masses. This was not likely to satisfy those who believed in political action, and it was inevitable that after a wave of direct action, which had not succeeded, there should be a phase of parliamentary activity. Even this activity was envisaged by Deshbandhu Das and my father, the leaders of the new movement, as one of obstruction and defiance and not of cooperation and construction.

Mr. C.R. Das had always favoured entry into the legislatures for the purpose of carrying on the national struggle there also. My father had more or less the same outlook, his acceptance of the Council boycott in 1920 was partly a subordination of his own viewpoint to Gandhiji's. He wanted to throw his full weight into the struggle and the only way to do it then was to accept the Gandhi formula *in toto*. The minds of many of the younger people were full of the tactics of Sinn Fein in so far as they had captured the parliamentary seats and then refused to enter the House of Commons. I remember pressing Gandhiji in the summer of 1920 to adopt this variant of the boycott, but in such matters he was adamant...He was the author of the movement, and it was felt that he must be given freedom as to the details. His chief objections to the Sinn Fein method were (apart from its association with violence) that it would not be understood by the masses as much as a straight call to boycott the polling-booths and the voting. To get elected and then not to go to the Councils would create confusion in the mass mind. Further, that once our people got elected they would be drawn towards the Councils and it would be difficult for them to keep out of them. There was not enough discipline and power in our movement to keep them out for long, and a demoralizing dribble would set in towards the many direct and indirect ways of taking advantage of Government patronage through the Councils.

On my discharge from gaol I cooperated with a few others who were trying to bring about an understanding between the rival groups. We met with little success, and I was fed up with the pro-change and no-change politics . . . . Mentally I was at a loose end. . . . .[1]

1. Jawaharlal Nehru, *An Autobiography*, Delhi, 1968, pp. 98-99.

SIMON COMMISSION'S VIEWS ON SWARAJ PARTY

The success of the Swaraj Party was admitted by the members of the Simon Commission in their Report. "The only really well-organised and disciplined party with a definite programme (though, it is true, a negative one) is that of the *Swarajists*. Only in Bengal and the Central Provinces did they, even temporarily, achieve their initial object of making dyarchy unworkable, and in the provinces they have tended everywhere, in varying degrees, to be transformed into an opposition of a more constitutional kind and, have not infrequently played a useful part as keen and vigilant critics."[1]

1. *Report of the Indian Statutory Commission*, Vol. I, p. 209.

CHAPTER 3

IDEOLOGY OF GANDHI

GANDHI'S VIEWS ON GONGRESS ORGANIZATION

As I have said in my statement to the Press on the question of Council-entry, it is not complete without an examination, in the light of my views, of the working of the Congress organization. The difference between the Swarajists and myself is honest and vital. I believe 'that the frank recognition of honest differences will accelerate the country's progress, as a patched-up compromise designed to hide differences would have retarded it. Each party is now free to give the fullest play to its views unhampered by any consideration save that of common cause.

It is, therefore, necessary to consider the way the Congress organization is to be worked. It is clear to me that it cannot be jointly worked just as a government cannot be jointly and efficiently carried on by two parties with opposite views. I hold the boycott of titles, etc., to be an absolutely integral part of the Congress programme. The boycott has two objects : first, to persuade those who hold titles, etc., to give them up; secondly, to keep the Congress pure from the influence of the institutions boycotted. If the first had been immediately successful, we should have attained our goal at once. But the second is equally necessary, if we are ever to reach our goal through the programme of non-violent non-co-operation. For me the boycott is national so long as the National Congress enforces it in its own organization. It cannot undermine the influence, the glamour and the prestige of Government institutions, if it cannot be run without the presence in it, as administrators, of title-holders, lawyers, schoolmasters and councillors who represent, as it were, the voluntary branch of the Government administration. The idea running behind the programme of non-co-operation was that if we could honestly, non-violently and successfully work the Congress organization without such influence, and nay, even in spite of it, that fact by itself would be enough to give us *swaraj*. Our numerical superiority is so great than an effective boycott carried out by the national organization must make the Congress an irresistible power. It follows, therefore, that the executive organization of the Congress must not contain titled persons, Government schoolmasters, practising lawyers and members of legislative bodies and persons who use foreign cloth or cloth manufactured even in our mills, and those who deal in such cloth Such persons can become Congressmen, but cannot and should not become members of executive organizations. They can become delegates and influence the Congress resolutions, but once the Congress policy is fixed, those who do not believe in that policy, in my opinion, should stand out of the executive bodies. The All-India Congress Committee and all the local executive committees are such bodies, and they should contain only those members who whole-heartedly believe in and are prepared to carry out the policy. I am the author of the introduction into the Congress organization of the system of single transferable votes. But experience has shown that, so far as the executive organizations are concerned, it cannot work. The idea that all opinions should be represented on these bodies must be abandoned if the executive committees are to become bodies for the purpose of carrying out the Congress policy for the time being.

One of the most important reasons why we have not been wholly successful is that the members of these executive bodies have not believed even in the Congress creed. I stand where I did when I wrote my impressions of the All-India Congress Committee, which met at Delhi soon after the Bardoli resolutions were passed by the Working Committee I saw then as clearly as possible that many members, if not indeed the majority, did not believe in non-violence and truth as an integral part of the Congress creed. They would not allow that 'peaceful' meant 'non-violent' and that 'legitimate' meant 'truthful'. I know that today there is more of the violent and the truthful spirit in us than we had in February 1922. I would, therefore, urge that those who do not believe in the five boycotts and non-violence and truthfulness should resign from the Congress executive bodies. This is why I have said in my statement on the Council-entry that the constructive programme should be worked by different parties through their respective organizations. The thorough believers, if there are any, in the five boycotts and non-violence and truth, have no organization other than the Congress. The most natural thing, in my opinion, therefore, is for the Swarajists to work the constructive programme through their own organizations. So far as I can see, their method of working must be different from that of the boycotters. If they are to make the Council-entry successful, they must devote the whole of their energy to that purpose, and, therefore, they can help the constructive programme by working it mainly through the Councils and the Assembly.

I for one can be no party to a tug of war in which each party tries to capture the Congress executive. That war may be fought out if at all necessary without heat and bitterness at the forthcoming session in December. The Congress is the debating and legislative body. The permanent organizations are purely executive bodies to give effect to the resolutions of the Congress. I am in a desperate hurry. I believe implicitly in the full and undiluted non-violent non-cooperation programme as passed by the Congress and no other. If I can get really non-violent and truthful workers who share my belief in the boycott, in the potency of *khaddar*, in Hindu-Muslim unity and in removal of untouchability, I would again feel *swaraj* coming to us much quicker than most of us think possible. But if we wrangle on in the All-India Congress Committee, we can only discredit and obstruct one another. Each party honourably and without jealousy and ill-will working separately (because they cannot do otherwise) can help one another.

I trust that all the members of the All-India Congress Committee will attend the forthcoming meeting. If we can discuss the plan of action in a calm manner without imputing motives and make the composition of the All-India Congress

Committee homogeneous, we can do a tremendous amount of work during the forthcoming six months. I would respectfully invite each member to consider for himself or herself where he or she is in respect of the programme. If they do not believe in the programme as it is and in its capacity unaided to secure *swaraj*, and if they really voice the feelings of their electors, I would not hesitate to advise the Committee even to take the risk of revising and radically altering the programme in anticipation of endorsement next year. No doubt for such a drastic change there must be a clearly made-out case, there must be real public opinion behind it. Granted these two conditions, I have no doubt that, in spite of anything to the contrary in the constitution, it is the duty of the All-India Congress Committee to reverse the Congress policy at the risk of incurring condemnation and show useful and substantial work at the end of the year. Stagnation must be avoided at all cost.

After I had finished the foregoing, it was pointed out to me that it was possible that my views might tend to make *Swarajists* appear weaker than or inferior to the No-changers in the estimation of the masses. Nothing can be further from my thought than any such idea. There is no question of quality. It is purely a question of temperamental differences. I have written simply with an eye to effective working of the Congress executives. That working is possible only if the executives are run only by one party. If the *Swarajists'* view is more popular, the executive bodies should be solely in their hands. The Congress must always represent the popular view whatever it may be, whether good or bad. And it is the duty of those who hold contrary views, not necessarily weak or inferior, to stand out and work on the popular mind from outside. The No-changers will be belying their trust if they regard pro-changers as in any way inferior to them by reason of their holding dierffent views.

It has been further pointed out to me that, in arguing for exclusive control of the executives, I am departing from the spirit, if not the letter, of the Delhi resolution reaffirmed at Cocanada. I have read both the resolutions carefully. In my opinion, the Delhi resolution and, more specially the Cocanada resolution, does not contemplate joint control of the executives. The Cocanada resolution is not a mere reaffirmation, but it emphasizes the principle of non-co-operation. But even if my reading of the resolutions is incorrect, my argument remains unimpaired. Mine is only an opinion to be accepted or rejected by the members of the AICC. And it is actuated by the sole consideration of expeditious working. I feel that both the parties can effectively help each other only if they work separately.

1. *Young India*, 29 May 1924.

OPINION ABOUT SWARAJISTS[1]

In *Young India* dated 4th September 1924, Gandhi gave his opinion about the *Swarajists*, 'People are however asking, "When will this suspense all end ?" So far as I am concerned it is all ended. I have no fight left in me. I do not propose to fight the *Swarajists* at the forthcoming Congress...I have no terms or my only terms are the beggar's bowl. I ask the *Swarajists*, the Moderates, the Liberals, the Conventionists to throw into it yarn of their own spinning. Such being my mental condition I can but advise all the national workers simply to concentrate their effort on spinning, on promoting unity and, if Hindus, on removing untouchability.'

1. *Young India*, 4 September 1924.

RADICAL CHANGE IN CONGRESS[1]

...It is necessary to say a word about the proposed radical change in the Congress constitution. I may be pardoned for saying that I am the principal author of the Congress constitution. It was intended to be the most democratic in the world, and if successfully worked, to bring *swaraj* without more. But it was not so worked. We had not sufficient honest and able workers. It must be confessed that it has broken down in the sense in which it was intended. We never had even one crore of members on the roll. At the present moment probably our nominal roll does not exceed two lakhs for all India. And the vast majority of these too are as a rule not interested in our proceedings save for paying four annas and voting. But what we need is an effective, swift-moving, cohesive, responsive organization containing intelligent, industrious national workers. Even if we are a few only, we should give a better account of ourselves than a cumbrous and slow body with no mind of its own. The only boycott proposed to be retained is, that of foreign cloth and if we are to make it successful, we can only do so by making the Congress for a time predominantly a spinners' association. It will be a great triumph and a great demonstration, if we succeed in one constructive item of a striking magnitude. I hold that the only possible thing of the kind is hand-spinning and hand-spun *khaddar*. If we are to make of *khaddar* a national success, the spinning-wheel is the only thing. If we are permanently to interest the masses in the national welfare of the country, the spinning-wheel is the only medium. If we are to branch pauperism from the land, the spinning-wheel again is the only remedy.

The implications of my proposals are that—

(a) the *swarajists* should be free to organize themselves without any opposition from the Congress or No-changers;

(b) the members of other political bodies should be invited and induced to join the Congress;

(c) the No-changers should be precluded from carrving on any propaganda either direct or indirect against Council-entry;

(d) those who do not personally believe in any of the four boycotts will be free, without any disgrace whatsoever, to act as if they did not exist. Thus non-co-operating lawyers will be free to resume practice if they chose and title-holders, school-masters, etc., will be free to join the Congress and be eligible to the executive.

The scheme enables all the political parties to work unitedly for the internal development. The Congress presents a suitable opportunity for a conference of all political parties and outside the Congress to frame a *swaraj* scheme acceptable to all and for presentation to the Government. Personally I am of opinion that time has not arrived for any such presentation. I believe that it would increase our internal strength beyond expectation if we could all simply unite to make the forthcoming constructive programme a success. But a large number of those who have hitherto led the country think otherwise. In any event a *swaraj* scheme for the sake of ourselves is a necessity. As the reader will remember, I am in this matter a complete convert to Babu Bhagwandas's view. I would therefore join any such conference, if my presence was required, and assist at framing the scheme. The reason for insisting on this matter being treated as an activity outside the Congress is to keep the Congress purely for internal development for full one year. When we have achieved a measure of success commensurate with the task before us, the Congress may function for outside political activity.

What if the proposal is not accepted and it is found difficult to bring together all parties on the Congress platform and to heal the breach between the *Swarajists* and ourselves ? My answer is simple. If the whole fight is for "capturing" the Congress, I must refuse to enter upon it. I would advise all who think with me to do likewise. I would advise handing the Congress over to the *Swarajists* on their terms and leave the *Swarajists* to work the Councils programme unhampered by any counter-propaganda. I would engage the No-changers purely on the constructive programme and advise them to seek such help from the other parties as they can give.

Those who depend for national regeneration solely on the constructive programme may be expected to lead in the matter of self-sacrifice. Not one of things we hold dear can be achieved by trying to retain power in the Congress in opposition to the *Swarajists*. We must hold it on their sufferance. Both parties will be guilty of corrupting the simple people who worship the name "Congress", if they are made at our bidding to engage in a suicidal tug-of-war. Power that comes from service faithfully rendered ennobles. Power that it sought in the name of service and can only be obtained by a majority of votes is a delusion and a snare to be avoided, especially at the present moment.

Whether I have convinced the reader of the soundness of my proposal or not my mind is made up. It hurts me to think that those with whom I have hitherto worked hand in glove should be working in a seemingly opposite direction.

What I have sketched above is not conditions of surrender.

Mine is an unconditional surrender. I would guide the Congress next year only if all parties wish me to. I am trying to see it dimly. But I may be still wrong. All I know is that there is no fight left in me. This is much for a born fighter to say. I have fought my dearest ones. But I fight out of love. I should fight the *Swarajists* too out of love. But I must, I see, first prove my love. I thought I had proved it. I see I was wrong. I am therefore retracing my steps. I ask everyone to help me to do so and to reunite the two wings on a common platform. The Congress must, for some time to come at least, remain largely a homogeneous body.

1. *Young India*, 11 September 1924.

GANDHI'S SURRENDER TO SWARAJISTS[1]

Gandhi opined, "So far as I am concerned, being an out-and-out believer in non-violence, my position remains the same as at Amritsar in 1919. I do not believe in obstruction in any shape or form within the Councils. It appears to me to be an utter waste of time. I would enter the Councils only if I believed that I could make use of them for the advancement of the country. I must, therefore, have faith in the machinery and those in charge of it. I cannot be part of the machinery and still want to destroy it.

"I am therefore engaged in surrendering to the utmost of my capacity to the *Swarajists*. . . . We must not hinder the *Swarajists* in their very difficult task. Wherever No-changers cannot have a majority without a bitter struggle, they must gladly and willingly and gracefully yield to the Swarajists . . . I would like No-changers so to behave as to be wanted by Swarajists, Liberals and all others."

1. *Young India*, 23 October 1924.

DISCUSSION WITH NO-CHANGERS[1]

7 November 1924

Explaining his own feelings at the outset, Gandhiji said :

I myself have no doubts as to the rightness of my action. I was caught in a whirlpool of doubt regarding my duty; but now I feel relieved. I am certain that I could not have done otherwise than what I have done. It is the very dharma of an advocate of non-violence that he should renounce till he has nothing further to renounce. Hence I have arrived at the final decision. I should practise surrender to such an extent that my opponent would see, it is the limit and would be taken aback by it. Moreover, this is not my first experience. The ethics of giving suggests this. Give till the receiver is satisfied. Still, the surrender that I have practised in this case is not of that kind, it is not renunciation in that sense. I have surrendered whatever I did after arguing and higgling. I have retreated inch by inch, gradually, by degree. Of course, some people believe that I have yielded more than they had expected of me.

Once you realize that non-cooperation cannot be carried on, you will see at once that there is no alternative but to retreat to the point where I have arrived. Wherever I go, I come across nothing but violence. It is so deeply embedded in the hearts of people that it would be a crime to carry on non-cooperation on a national scale. There is, however, a distinction between "national" and "individual" non-co-operation. In other words, individuals should continue to non-cooperate to the same extent that they have done so far; if, on the contrary, they give it up, their initial non-coopera-tion would be deemed meaningless.

Much discussion has arisen over the spinning franchise. You feel that I have surrendered a great deal, that I have turned *khadi* into a kind of ritual. However, that is not so at all. If you examine history, you will realize how much we have gone ahead. At the outset, there were merely pledges, pure, mixed, and so on. After that, mill-made cloth was discarded and *khadi* came along. Later, the spinning-wheel was introduced. *Khadi* was then made compulsory for volunteers. Then again proficiency in spinning was made compulsory. Going still further, everyone was called upon to spin. After this, resolutions were passed making it compulsory for workers to spin and today we have introduced spinning as a condition to enable one to vote.

It is true that every single member may not spin. But those who spin today will cease to do so. On the contrary, there will be an increase in the number of spinners. How many persons will be able to get yarn spun for payment ? Hence the majority of members will contribute their own yarn. Those who have not themselves determined to spin, how can we force them to do so ? However, we should be satisfied if they bring in yarn spun for them by others. Moreover, if you consider the matter a little more carefully, it was never accepted as a principle that every member of the Congress must spin. I should also add that many persons did not share this idea; it was mine alone; I could even say that even for me it was an ideal. It is a fact that long ago a gentleman had written to me from Ceylon asking me why every member should not be compelled to spin. However, at that time I had not given any thought to the proposal, regarding it as unfeasible. Later I considered it feasible and placed it before the country. Hence if anything has been given up, it has been taken away from my ideal, from something that I myself had conceived.

Then, again, do you feel that *khadi* has been reduced to a more formality ? Even that fear is groundless. It is one thing to pass a resolution in favour of *khadi*, it is another to say that anyone who does not wear *khadi* cannot become a member of the Congress. The act of voting is a very definite one, the condition for voting should not be very rigid and difficult to fulfil. Mr. Suhrawardy—the Deputy Mayor of the Corporation—came yesterday dressed from head to foot in *khadi*. He does not wear *khadi* regularly; but he felt that yesterday the occasion demanded that he should. Now, how can I say to people like him that even when they stand up in court, they should wear a *khadi* gown ? I can but hope that if on national occasions he wears *khadi*, he will not start using foreign or mill-made cloth on private occasions through sheer waywardness. Those who are using *khadi* will continue to do so; those who never use it will get the opportunity of entering the Congress temple after being purified by *khadi*. Today even the delegates who come to the Congress do not wear *khadi*. Ninety per cent of the people today come to the Congress session clad in *dhotis*[2] made not of *khadi* but of mill-made cloth. This would not happen if this condition is laid down.

The question of uniting with the Swarajists came. Gandhiji has fully discussed that question in his own article. He wound up that argument by saying : I cannot be persuaded to believe that the Government has arrested the Swarajists for the good of the people. My conviction is getting stronger every moment that the Swarajists have been arrested only in order to crush them.

In conclusion he said :

I believe that my sacrifice involves surrendering a part of my ideals as outlined in *Young India.* It does not involve sacrificing anything that is basic nor is it a sacrifice of any principles. However, if you feel that I have sacrificed the essence, if you feel that my sacrifice is unjustified, you should oppose me vigorously. I had informed Shyambabu of my objective. My object today is to end chaos and bring order, to put an end to disputes and bring about harmony, to unite a lifeless people and infuse them with strength and fearlessness. If I have given rise to a party which is nurtured on blind faith alone, it is harmful to the country. I can excuse the ordinary people, but you are writers, orators and debators. You should act only in accordance with the dictates of your reason. I am not infallible. Of course, I may make fewer mistakes as I am more experienced than you. It may well be, though, that one who seldom makes a mistake, makes a terrible one when he actually does make one. It is possible that I am giving unnecessary importance to the work of Swarajists, that I am laying undue stress on Hindu-Muslim unity—in that case you should unhesitatingly choose a new path and follow it. By doing so you will show your self-respect. There are two kinds of sacrifice : that of one's individual opinion and that of basic principles. Shri Gokhale used to say that the former can be sacrifed in public interest, but the latter cannot. In view of this, you may feel free to act in whichever way you wish.

This was followed by a large number of questions and answers.

Q. The Congress will no longer belong to the poor, if till belong only to the well-to-do class. This will be so as the latter can buy yarn anywhere.

A. No, it will belong wholly to the poor. It is the duty of the Congress to provide cotton to the poor; it is for the latter to contribute their labour. The common people will not buy yarn, they will spin it themselves. Those who have an aversion to spinning or are lazy may get others to spin for them.

Q. You began non-co-operation with this wicked Government and now you are gradually giving it up. In addition to it, you now advocate co-operation with wickedness; the *Swarajists* have practised such deceit and lies; how can there be any co-operation with them ?

A. I have never said that non-co-operation should be preached everywhere. It should be preached if otherwise we would have to participate in the wicked deeds of the opponent. Even if the allegations you make are true, we do not wish to be partners in their lies. Moreover, you tend to forget that we have resorted to non-co-operation with the Government after having co-operated with it for thirty years. There was no occasion for non-co-operation with the *Swarajists* or our brothers. We have hardly co-operated with them; so the question of non-co-operation does not arise. Today my only task is to bring about a change of heart among Hindus and Muslims. I seek help from all in that task only. When this has been achieved, my hopes for the immediate attainment of *swaraj* will multiply.

Q. You want to include even Moderates and also to find a way for those who advocate violence. What is this and how could all these be reconciled ?

A. I wish to live and die for truth. I hope that people will become truthful and honest. Making everyone accept the ideal conditions that I desire would not lead to any increase in honesty, but would rather give rise to hypocrisy. The resolution that has been taken up today will promote honesty. I only want that people pledge themselves to the minimum and fully abide by it. I said therefore that the words "peaceful and legitimate" should be taken out of the Congress resolution. Rather than practise violence after taking the pledge of non-violence, would it not be better not to pledge oneself to non-violence ? The country should accept my ideals if it approves of them. I shall have to put them in my pocket if the country disapproves of them. Nevertheless I did not sacrifice those points which could not be sacrificed.

Supposing a Hindu comes to me and asks me to give up Hindu-Muslim unity from among the objectives, would I agree to it? Similarly, I could not possibly have accepted the use of mill-made cloth among the conditions to be fulfilled by voters, because by doing so I would certainly have ruined [the cause] of *khadi*.

Q. At one time you used to say that an honest shoeblack was preferable to a co-operating lawyer. Today you are prepared to side with the lawyers and the big wigs.

A. Yes, you are right. What I had said was literally true. There is no non-co-operation today. If it had been widespread, if even shoeblacks had offered non-co-operation, they could keep off the co-operators, However, I am not master of the Congress. Should I wish to become a leader, it would not be by imposing impossible conditions but, rather, by laying down such conditions as can easily be fulfilled. I would have persisted on the same old path, had there been no misunderstanding, no widespread bitterness. However, those conditions no longer prevail and so I felt that I must exercise patience and forget about the struggle.

1. *Navajivan*, 16 November 1924.

2. Garment worn by men.

GANDHI ON TRIAL[1]

It is not to be wondered at that No-changers are intensely dissatisfied with the agreement arrived at between the *Swarajists* and myself. I have repeatedly admitted that I am but an humble explorer of the science of non-violence. Its hidden depths sometimes stagger me just as much as they stagger fellow-workers. I observe that the agreement seems just now to satisfy no one but the parties to it. Many Englishmen regard it as an ignominous surrender to the *Swarajists* on my part. Many No-changers regard it as a lapse, if not a betrayal. A friend says that it has caused consternation among students. Why, they ask should they remain in national schools if non-co-operation is suspended? They are the greatest sufferers and they have not been considered in the past at all. I hold a letter from an Andhra friend which arrests attention and calls for a reasoned reply.

Surrrender on my part it undoubtedly is. It is a conscious surrender, but not, as an English paper puts it, to the party of violence. I refuse to believe that the Swaraj Party is a party of violence. Such charges were I know levelled against even the late Dadabhai Naoroji and Justice Ranade. They were suspected and shadowed. Lala Harkishen Lal who had no more to do with any party of violence than Sir Michael O' Dwyer himself was arrested and imprisoned by that satrap. I would have been false to the country if I had not stood by the Swaraj Party in the hour of its need. Let it be unequivocally demonstrated that it has had anything to do with violence, and I shall be prepared to denounce it in as strong language as is open to me to use. On such proof I shall sever all connections with it. But till then, I must stand by it even though I do not believe in the efficacy of Council-enty or even some of the methods of conducting Council-warfare.

But recognition of the party as an integral part of the Congress does not mean surrender by individuals of their non-co-operation. It means an admission that the Swaraj Party is a strong and growing wing of the Congress. And if it refuses to take a back seat without a fight, and if it is necessary or even expedient to avoid a fight, the claim to a definite official recognition is irresistible. Every Congressman, however, is not, by reason of his being a Congressman, assumed to be a believer in all the items of a Congress programme. My own position, I admit, is somewhat different. I have made myself instrumental in bringing the agreement into being. I am not sorry for it. Rightly or wrongly, the country expects me to give it some guidance. And I have come to the conclusion that it is in the interest of the country to give the Swaraj Party the fullest possible chance of working out its programme without let or hindrance from No-changers. The latter are not bound to participate in its activity, if they do not like it. They are free and bound, as the *Swarajists* are bound, to pursue the constructive programme only. They are free also to retain their individual non-co-operation. But suspension by the Congress means that non-co-operators can derive no support or strength from the Congress. They must derive all their strength from within. And that is their test and trial. If their faith abides, it is well with them and non-co-operation. If it vanishes with suspension, non-co-operation dies as a force in public life. But a friend says : "If you waver, what about lesser men?" I have not wavered. My faith in non-co-operation is as bright as ever. For it has been with me a principle of life for over thirty years. But I cannot impose my personal faith on others, never on a national organization. I can but try to convince the nation of its beauty and usefulness. And if I find in reading the national mind, that the nation in so far as it is represented by the Congress must have breathing time, I must cry halt. I may misread the mind of the Congress. When that happens, I shall cease to be any force in the Congress That will be no calamity. But it would be a calamity if by my obstinacy I stand in the way of the country's progress by other means, so long as they are not positively mischievous and harmful. I should for instance rise, even if I was alone, against methods of actual violence. But I have recognized that the nation has the right, if it so wills, to vindicate her freedom even by actual violence. Only, then India ceases to be the land of my love even though she be the land of my birth, even as I should take no pride in my mother if she went astray. But the Swaraj Party is a party of orderly progress. It may not swear by non-violence as I do, but it accepts non-violence as a policy and it discountenances violence, because it considers it to be useless if not even harmful. It occupies a prominent position in the Congress. I do not know that if its strength was tested, it might not be found even to occupy a predominant position. It is easy enough for me to secede from the Congress and let the party run the Congress. That I will do when I find that I have nothing in common with the party. But so long as I have the faintest hope of its redemption, I shall cling to it like a child to its mother's breast. I will not weaken it by disowning or denouncing it or by retiring from the Congress.

I have used the word "redemption" in no offensive sense. I have too my method of *shuddhi*[2] and *tabligh*. It is the best the world has yet seen. Conscious of my own ground and strength, I let the party act upon me and influence me as much as it will. It enables me to know it at its best. I make no secret of my intention that by coming under its influence, I hope to influence it in favour of my method. If in the process, it redeems me and converts me, all honour to it. I should then declare my conversion from the house-top. It is *shuddhi* by reason appealing to reason and heart speaking to heart. It is the non-violent method of conversion. Let non-co-operators join forces with me. At the same time let them remain firm in their individual conduct. If their non-co-operation springs from love, I promise that they will convert the *Swarajists*, and even if they don't succeed, they will have lost nothing, personally. If the country is with them, the *Swarajists*, if they do not follow, will naturally take a back seat. And if the latter gain ground during the twelve months of grace, they must be undisputed masters of the Congress, and non-co-operators must be content to be in a minority. They may register me in advance as one of that minority.

The problem with the students is the same. Non co-operation may be suspended, but schools will not be suspended. They are an accomplished fact. They are among the best fruit of non-co-operation. The studends are, therefore, expected to keep the flag flying and show to the country that they can flourish even though the Congress may suspend the non-co-operation programme. It is poor faith that needs fair weather for standing firm. That alone is true faith that stands the foulest weather.

1. *Young India*, 20 November 1924.
2. Purification.

GANDHI IN SWARAJ PARTY

In a speech at the session of the AICC held in Bombay on 23 November 1924, Gandhi clarified certain doubt lurking in the minds of no-changers. He stated that he could not afford to neglect the *Swarajists*. He admitted that they represented a very strong body of public opinion in favour of council-entry. They also possessed the best intellect in the country. He had the apprehension that without the coopera-tion of such a body, he would not be able to make any head-way. "The *Swarajists*, in their own way, are an advanced party. They have evidently influenced the atmosphere of Councils and of the Legislative Assembly. I could not—nobody can—defy their political sentiment.. I practically confess that I consider it impossible to lead the battle of non-cooperation or of civil disobedience, unless we have by us the intellect of the country...That we cannot expect unless we yield to them in some respects. In making this concession about Council-entry, we find that we have got with us the Council programme workers, who are wise men, men whom I claim to be practical men,..., I believe that spinning should be a part of the *Swarajists*' programme like the Council programme, that we should introduce *khaddar* and spinning-wheel into the franchise...I do not believe that the spinning-wheel give anything substantial to India. But is it a sin to spin ?...I have affection for the spinning-wheel, but there are other countrymen of ours who have real disinclination to spin; for them I have given way in regard to the spinning franchise. Therefore I had no hesitation in subscribing to the spinning franchise in the way I did to meet some of the unwilling *Swarajists*. I want to make this franchise a living thing in the Congress. I want to make it successful with the help of the Swaraj Party...My appeal is to the No-changers. It is equally to the *Swarajists*... Accept it even for the sake of discipline. Accept it as an article of faith.

"The *Swarajists* are not idiotic, the *Swarajists* are not unpatriotic. They have got their own duty to perform according to the best of their ability. If they consider that it is necessary to give battle to government by going to the Councils, let them go and make the Councils workable. They do not go to Councils to spite the No-changers. They do not go there to make harangues. They have a purpose in view. Suppose you do not allow them to go to the Councils, what are they going to do ? Are they going to rot ? The No-changers should believe that the proper place for the *Swarajists* is inside the Councils and not outside.

1. *C.W.M.G.*, Vol. XXV.

VIEWS ON SWARAJ[1]

During last month I had a hearty discussion with an English friend who takes deep interest in matters Indian and who is anxious to serve India to the best of his ability. He asked me whether I would publish the gist of of our conversation. I readily agreed but asked him to jot down the points he raised which he gladly did. I do not disclose the friend's name as the name does not matter. It is my views that matter because they are exciting some interest at the present moment. If I am a friend of Englishmen, as I claim to be, I must patiently answer all the doubts that may arise in their minds. The English friend put the questions not all on his own behalf but mostly on behalf of those Englishmen who had originally raised them.

Here are the questions with answers.

What is the real purpose of your insistence upon the *khaddar* programme as a means of obtaining *swaraj* ?

I am interested in the attainment of *swaraj* only by non-violent and truthful means. This is possible only through a diligent and successful prosecution of the *khaddar* programme. *Swaraj* can be peacefully attained only if the whole Indian mass work as one will, be it on ever so little a constructive and useful thing for ever so little a time. Such an effort presupposes national consciousness This is possible only through the spinning-wheel. It is not remunerative enough for individuals. It is, therefore, not enough incentive for an individual selfishly inclined. It is however enough to raise at a bound the national prosperity in an appreciable manner. An increase of one rupee per head per year may mean nothing to the individual. But Rs. 5,000 in a village containing a population of many would mean the payment of land revenue or other dues. Thus the spinning-wheel means national consciousness and a contribution by every individual to a definite constructive national work If India can demonstrate her capacity for such an achievement by voluntary effort she is ready for political *swaraj*. Any lawful demand of a nation with a will of its own must prove irresistible. I have hitherto said nothing of the immense economic value of the wheel and its product *khaddar*. For it is obvious. The economic prosperity of India must indirectly affect the course of her political history—even using the word "political" in its narrow sense. Lastly, when the exploitation of India by Lancashire ceases by reason of the ability of India through the wheel to clothe herself and consequently to exclude foreign cloth and therefore also Lancashire cloth, England will have lost the feverish anxiety at any cost to hold India under subjection.

This means revolutionizing the national taste ? Do you expect to persuade your countrymen to give up the use of foreign cloth ?

I do. After all I am asking for very little. Millions are indifferent as to what they wear. They merely look to the cheapness of the articles they buy. It is the middle class whose taste has to be revised. I do not think that the substitution of foreign cloth by *khaddar* is an impossible task for them. Moreover it should be remembered that nowadays it is possible for *khaddar* to suit a large variety of taste. And improvement in fineness is making steady progress. I am, therefore, of opinion that if any constructive work is capable of success, it is the *khaddar* programme.

What do you mean by *swaraj* and what are its limitations, if any ?

By *swaraj* I mean the Government of India by the consent of the people ascertained by the vote of the largest number of adult population, male or female, native-born or domiciled who have contributed by manual labour to the service of the State and who have taken the trouble of having their names registered as voters. This Government should be quite consistent with the British connection on absolutely honourable and equal terms. Personally I have not despaired of the substitution for the present servile condition of equal partnership or association. But I would not for one moment hesitate to countenance or bring complete severance if it became necessary, *i.e.*, if the connection impeded India's full growth.

To what extent are you committed to the programme and methods of the Swaraj Party ?

I am personally committed neither to the programme nor to the methods of the Swaraj Party. As a Congressman I recognize its undoubted influence in the country and therefore its right to represent the Congress—a right which it now enjoys by arrangement but which it otherwise might have secured by a party vote.

What are the relations between you and the leaders of that party ?

They are of a most cordial character. I give them the same credit for patriotic service and sacrifice that I would like to claim for myself.

It has been stated that you have surrendered to Mr. Das ?

The statement is true in the sense that I have avoided a quarrel among Congressmen. But it is not true if it is intended to convey the meaning that I have surrendered an iota of my principle.

Was not your attitude on the Saha resolution different from the one you have now adopted ?

Not in the least. At the time of the Saha resolution I was opposing an internal error. At the present moment I am resisting external oppression based on erroneous assumptions. Moreover, my attempt then to secure consistency of conduct and control of the Congress executive by one party must not be confined with my action on the Saha resolution. The two things were totally different and were not even inter-related. As soon as I discovered that the attempt to secure unity of control led to bad blood, I retraced my steps and declared complete surrender to the Swaraj Party.

It has been stated that you have lost your moral authority by your surrender ?

Moral authority is never retained by any attempt to hold on to it. It comes without seeking and is retained without effort. I am not conscious of loss of moral authority, for I am utterly unconscious being guilty of any single act compromising my moral conduct. What I have undoubtedly lost is the intellectual co-operation of a large number of educated men in my presentation of the means of attaining *Swaraj*, *e.g.*, the spinning-wheel.

Why do you insist upon non-co-operation while every one of the activities has failed ? What is the purpose in speaking of its suspension ?

I do not insist now. But I do not admit that every one of the activities has failed. On the contrary, every activity of non-cooperation succeeded to an extent. I can speak only of its suspension because to me non-co-operation is a vital principle of life and because in my opinion it had done India and, if you will, the world an amount of good of which, at present, we have not adequate conception and also because, if found an atmosphere of substantial non-violence and real co-operation among the people and if the end remained still unattained, I should not hesitate to advise its resumption by the nation.

How do you propose to solve the Hindu-Muslim problem ?

By constantly insisting upon both the communities cultivaing mutual respect and trust and by insisting upon Hindus surrendering out of strength to the Mussalman in every mundane matter and by showing that those who claim to be nationalists and are in an overwhelming majority should stand out in any unseemly competition for legislative or administrative control. I hope also to achieve the end by demonstrating that real *swaraj* will come not by the acquisition of authority by a few but by the acquisition of the capacity by all to resist authority when it is abused. In other words; *swaraj* is to be attained by educating the masses to a sense of their capacity to regulate and control authority.

What is your own real attitude towards the English and your hope about England ?

My attitude towards the English is one of utter friendliness and respect. I claim to be their friend, because it is contrary to my nature to distrust a single human being or to believe that any nation on earth is incapable of redemption. I have respect for Englishmen, because I recognize their bravery, their spirit of sacrifice for what they believe to be good for themselves, their cohesion and their powers of vast organization. My hope about them they will at no distant date retrace their steps, revise their policy of exploitation of undisciplined and ill-organized race and give tangible proof that India is a friend and partner in the British Commonwealth to come. Whether such an event will ever come to pass will largely depend upon our own conduct. That is to say I have hope of England because I have hope of India. We will not for ever remain disorganized and imitative. Beneath the present disorganization, demoralization and lack of initiative I can discover organization, moral strength and initiative forming themselves. A time is coming when England will be glad of India's friendship and India will disdain to reject the proffered hand because it has once despoiled her. I know that I have nothing to offer in proof of my hope. It is based on an immutable faith. And it is a a poor faith that is based on proof commonly [so] called.

1 *Young India*, 29 January 1925.

AN INTERVIEW TO *SWARAJYA*[1]

Madras
7 March 1925

Questioned by the *Swarajya* representative whether the acceptance of office by the *Swarajists* would in any way affect the relations between the Congress and the Swaraj Party, Mahatmaji answered with a decisive "No" and added that the Congress had given a *carte blanche* to the *Swarajists* in regard to their activities in the Councils.

On his attention being drawn to the Viceroy's assent to the Hindu Religious Endowments Act in spite of opposition from the elected Hindu members, Mahatmaji stated that he had not studied that Act or its implications, and added that in case it became absolutely necessary for him to do so he would pay his attention to it and express his opinion in course of time.

Questioned whether it was consistent with the policy of the Congress for the President of the Tamilnad Congress Committee to openly support the Act, Mahatmaji replied that he saw no objection to any Congressman supporting the Act who also accepted the principle of entry into the Councils.

To another question Mahatmaji replied that he would certainly avail himself of the opportunity of his visit to Vykom to see the Maharani Regent if he could.

He also confessed with regret that the prospects of Hindu-Muslim unity in the North which he lately visited were not very bright. He said that on his way to Bombay he had written on the subject to Dr. Kitchlew and other Muslim leaders and he was expecting a reply from them. Mahatmaji expressed his satisfaction at the cordial relationahip existing between the two communities in this province.

The only message he could give to the South was :

I ask them to spin, that's all.

1, *The Bombay Chronicle*, 12 March 1925.

AN INTERVIEW TO *THE BOMBAY CHRONICLE*[1]

Bombay
13 April 1925

Questioned whether there was any truth in the suggestion that he had purposely avoided calling the meeting of the All-India Congress Committee, although more than three months had elapsed since the Congress session, Mahatma replied :

The charge is baseless. I have not convened a meeting of the A.I.C.C. for the simple and obvious reason that I have no new policy or new programme to place before the country. Nor have I heard of any new programme to be placed before the Committee by any member. The one that was mapped out at Belgaum is incredibly simple. It has only to be worked out by each province to the best of its ability. If, however, there is a desire on the part of any member for the A.I.C.C. to meet, I shall gladly ask Pandit Jawaharlal Nehru to convene the meeting.

Is it true that some Committees are accepting cash value for yarn as subscription from members ?

I know, that some Committees are doing it, and my own personal opinion is that it is wrong.

I understand that the secretaries of some Committees act as the buying agents of the members from whom they accept cash and purchase yarn on their behalf to be tendered to the Committees. Would there be anything wrong in such a practice ?

It is not a desirable practice for secretaries to encourage.

Questioned whether there was any movement to challenge the representative character of the *Swarajists* in the Councils and the Assembly, Mahatmaji said that he had not heard of a single No-changer wishing, in any shape or form, to reopen the question. Even if any member desired to reopen it now at a meeting of the A.I.C.C., it was not open to him to do so at this stage. It could only be done at the next session of the Congress.

Asked to state his views on the Das-Birkenhead statements, Mahatmaji replied that he had absolutely nothing to say, as he had not so far taken any part in the discussion.

Do you agree with the interpretation put by the Anglo-Indians and Europeans on Mr. Das's manifesto on non-violence ?

No. I don't think it is a recantation of his former views on the subject. Mr. Das has merely reiterated his faith more clearly and more precisely.

What you to say regarding Earl Winterton's[2] suggestion that Indians must first enlist the support of the Government of India and the local Governments for any proposals they have to make before approaching the Imperial Government or British Parliament ?

In my opinion, the suggestion is a euphemistic way of saying that no proposals coming from the Nationalists would be considered by the India Office. Virtue lies in the India Office considering suggestions, irrespective of the *imprimature* of the Government of India, and even though they may come from, say, the revolutionaries.

What are the prospects of inter-communal unity at present?

I do not see any immediate prospect of achieving much. I am inclined to leave the question to work itself out. There are some diseases which, medical men tell us, are best left alone. The more thay are pampered, the worse they become. This communal trouble appears just now to have developed that character.

1. *The Bombay Chronicle*, 13 April 1925.
2. Under Secretary of State for India. On 6 April he had rejected in Parliament a suggestion that C.R. Das, Gandhiji and other Indian leaders should be called to London for consultations during the Viceroy's visit.

GANDHI'S IDEOLOGY

It was for the first time and in Bombay that I heard, the other day, some complaint about my not having called a meeting of the A.I.C.C. A press reporter came to me and tackled me on the question to which he seemed to attach the highest importance. I could not understand his agitation for some minutes for I was innocent of any newspaper controversy on the subject. My incessant travelling has practically cut me off from the newspaper world. It was only when Mr. Shastri told me in Madras, some days after the event, that I knew Sir Abdur Rahim was superseded. I do not regret this gross ignorance of mine on current events. I know that I am apparently useless for making any impression on such events. I can show no immediate remedy for such ills as the supersession of Sir Abdur Rahim. My ignorance of current events, therefore, does not matter much. I must apply myself to preparing efficient non-violent self-sacrificing workers with a living faith in hand-spinning and *khaddar*, Hindu-Muslim unity and, if they are Hindus, in removal of untouchability also. For the current year at any rate, this is the national programme and no other.

I do not need to worry about the purely "political" programme which the Congress has entrusted to the *Swarajists* who are an integral part of it. As a time economist I would be foolish if I bothered my head about things which with my eyes open and full trust I have handed over to a body of men who are at least as capable as myself, if not much more, in the domain which they have specially selected for themselves. It is enough for me to watch from a distance with admiration the valiant effort of Pandit Motilal Nehru in the Assembly, the brilliance of Deshbandhu who at the cost of his health pitted himself against an all-powerful Government and came out victorious each time the Government gave him battle, or the marvellous cohesion of the *Swarajists* in the Central Provinces or the courteous and almost unperceived encroachments of Mr. Jayakar. I would not insult these great workers by my officious and indifferent attention. I help them by my prayers for their success and by ceaseless effort to prepare the nation from within in the only manner I know.

I know of no division in the Congress ranks. I shall be party to no division. The Working Committee has a majority which does not wholly share my views. It is there to keep me straight, I shall never do a single thing during the year which my precious colleagues do not endorse. I am in correspondence with them as to the advisability of holding a meeting of the Working Committee. I am anxious not to take their time unnecessarily. Similar considerations guide me in not worrying the A.I.C.C. It is a body which has to be summoned only for giving new directions or framing new programmes. There are no new directions to be given, no new programme to be settled. It is no light thing to bring from long distances nearly four hundred men, the majority of whom are poor and all of whom are or should be busy. I have, therefore, purposely refrained from convening the A.I.C.C. But if there is a large body of members who wish to have a meeting called, and if they would name the purpose, I would have it summoned without avoidable delay.

What is most necessary, however, is for Provinces to organize themselves. Their Committees may meet frequently. We have practical provincial autonomy in the Congress. Let each Province honestly and industriously work the franchise. There seems to be a disposition to regard its failure as a foregone conclusion. Let me inform the pessimists and alarmists that the spinning movement is gaining, not losing, ground. There are workers all over India who are working at it silently, surely and effectively. The production and quality of *khaddar* have considerably improved. Many interesting experiments are being made to make *khaddar* cheaper and more durable. Tirupur perhaps heads the list. But Tirupur is only a sample of what is going on. The Gujarat experiment has only just begun. It has in it immense potentialities. It is an attempt to reduce the price of *khaddar* from nine annas to three annas per yard and at the same time to improve its quality. The indirect effect of the franchise has been already great. The direct effect depends upon the capacity and integrity of those who are working it. My advice to them is :

1. Canvass only for those who would spin themselves, but take in all who would bring their own yarn.

2. But be detached even regarding self-spinners. You must not pamper them. The franchise is a privilege. Those only are to be valued who will value the privilege and work to retain it.

3. Do not be disappointed if you have only a few members so long as they are true members.

4. Do not take money for yarn for you to convert it into yarn. Throw the burden of supplying the yarn on those who want to become members. You may open yarn depots for the sake of those who want yarn. Let the Provincial Khaddar Board undertake the supply of yarn.

Let me make my position clear. I am wedded to the three-fold programme. I cannot tease Hindu-Muslim unity into life. It, therefore, requires no outward activity from me. As a Hindu I shall serve as many Mussalmans as will let me serve them. I shall advise those who seek my advice. For the rest, I cease to worry about what I cannot mend. But I have a living faith in unity coming. It must come even if it has to do so after a few pitched battles. If there are men who will fight, nobody on earth can prevent them.

Untouchability is doomed. It may take time. But the progress made is truly marvellous. It is more still in the thought world. But in action too one notices the effect everywhere. It was a glorious sight, the other day, to see in Mangrol not one of the ladies raising her hand against untouchables sitting side by side with them. And when they were actually brought in, none of these brave women moved. It is not a solitary instance. But I know that there is a dark side to the picture. Hindus must unremittingly toil away at the reform. The larger the number of workers the more substantial the result.

But the most encouraging results are to be seen in spinning. It is spreading to the villages. I make bold to say that it is the most effective method of village reconstruction. There are thousands of women hungering to spin, because they want a few coppers to find them food. There are no doubt villages where the villagers do not need any supplementary income. I would not touch them for the time being. Just as I would not pamper self-spinners for the franchise, so would I not pamper spinners for money. They must spin if they need, not otherwise. The greatest difficulty in the way of workers is to induce men and women to spin or to do any other work even though they need some work. They either live on charity or are content to starve to death. There are millions in India who have lost all interest in life. We can only touch them by ourselves spinning. I am interested in producing the spinning atmosphere. When many people do a particular thing, it produces a subtle unperceivable effect which pervades the surroundings and which proves infectious. I want that atmosphere so that the idle hands I have described will be irresistibly drawn to the wheel. They will be so drawn when they see people spinning who do not need to. Hence the franchise.

But if the Congress workers do not wish to take part in the work, let them revise the programme next year. I shall resolutely refrain from any fight next year either. I shall swear by the franchise even if only a few spin to become members. But I have no desire to retain my hold on the Congress by mechanical means. I simply state my limitations. I cannot work at the reforms without any power behind. That power can only come by organizing the people either for violence or non-violence. I can only try to organize them for non-violence or fail. There is no indication of failure yet. There is every hope of success. Organization for non-violence means giving villagers remunerative work to do and inducing them to give up some of their bad habits and to bring into being consciousness of one nationality by making untouchables proud of their Hinduism and bringing Hindus, Mussalmans and others to believe in and to work for the common cause with a full heart. I have no aptitude for any other work along political lines till the three things are done. I am as keen as the tallest among us to establish *swaraj* at the earliest moment. I am as impatient of wrong as the most ardent patriot But I recognize the nation's limitations. It may be a long and dreary route but I know that it will be found to be the shortest. But all need not think alike, do not think alike. If there is an overwhelming body of opinion in the country that requires a change of methods and change of the franchise even during the current year, they can have it if they can ensure a full house of the A.I.C.C., and secure an overwhelming majority. Though it may be a straining of the Congress constitution I will not stand in the way of a vast majority of the members of the A.I.C.C. altering even the constitution. The A.I.C.C. can take such a drastic step if this urgency can be demonstrated and an overwhelming majority demand it. But if there is nothing to warrant such a change, then it behoves every one of us to rivet our attention to the franchise without interfering with the *Swarajist* part of the Congress activity in any shape or form. Half an hour to be honestly given by every Congressman and Congresswoman to the wheel and whole time to its organizing by those who have an aptitude for it, is not an exorbitant demand for the national cause.

1. *Young India,* 16 April 1925.

PROGRAMME OF SWARAJISTS[1]

There is at the present moment a note of despodency in the air over the number of Congress members. The complaint is that the members have been never so few as today. The complaint would be reasonable if the franchise being the same, the response was less than before. It would also be reasonable if the influence of the Congress was to be measured by the number of members. Opinions would undoubtedly differ as to the measure to be applied for gauging the Congress influence. For me there is one measure. I attach the highest importance to quality irrespective almost of quantity, the more so for Indian conditions. In the midst of suspicion, discord, antagonistic interests, superstition, fear, distrust and the like, there is not only no safety in numbers, but there may be even danger in them. Who does not know how often numbers have embarrassed us during the past four years? Numbers become irresistible when they act as one man under exact discipline. They are a self-destroying force when each pulls his own way or when no one knows which way to pull.

I am convinced that there is safety in fewness so long as we have not evolved cohesion, exactness and intelligent cooperation and responsiveness. One virtuous son is better than one hundred loafers. Five Pandavas[2] were more than a match for one hundred Kauravas.[3] A disciplined army of a few hundred picked men has times without number routed countless undisciplined hordes. A few members fully satisfying the Congress test can give a good account of themselves, whereas one million members nominally on the Congress register may not be worth the register itself. I do not for one moment suggest that those whom we have now on the register are sound or even sounder than those whom we had before. That can only be verified at the end of the year.

What I would like to drive home is that we should know what we want. Do we believe in the paramount value of the spinning-wheel ? Then we must adopt it whether we are few or many. Do we believe in the necessity, in terms of *swaraj*, of removing the curse of untouchability ? Then we may not surrender, though we may be overwhelmed. Do we regard Hindu-Muslim unity as absolutely necessary for the attainment of *swaraj* ? Then we must stake much to achieve it. We may not be satisfied with a sham. We must have the real coin or none.

"But these are not politics. There is no giving battle to the Government in all this", say some friends. My answer is we cannot give effective battle to the Government till we achieve these things. "But we shall never achieve any single one of these things till we attain *swaraj*", say others. I answer that we must evolve the ability to achieve these things notwithstanding Government indifference or opposition, secret or open. Achievement of these things to me means half the battle, if not the whole of it.

"What then of the *Swarajist* programme ?", say they. That programme must go on side by side with the development of internal strength. The *Swarajists* are an integral part of the Congress. They are able, they are on the alert, they will shape their policy in accordance with the exigencies of the situation. Let those who have the aptitude prosecute that programme as well. But let them not forget the internal work. If twelve thousand men and women, nay, two thousand men and women, can be induced vigorously to work the constructive programme, things will immediately wear a different aspect. Throughout my wanderings, I have noticed a lamentable dearth of workers—brave, honest, self-sacrificing, self-reliant and with confidence in themselves and the mission. The harvest is indeed rich but the labourers are few.

Sjt. Srinivasa Aiyenger and I were attending a meeting in Madras. People were bubbling with enthusiasm. We were driving to keep time for another meeting But my 'admirers' insisted on exhibiting me through a street which was not on the programme. He pleaded, I pleaded, want of time. Sjt. Aiyenger pleaded on behalf of my health. It was all to no purpose. We were driven !—shall I say compulsorily ? Both of us realized that these men were no help to the cause, they were a positive hindrance. Things were set right only when I took the law in my hands, declined to be driven, actually got out of the car and defied the crowd to carry me bodily if they wished. Here there was an ocular demonstration of danger in numbers. I can cite a score of such experiences. The people are well-meaning but ignorant and thoughtless. How many well-meaning mothers drug their children to death ?

We want not excitement at the present moment but calm constructive work. It is a laborious task, it is stupendous. But is not beyond our capacity. It need not even take time. What hinders progress is indefiniteness. The verbal assent without practical performance embarrasses. I plead for quality and quality alone. I must, therefore, refuse to trouble the All-India Congress Committee unless I receive a requisition to summon it. The present programme has been framed to arrive at the requisite quality. And so long as it remains, I can but advise every Congress worker to put his or her whole soul into its working so that we might have, at the end of the year, if it is at all possible, a compact body of men and women possessing the requisite qualifications, be the number ever so small.

1. *Young India*, 30 April 1925.

2. Five brothers, heroes of the Mahabharata.

3. Cousins of the Pandavas.

SPEECH IN CALCUTTA[1]

1 May 1925

Friends,

I have spoken sufficiently in Hindustani and I hope that a large part of this audience has followed my broken Hindustani. It is always a matter of deep grief to me that, whenever I go to the South or I come to Bengal, I am obliged in order to be able to make myself understood by my educated countrymen to speak in English. I wish that the people of the South and the people of Bengal would rid themselves of this laziness and make up their minds once for all to add to a knowledge of their own mother tongue a passable knowledge of Hindi or Hindustani which, and which alone, can become the language of internal commerce in India. Let English be, as it ought to be, language of international diplomacy, the language of intercourse between all the different nations of the world. But English can never usurp the function that specially belongs to Hindi or Hindustani. You ought to know that nearly twenty crores of the people of India can understand my broken Hindustani. Let it not be said that ten crores of India want to impose their speech or English speech on the twenty crores of India.[2]

I have said in my opening remarks with a deep grief it was to me this morning to enter 148 Russa Road. I know that that house no longer belonged to Deshbandu Das. I knew that he contemplated making over that beautiful mansion to trustees in order to divest himself of the last vestige of wealth that he possessed in this world. But, man of the world, living still in the world as I am doing, when I actually entered the house with the knowledge that its distinguished owner had voluntarily dispossessed himself of it, I could not help shedding a tear. I felt a wrench within me that the house was no longer Das's, and when I heard that he had not yet been able to repair his broken-down constitution, I felt doubly grieved and my grief was still further increased when I received a brief but beautiful and loving message from him, written by him in pencil hand, telling me how it was impossible for him to stand the double strain and why therefore he had gone away to Faridpur in advance. May God grant him health and long life to serve the country which he loves so dearly.

You will not expect me to tell you anything on what is called the political situation. A newspaper reporter told me today about the negotiations that are going on between Lord Birkenhead and Deshbandhu Das. I am totally unaware of any such negotiations. I have no knowledge of any such negotiations whatsoever; but I do not know that there is what may be called a political situation in this country today. But that political situation does not interest me sufficiently today. I am an economist of time; I have deliberately given me my general power of attorney to the Swaraj Party which is an integral part of the Congress. The Swaraj Party is in-charge of the political programme of the Congress and, seeing that I have the fullest faith in the ability of the Swaraj Party to handle the political situation, seeing that I have the fullest faith in the wisdom of Deshbandhu Das and Pandit Motilal Nehru, so far as the Council programme is concerned, it would be impudence on my part to concern myself about it unless they want me to do so and there is absolutely no reason for them to want my interference or to desire my opinion. When they do so you may depend on it that I am always at their service but, what is more, it would be impossible for me to make any effective statement on the political situation unless I have had a consultation with Deshbandhu Das. I have not come to Bengal, I am not travelling throughout the length and breadth of India to embarrass the Swaraj Party or to embarrass Deshbandhu or a single member of that party. I am pledged in the name of God to help that party to the best of my ability. I am pledged not even mentally to interfere with its programme and, if I do not throw myself heart and soul into that programme, it is because of my limitations. it is because I do not see eye to eye with them in their policy. But that does not mean that I must not help them. That does not mean that their policy is inimical to the country. It simply means that there is a difference of opinion as to the weight and the relative importance to be attached to the political programme and the constructive programme. I swear by the constructive programme; the more I examine myself the more I feel that I am more fitted for handling the constructive programme for developing our own power from within than for engaging into diplomatic relations with the matchless diplomats from England. I confess to you that I will be ill at ease in carrying on negotiations with any of those officials unless I feel that we have power from within and I am here to confess to you that we have lost today the power that we thought in 1912 we had in abundance, and therefore I propose to the best of my ability to concentrate solely and exclusively upon the constructive programme. That will be my best contribution to the country and to the Swaraj Party, and I promise to you that if you, the young men and the young women of Bengal, will help me—no matter to what political party you may belong—if you will kindly help me in making this constructive programme a living, a swinging success, you will find that our fetters automatically drop. You will find that those whom we consider unjustly incarcerated and kept under detention, that those are today pinning away in the Jail at Mandalay, you will find that, if you can make the constructive programme a success, they will be discharged without your asking for their discharge. What is that constructive programme by which I swear ? Let me take you through these three items as rapidly as I can. Hindu-Muslim unity, meaning unity between all the races that inhabit the fair land of ours. Is that programme unattainable by us ? Is that programme undesirable ? But I have admitted my incompetence. I have admitted that I have been found wanting as a physician prescribing a cure for this malady. I do not find that either the Hindus or the Mussalmans are ready to accept my cure and therefore I simply nowadays confine myself to a passing mention of this problem and content myself by saying that some day or other we Hindus and Mussalmans will have to come together if we want the deliverance of our country; and, if it is to be our lot that before we can come together, we must shed one another's blood then I say the sooner we do so the better it is for us. If we propose to break one another's head, let us do so in a manly way, let us not then shed crocodile tears, let us not ask for sympathy from any quarter if you do not propose to give any quarter. That is what I have to say about the Hindu-Muslim unity.

Is it a long drawn-out programme or an impossible programme that we Hindus should rid ourselves of the cure of untouchability ? So long as untouchability disfigures Hinduism, so long do I hold the attainment of *swaraj* to be an utter impossibility. Supposing it would be a gift descending from Downing Street to India that gift would be a curse upon this holy land. If we do not get rid of this curse, it would be a curse added to curse, *swaraj* without the freedom of the untouchables. But what are the implications of this removal of untouchability ? Let the *Sanatani* Hindus understand from me who claims to be a *sanatani* Hindu. I do not ask you to interdine with anybody; I do not ask you to exchange your daughters with the untouchables or with anybody, but I do ask you to remove this curse so that you may put him beyond the pale of service. For me the removal of untouchability is the acceptance of the privilege of service to people whom we have kept under bondage in the sacred name of religion. Listen to me the *sanatani* Hindus of Calcutta, that this Hinduism is in the balance and it will go down to predition if you do not get rid of this untouchability. So much and so far for untouchability.

Then take the third item in your programme, the spinning-wheel and the *khaddar*. What do I ask of you ? The millionaires of Calcutta, the barristers, the M.L.As. and the M.L.Cs. of Calcutta, what do I ask of you ? The women of Calcutta, what do I ask of you ? Half an hour, in the name of God, for the sake of perishing and famishing humanity of India. Is it too much for you to give half an hour of your time to doing that—to spinning for the sake of these poor people so that you can cheapen *khaddar*, so that I can tell the villagers of Bengal that the daughters and sons of millionaires are spinning ? Why will you not spin ? Do you know that the villagers have lost faith in us, in themselves and in God Himself ? Because they find that we often go to them, sometimes to collect money, sometimes with one programme and sometimes with another programme. They do not know where we want to lead them and so they are distrustful of us and when we take in our simplicity, the spinning-wheel to their homes, they smile at us the smile of no-confidence, They do not say : "We do not understand this instrument of yours. We do not know what that meaning lies behind the spinning-wheel." So when the villagers have forgotten the use and the beauty, the life-giving beauty of the spinning-wheel, they do not take to it kindly. If you want them to take to this home industry of yours kindly, then it is necessary for you to spin the wheel yourselves, you will not be able to make necessary improvements on it, you will not be able to re-establish this almost lost industry of India. No agricultural country in the world has yet lived which has not added a supplementary industry to it. And I defy any Indian, no matter how distinguished an economist he may be to show me an effective substitute for the millions of India who are scattered all over the land which is 1900 miles long and 1500 miles broad and scattered in 700 thousand villages most of which are outside even the railway tracts. I defy anybody to propose or to show any effective substitute. But till such an effective substitute is placed before you, do not idle away your time, do not grudge the poor, down-trodden humanity of India, the half an hour that I ask of you, the Congress asks of you. And then, if you take to the spinning-wheel what about its product ? Why is this spinning-wheel a necessity ? Because we want clothes made not in Manchester or Japan, made not in Ahmedabad or Bombay which did not stand Bengal in good stead at the time of Partition, but we want beautiful *khdddar* manufactured in our own village homes which always stands us in good stead. We want the villagers to be smiling with plenty; we want the people of Khulna, when again they have got famine, to know that they are not to live on the doles of rice thrown at their face by a Dr. Ray, but I want the people of Khulna to feel that they do not need the assistance of even a Ray, because they have got the spinning-wheel to fall back upon. Let them not become beggars when they have got ready in their hands an instrument of living, an instrument which shall be an insurance, a permanent insurance against famine. That is why I ask you to take up the spinning-wheel and *khaddar* and that is what has brought me to Bengal.

I do not want to interfere with the politics of Bengal or India today. There are men who are able enough to handle it, but I regard myself as a *charkha* expert; I regard myself as a *khaddar* expert. I believe that I have something to say to every man and woman in connection with this message of *khaddar*, and therefore, while I have yet life left in me, whilst Bengal is yet ready and willing to listen to me, I want to re-deliver my message to Bengal with all the power at my command and say if you want freedom for your country do anything else you like but at least lay a firm and stable foundation on which you will be able to erect a proper and firm structure, and remember the words of this old man speaking to you again and again in Calcutta and will speak again and again throughout his tour in Bengal that, if you do not lay this sure and certain foundation, remember that any reform that you get, any liberty or freedom that you think you possess will be nothing but a house built of cards which is going to topple down under the first gust of wind. Therefore, I pray of you to work up this message, the living message of *khaddar* and spinning-wheel. Hindus, remove this curse of untouchability. Hindus and Mussalmans, if it is at all possible for you without shedding a drop of blood, do come together and embrace each other as brothers in arms.

I thank you for the patience with which you have listened to me.

1. *Amrita Bazar Patrika*, 2 May 1925.
2. The meeting was attended by 10,000 persons. Dr. P.C. Ray presided.

INTERVIEW TO ASSOCIATED PRESS[1]

Calcutta,

1 May 1925

Mahatma Gandhi was spinning when a representative of the Associated Press called on him this afternoon. Referring to the Das-Birkenhead discussions, Mahatmaji refused to make any statement until he had seen Mr. Das personally. He did not want to embarrass his position by any statement at present :

I have come to Bengal not to hinder, but to help Mr. Das, as far as it lies in my power.

As regards the object of his extended visit to Bengal, Mr. Gandhi said he had come here to study the possibility of Bengal so far as *khadi* is concerned, to study the untouchability problem and to know the Hindu-Muslim relations here. He had been for a long time under a promise to visit certain places in Bengal. As soon as he finished his Southern India tour he took the first opportunity of coming to Bengal. Mahatmaji said that he was feeling well and he expressed confidence that he would be able to fulfil his Bengal programme.

Asked by the representative what attitude he would take

if more power was given to the transferred department and the possible date of Dominion Status was announced, Mr. Gandhi smilingly replied :

Why should I accept a mere supposition when I know that I can see Mr. Das tomorrow and discuss with him ?

1. *The Hindu*, 2 May 1925.

INTERVIEW TO *THE STATESMAN*

Calcutta

1 May 1925

In a room practically devoid of furniture, on the floor of which were lengths of carpet, Mr. Gandhi, clad only in loin-cloth, sat cross-legged and, after a greeting, asked to be excused while his spinning-wheel was adjusted. He then expressed his readiness to convese, and proceeded to do so, spinning rapidly and skilfully the while.

Seldom taking his eyes from his work, he answered questions without the slightest hesitation, although his voice, soft and musical, was sometimes almost inaudible through the gentle whirl of the *charkha*. At the outset he similingly acquiesced in a suggestion that the *charkha* was the machine on which he pinned his political faith.

Mr. Gandhi was first invited to express an opinion regarding the attitude of Europeans in the present political situation and the difficulty which many people experienced in defining a clear-cut policy from the maze of political panacea enunciated from time to time.

He replied that there must be some organization to guide political thought and the National Congress ought to represent the national feeling. There were two sides to the present programme—the internal and the external. The object of the former was to achieve unity among all races, "Hindu-Muslim unity" being a short term to cover all classes—the removal of untouchability by the Hindus, the spinning-wheel and *khaddar*.

On the external side, there was activity in the Council represented by the Swaraj Party, which was an integral part of the National Congress. That was the whole of the national programme.

Asked to express his opinion on the general political situation in India, Mahatma Gandhi said :

I am certainly not a pessimist, but I do not see much sign of hope. I shall begin to hope when we meet with demonstrable success in our external programme...meaning thereby the unity of all races in India, the removal of untouchability and the development of spinning and the use of *khaddar*.

As a declared "friend of the British", Mr. Gandhi regretted that he was unable to see a change of heart on their part.

Europeans may well co-operate on the internal as well as on the external side, and I invite them, as I have always invited them, to examine the programme in both its aspects. As regards the external side, if they are satisfied that we mean what we say, that we have absolutely no desire, if we could, to drive out the English, or to end the British connection they should make common cause with us.

Touching on the question of non-cooperation, Mr. Gandhi said :

The programme of non-co-operation, so far as the nation is concerned, is suspended, but so far as I am personally concerned, it is not suspended, although the individual suspension had little meaning in it today. I never was a Council-goer, but I suppose at the present moment with me it is a virtue of necessity, because my late imprisonment debars my entry into the Councils. I had long suspended my practice, but the Society of the Inner Temple has removed the last vestige of temptation from me.

What, therefore, remains of non-co-operation in me is as Mr. Das would put it, a matter of "mental attitude". But it is an attitude that I personally prize because, claiming as I do, to be a friend of the British, I want to tell them that I see no trace yet of any real change of heart.

I am a born co-operator, but non-co-operation with me became a necessity; but I am waiting for the opportunity when I can declare that I will again become a hearty co-operator.

Referring to the problem of Hindu-Muslim unity, Mr. Gandhi said :

My travels have shown me that both communities are filled with mutual distrust and fear, but I have not a shadow of doubt that unity is coming in the near future. Each party regards it as a national necessity.

Mr. Gandhi added that there might be a clash before that came about, but whether they escaped that calamity or had to face it, unity was eventually a certainty.

On the subject of Mr. Das's manifesto and his terms on which a settlement might be reached. Mr. Gandhi said :

I prefer to say nothing until I have had a consultation with Mr. Das. But I can say generally that I am bound under the agreement, and even without it, not to embarrass the Swaraj Party or Mr. Das personally in their political activity.

Asked to give his view regarding His Excellency the Viceroy's visit to England, Mr. Gandhi said :

I know nothing of the nature of the negotiations and I do not want to go by the newspapers, especially as I have become, again of necessity, an indifferent reader of newspapers and bazaar talk had never interested me. I do not know what Lord Reading's mission is, I do not know thc implications in Lord Birkenhead's speech, much less do I know what is going on behind the curtain.

1. *The Statesman*, 2 May 1925

SPEECH AT BENGAL PROVINCIAL CONFERENCE, FARIDPUR[1]

3 May 1925

President and Friends,

I am supposed to be speaking to you to return thanks for the very kind and generous words spoken about me by the Chairman of the Receptien Committee and our worthy President. At the outset I want to tender my congratulations to the Subjects Committee on having finished its deliberations in perfect harmony. It is an open secret—and latterly we have ceased to have secrets whatsoever in connection with our politics and, therefore, we have been welcoming, and even inviting, detectives so as to enable them to detect flaws in our policy, detect flaws in our doings and in everything that we may do in connection with the national policy and even outside the national policy. But still, as I said, it is an open secret that there were some disputes or differences or dissensions in connection with the resolutions that will be brought before this House this afternoon. But all's well that ends well. I do not recall any Subjects Committee in which there have not been little differences or little jars. I suppose, they will abide with us to the end of time whether they are in India or elsewhere. European Cabinets have their secrets, but if we are permitted to pry into their secrets and into the secrets of their Subjects Committees, I suppose, we would have about the same kind of reports as reports are to be found in connection with our dissensions and disputes. Let us not, therefore, exaggerate those dissensions and differences, but let us treasure the thought that, after all, in the end we can unite and we can unite to a purpose.

I read the address of Deshbandhu Das and I have had the privilege and pleasure of reading the English translation. I do not know which is the original, whether Bengali or the English translation, because Bengali scholars tell me that the Bengali version reads as sweet and as eloquent as the English version, but, in any case, I had the pleasure and privilege of having an advanced copy of the English address when I was in Calcutta with a brief, little, loving, sweet note from Deshbandhu that, if I could spare a few minutes, I should read that address. Well, I read from the start to the finish and I was wondering whether he had pilfered every sentiment from me. But I must confess to you that I saw that the language was not mine. The language was that of a scholar and not of a rustic who delights in calling himself a spinner, a scavenger, a weaver, a farmer and now even a *Namasudra*. And so I saw that the language was not mine, but the thoughts seemed to have been pilfered and so immediately I said to myself, if he would ask me to subscribe to it, I would have no hesitation in doing so without perhaps altering a single word or a single phrase. But, perhaps, some of you will consider that this is no recommendation whatever for that address, but on the contrary that is the surest guarantee that the address is as dull as ditch water. Well I assure you that it is not as dull as ditch water. And why do I want to give you that assurance? You have listened to it. You read it. And when a thing is not dull in reading, you may depend upon it.

I want to look not at phraseology. I do not want to look at the language. I only want to look at the thoughts that underlie it and what he has said to us in that address. If we are true to ourselves, if we are true to the nation, if we are true to the policy that was enunciated for the first time in Calcutta in 1920 with all the great deliberation that we could bring to bear upon that policy, if we are to be true to that, there is absolutely nothing in that address to cavil at. And that address is a re-enunciation and an emphatic and unequivocal re-enunciation of the policy that was laid down for the first time in the history of the Congress in 1920. When I say laid down for the first time in the history of the Congress, it is not that the Congress ever believed in a policy of violence, nor that the Congress ever believed that we should follow anything but legitimate methods, but that the Congress never made that declaration. But in 1920 we chose deliberately to tell the world that we intended to attain goal of *swaraj*, that in order to attain that goal we intended to follow a means that was absolutely peaceful and legitimate. And as I have translated these two phrases or these two words or paraphrases, "non-violent and truthful" means, do you abide by that interpretation or that paraphrase or these two words? And during the four or five years that have intervened, Deshbandhu has been one of those who have had a part in the shaping of the national policy in those terms—and you have no right to expect anything else from him and you have no right to expect anything more from him today. Anything more I say, because some of us like pepper and salt eschewed from our programme for the time being, at any rate. We have considered it, everyone of the leaders has considered it, that it is not possible for us to attain our freedom with pepper and salt or with fire and brimstone. We shall be able to attain our national regeneration—shall we say, nation salvation—only by mean that are absolutely non-violent and truthful; not that it need be the religion of any single one of us—it is sufficient if it is our policy, it is sufficient if we accept it from motives of expediency and no other or no higher motive.

We have problems in India to deal with which no other nation on the earth has. We have, if we are Hindus, to deal with our Muslim countrymen, with our Christian countrymen, with our Zoroastrian countrymen, with the Sikhs and so many sections and sub-sections of Hindus, which dignify themselves by a name which does not belong to Hinduism. How are we to achieve the unity of action between the diverse elements except by means which are not open to any question, namely, non-violence and truthfulness ? We will not be able to deal with our Muslim countrymen or with our Hindu countrymen on any other terms. And then we have our provincialism. Bengal thinks that she must rule the whole of India and that the whole of India is to be merged in that little province called Bengal, and Gujarat probably thinks likewise. Gujarat, which is merely a drop in the ocean compared to Bengal, thinks it must rule the whole of India and India should be merged in Gujarat. Then take the brave Mahrattas with their recent traditions. Why should they not think that they must shape the destiny and policy of India ? The Muslim with his still later traditions thinks that he must establish or re-establish a Muslim empire. From these diverse elements and provincialism there is no escape for us except through non-violent and truthful means because, otherwise, we are sitting on a mine which is likely to explode at any moment. The slightest trace of dirt in us is likely to make us perish and that is why I have insisted in season and out of season upon a policy not of religion but a policy of non-violence and truthfulness. You may do anything you like with your country after you have attained your goal.

You may resort to any means that you consider legitimate or proper for the vindication of your country's honour, but for me I make no secret. It is the first and the last. It is my religion. It is the breath of my nostrils—non-violence and truthfulness, and I wish, I could infect every young man in this hall with that zeal and with that devotion for this non-violent and truthfulness.

I know many a Bengali youth. I know that he has got courage which is matchless; I know he is eager to die for the freedom of his country as he is today living for the country. I claim, if it is not impertinence on my part, that I have also the ability to die for the country as I am today living for the country. But, as I have said, it is for me a living death. Death on the gallows has absolutely no terror for me. I believe I have got the capacity for dying on the gallows with a smile on my lips if I am innocent. If my hands and my heart are as white as snow, then death has no terror for me. Let it be so with every young man in Bengal. And Deshbandhu has re-enunciated and re-stated that policy for you. Did he not say the same thing in his beautiful address[2] at Gaya ? I have not read that address even now, but I heard the echoes of that address delivered to me at the Yeravda Jail.[3] I did not pilfer that news. I may tell you I carried out every instruction of the Jailor's, but the Jailor and visitors sometimes told me what was passing outside the walls of that prison and I came to know in ordinary course that Deshbandhu had enunciated in emphatic terms the policy of non-violence and the policy of truthfulness. He thinks likewise for you, for me, for himself and for the whole of the country. You know how he has been assailed. You know how many detractors he has, not merely amongst Europeans but amongst our own countrymen. He has detractors in his own camp. What is he to do ? Is he to sit on the fence ? Yes, he might have sat on the fence if he had not his country's interest in all his heart—if he did not dream about the deliverance of his country, and if he was not prepared to say in most loving manner : I cannot possibly wish you, Mahatma Gandhi, a long life because you are destined to die the moment we have achieved *swaraj*, because you are living for *swaraj* and *swaraj* alone and as I want my *swaraj* for India today, I cannot pray to God that Mahatma Gandhi may live long lest my *swaraj* be delayed. I treasure that thought and in that thought, although humorously uttered, is the highest compliment that he is capable of paying me or you are capable of paying me because it is right.

I am as impatient as any single one of you to attain *swaraj*. But I am understanding our functions, know what we have got to do. If we could get *swaraj* by a doze of intoxicating medicines, I would today hurl defiance at the great British throne and say out with you I want my *swaraj* today. But I cannot do that today. I cannot hurl that defiance. I admit my incapacity. I admit the incapacity of my country today. Yes, I am certainly take off a few English heads as anyone can. It does not require strong arms. It requires a strong heart. A little bit of revolve can be manipulated by me just as [by] any one of you. But what is the use of my taking off the head of Lord Reading or Lord Lytton or of any Englishman ? But I canot possibly put that head on a charger and say that here is the deliverance of my country. Deliverance of the country requires a sterner stuff. We have got to evolve not merely the capacity for dying. We have got to evolve not merely the capacity for killing, but, as Dr. Besant once said, it required some amount of courage, even to live in the face of odium, censure, neglect and boycott—even from those whom you have treasured as nearest and dearest to you. And she was right. I say that every moment of my life it requires some degree of courage even to live in the midst of such storms and strife.

But, how, then, are we to attain freedom of our country ? Not cartainly by killing, not certainly at the present moment even by dying, but by pleading, and that is the reason why I have humbly ventured to place before you these three things : Hindu-Muslim unity, removal of untouchability and the spinning-wheel. But the Hindu-Muslim unity cannot occupy a young man's whole twenty-four hours. It is our creed. Just as a Mussalman has said his *kalma*[4] it is finished and then he has got to live up to the implication of the *kalma*, just as I have recited a *gayatri*,[5] it is finished with me and I need not be reciting it fifty million times during the day, but I must live up to it—so this is but a creed—of Hindu-Muslim unity, removal of untouchability. But every one of us can put our hands to something tangible, to something feasible. Everyone of us can put our hands to be beautiful spinning-wheel and with every yard of yarn that you spin, you spin every yard of the destiny of India. That is the finest revolution that I know for India. I know that some of your laugh—the laugh of incredulity. Some of you will consider—here is an idiot speaking to us in season and out of season about the spinning-wheel. But I promise, I prophesy that a day is to dawn, and is not very far, when nobody will call me an idiot. But the finest testimony that will be given to me will be that I revived the cult of *charkha*—that Gandhi gave the simple message of the rustic when he asked us to spin—that he spoke in terms of *swaraj*—*swaraj* for the masses and millions of his down-trodden countrymen when he delivered the message of *charkha*. I have no misgiving about the future of my career. My career is ensured. My future is ensured so long as I swear by the *charkha* and I promise to you that [even if] everyone of the audience here, including Deshbandhu Das, says : "Gandhi is wrong; *charkha* is nothing, it is an idiotic thing in this age of machinery and speed", I will still say the same thing up the very last breath of my life : "Give me the spinning-wheel and I will spin *swaraj* for India."

You will not get *swaraj* for India on any other terms. We must become a nation of workers and not a nation of talkers or ideas. We are by nature not idle but, by force of circumstances, millions of our countrymen have to live in enforced idleness. You do not know the idle masses as I do. I have lived in the midst of the 17 lakhs of people of Champaran for six months or more, and I have seen them hovering round me from day to day without doing anything whatsoever. They were satisfied to draw a little of warmth from one whom they considered to be their true servant, but they would not work. But I had not, at that time, this spinning-wheel or I would have placed it before them, They were not famishing, not starving, but they had forgotten the use of their limbs. They would scratch a little bit of earth, grow indigo, reap corn, but would not spin. They had no industry in their homes and, having forgotten it for years, they now consider it perfectly useless. That is why I call it enforced idleness. Our limbs were cut off by the East India Company—that is one of the blackest crimes that I have charged the British Rule with and that is why I have said that, not until I see a change of heart amongst the Englishmen, and not until they feel in terms of the masses of India and say : "Yes, we repent, we ought to return to India what we have taken from her"—for me there is no hand extended; to them I say, "I cannot clasp your hand if you do not call me, 'my dear brother'." I cannot do that unless he sympathizes with the masses of India. He flings a little bit of sympathy in the face of masses from time to time.

It is not enough for me. I want him to read the hearts of the masses and understand their economy, not economics borrowed from Europe, no matter how distinguished a personage he may be. He must think in terms of the masses and, the moment the Englishman begins to think in terms of the masses, you will find me fall prostrate at his feet, because I know his virtues, his capacities. But I cannot do so unless he develops along right lines. That being so, unless he does so, what is the use of my speaking to the Englishman; for I charge him with a black crime in that he has robbed me of the spinning-wheel.

But why should I charge him when you, my countrymen, refuse to spin for half an hour, when you send messages or when you write sometimes that 'this fool of a Gandhi has imposed this cursed franchise on us; let us get rid of it as he has imposed the cursed burden upon us.' But does he ask you to do something marvellous, something beyond your capacity when he asks, in the name of God, for the sake of the country, to spin if it is only for half an hour ? Does he ask you to do something which you are incapable of doing when he asks you to be clad from top to toe in hand-spun and hand-woven cloth ? What shall I say to you, what shall I do with you or how shall I attain my *swaraj* if you cannot do this little practical thing ? They accuse you, they accuse the Bengalis, of want of practicability and in some respects they are right. We want everything, but without having to work for it sufficiently. If we speak about the thing sufficiently, if we pass resolutions, but immediately, when it comes to actual work, we shirk it, remember those who shirk work for the sake of the nation shall have no hand in shaping the destiny of India, shall have no hand in attaining *swaraj* for India. I ask you, therefore, to retain his "Yarn Franchise". Make it still more restrictive. If it is to be restricted, make it obligatory on every man and woman who wants to serve India through the Congress, a living organization, make it obligatory upon every man and woman, upon every girl and boy, to spin for at least half an hour and to wear *khaddar*, not only on ceremonial occasions, not for Congress work, but for all work. In your home also, you will wear nothing but *khaddar*. You will go stark naked rather than you should wear anything that is not hand-spun by your sister and handwoven by your brother in your home and not in the factory. That is the message of the spinning-wheel. That is the simple little demand I make of every man and woman who loves India and who wants freedom of India.

Would you be surprised if I tell you that, if you want to have the discharge of those prisoners who are cooped within the walls of the Mandalay Prison, if you want the release of Subhas Chandra Bose and others you must spin. Without work it is impossible. If you want him and his fellow-prisoners to be discharged with honour and with dignity, then I say, spin.

Promise me that every Bengali--man and woman—will henceforth wear *khaddar*, and nothing but *khaddar*, that every man and woman will go to the *charkha* with the same delight that he goes to his meal or with the same delight of a young lover who goes to his sweetheart. Then I promise deliverance of those young men in no time.

You will find that this incredibly simple thing will secure their deliverance, because that will be a sign of your determination to work for India without expecting any remuneration; because I have asked only for half an hour's free labour for the sake of India. It is not a mighty thing that I ask of you. But [it is] because you are of little faith, because you have no faith in your masses, because you have no faith in yourselves, because you have no faith in your country, that you decline to spin and still feel that Deshbandhu would secure the key of that prison, break their fetters and unlock those gates. It is impossible for him to do so.

Some of you consider that he is carrying on negotiations with the Government in secret. He has no secrecy whatsoever, so far as I know. Secrecy is prohibited in Congress politics. When somebody asked him what is at the back of all this, he said, "There is as much in the back of it as in the front". Lord Birkenhead has sent no secret message to him. He is not in secret negotiations with him. All that he had got to say, you will fid it in his beautiful address. You will find it in his writings and speeches. You will find it in his life when he is closeted in his own inner chamber or when he is in this big *pandal*.[6] If you scratch him, I know you find the same man wanting deliverance for the country. That is the link that binds me to him, that is the link that should bind the audience to him. That is the link which should bind you to him.

You may not be convinced with our reasons. You may say : "Our heart is satisfied that you are on the right track. We subscribe to your advice so long as we hold you to be our ideal." That is the way for you. That is way I would like you to treat those whom you love. You [are] like sepoys and soldiers, it is not for you to reason why after you have chosen your leader. If you have not made your choice and are called upon to make your choice, exercise your reason to its utmost. Scan the would-be candidate to leadership from top to toe. But after having made your choice and after having garlanded, like Sita, your chosen person, never flinch and, like Sita, go through the fire with him and all will be well with you.

1. *The Searchlight*, 8 May 1925
2. At the Congress session in 1922.
3. During 1922-24.
4. Religious recital of Muslims.
5. Vedic prayer to Sun-god.
6. A place of meeting.

NEW THEORY OF SWARAJ[1]

Gandhiji was inerviewed by Babu Hardayal Nag and gave replies to questions put to him.

Q. (Question) : Do you still hold that *swaraj* cannot come from abroad ?

A. (Answer) : Yest, most emphatically.

Q. Then why did you not controvert Mr. Das's new theory of *swaraj* by way of gift and necessarily within the Empire ?

A. I do not think that Mr. Das has said any such thing in his presidential address at Faridpur. I read the address quite differently from what you do. For Deshbandhu Das does not say that it is necessarily within the formula—"Within the British Empire". On the contrary, he adheres to the formula—"Within the Empire, if possible; without it, if necessary."

Q. Do you not feel that certain classes of people are trying to change the colour of administration only, but not its character ?

A. I know that some people merely want to change the colour but not the character.

Q. I venture to suggest that the Swarajists are trying to add another class to these classes for capturing the services with certain amount of false power transferred to them.

A. I hope not; nor do I believe it is so. I know Deshbandhu Das and Pandit Motilal Nehru. I am convinced that they will not be satisfied with mere change of colour.

Q. I cite the Calcutta Corporation as an instance. It is now manned by Swarajists, as far as possible. The Swarajists, I suggest, want to capture the provincial and local administrations only to man them with Swarajists.

A. I do not know what is happening in the Calcutta Corporation.

Q. I and many others think that *swaraj* must grow from within and it must be built in the village and we accept *charkha* as the only weapon for the foundation for it. Do you agree ?

A. I literally endorse your view. But we feel that our task is very difficult on account of the apathy of the Swarajists. In Bengal, almost all the Congress organizations are in their hands and they have no faith in *charkha*. That being the case, *charkha* is suffering most on account of want of provincial or district organizations.

Q. Do you approve of any separate organization in favour of *charkha* and *khadi* movement ?

A. I shall be very sorry if I discover that the Swarajsts have no faith in the spinning-wheel. I am aware that some of them do not possess the same faith in it that you and I have, but so far as my knowledge goes, I have not met a single Swarajist who has shown his disbelief in the spinning-wheel. Assuming that they do not believe in the *charkha* at all, I am still unable to understand your deduction that their apathy is hampering your or my progress. On the contrary, you and I should to that extent make greater effort. I, therefore, do not consider a separate organization for the development of spinning necessary, so long as the Swarajists do not repudiate the spinning-wheel.

Q. Do you recognize the fact that two parties are not pulling on well in their respective work?

A. I do not recognize the fact, but if the two parties are not pulling on well, I would then blame the non-Swarajists more than the Swarajists, for the simple reason that the former had not the slightest occasion to stand in the latter's path. They at least have, I expect, made their final choice. Let them abide by it and live up to it.

Q. But considering the fact that you are the accredited leader of both the parties, does your duty end in blaming this party or that party?

A. Yes, certainly, because though I may be the nominal head of both the parties, I am myself a non-*Swarajist*. Therefore, I am entitled to blame the non-*Swarajists* more.

Q. Many of us have of course individually implicit faith in non-violent non-co-operation as a means to win *swaraj*. Now it is evident that the *Swarajists* are trying to discredit non-co-operation only for their class or party purposes and have already made gestures for co-operation, of course on certain terms quite immaterial to the people of the country. Under the circumstances, in his presidential address at Faridpur, Mr. Das has declared non-co-operation as a failure. In your speech, subsequently made at Faridpur, you laid stress on non-violence and truthfulness, but you did not say a word to save non-co-operation from the attack of Deshbandhu Das. Will you illuminate us on this point?

A. I have discovered no attack on the part of Mr. Das on non-co-operation. Therefore, non-co-operation was not a relevant matter. Moreover, I have debarred myself from saying a word upon non-co-operation from the Congress platform, being the author of the resolution suspending non-co-operation at Belgaum. But my own individual view is known to the world and my personal abstention from co-operation is an ocular demonstration of my view.

Q. Of course at Faridpur you spoke not as President of the All-India Congress Committee, but in your individual character and the phrases you used there were non-violence and truthfulness but not a word about non-co-operation. To my mind, non-violence without non-co-operation is meaningless. There is non-violence even in cowardice. If you have a firm faith in non-violent non-co-operation, how can you allow any *Swarajist* to speak against it without any protest?

A. As I have told you there is not a word, so far as I am aware, said in Deshbandhu's address against non-co-operation. And we should also recollect that I was speaking on the creed of the Congress. The creed of the Congress makes no mention of "peaceful and legitimate means" and I took care in my speech to say that I paraphrased these two terms by the adjectives: non-violence and truthfulness.

Q. Your declaration at Faridpur is that you have given your general power of attorney to Deshbandhu Das to do what he is doing in the Council. Anyone can rake it by implication that his performances in the Council are on behalf of you as principal, he being only an agent of you. No one can be blamed for taking such a view of your statement according to the law relating to principal and agent. Is that the case? Do you support also what Deshbandhu Das does in the Council?

A. When I spoke of Deshbandhu Das or *Swarajists* being agents I spoke, as an Irishman once spoke of himself as one of the proprietors of the Empire, as one of the shareholders of the concern called the Indian National Congress. And the Congress having given authority to the *Swarajists* to prosecute their Council programme, I think I was quite correct in describing the *Swarajists* as holders of my general power of attorney, so far as their Council work is concerned. I need not, therefore, on that account endorse every detail of the *Swarajists*' policy in the povincial Councils or Legislative Assembly. As a wise and practical man, having one given my general power of attorney to the agents of my own choice, I do not bother my head about what they are doing.

Q. If the *Swarajists* succeed in obtaining a concession from the bureaucracy based on a certain agreement, will you be a party to that agreement?

A. Oh, when the terms of any agreement with the bureaucracy are out, I shall have to consider them. I have issued no power of attorney to anybody to conclude any settlement with the Government. I therefore reserve, like every individual

Congressman, my full right to scrutinize any terms of settlement that may be proposed for national acceptance.

Q. Do you understand what Deshbandhu Das means by provincial autonomy?

A. I can guess.

Q. Then what is it ?

A. I take the word in the dictionary sense of the term.

Q. Can't I expect a clear answer from you on this point?

A. That is the answer. For I have closely followed Deshbandhu's address at Faridpur, but he has not gone into details there. Therefore, I am entitled to give provincial autonomy the meaning that is given to it in the English language.

Q. Is not the Faridpur speech liable to the interpretation that Deshbandhu Das has changed his views with reference to provincial autonomy?

A. I should think not. That is certainly not my impression.

Q. Then why has he fought shy of the phrase in his presidential address.

A. Has he laid any stress on this matter, I mean upon provincial autonomy? There was no occasion. All that he has laid stress upon is *swaraj* and *swaraj* is a term which to me is more inclusive because it goes farther than provincial autonomy.

Q. But can you illuminate us why he studiously avoided the word which he has been preaching so long?

A. For the simple reason that he has used a more general term, an inclusive term.

Q. Can you guess the ultimate result of the work of the *Swarajists* in Council?

A. I do not need to. Because whenever I want to understand what they have done, I have got the newspaper records to fall back upon. Further, I have got my own measure for gauging the worth of all such work. And I know that it can be no more and no less than the work that you and I are doing outside and internally. Because those who have gone to the Councils have declared and must declare that their potency depends upon the work done by the people themselves and the power evolved by them for self-rule, I suggest that measure for your and everybody's acceptance. In that case, we need not search the newspaper files nor resort to the dangerous pastime of guessing.

Q. Do you not feel that non-co-operation is suffering most on account of your giving a long rope to the *Swarajists*?

A. I do not think so at all. Rather, I hold that it is suffering because of the weakness of non-co-operators.

Q. Are you aware that the *Swarajists* have not yet changed their methods?

A. What method?

Q. Their methods and procedure. I cite this instance. Do you know anything of the supersession of Dr. P.C. Ray's election as President of the Bengal Provincial Conference at Faridpur?

A. I know nothing of it. What was it?

Q. At the time of election Dr. Ray stood second, while B.N. Sasmal stood first. Mr. Sasmal having resigned, Dr. Ray's election was set aside and Mr. Das was elected President. Do you not know anything about it?

A. I know nothing about it.

Q. If I cite this as an instance of their method, what have you got to say?

A. I cannot give any opinion without hearing the *Swarajists* and without knowing the full facts.

Q. Are you willing to enquire?

A. I would not lose my time over a thing that is finished.

Q. I bring this matter to your notice as a vivid example of the *Swarajists*' method. What have you to say to this?

A. I know nothing of their methods whatsoever. Without examining the instances, I am not able to pass any opinion, as I do not want to sit in judgment on the *Swarajists* or anybody, specially where there is no necessity for it.

Q. When you find the *Swarajists* have not yet changed their methods, can you accuse the puritans of incompetency?

A. In the first instance, you are assuming that the methods of the *Swarajists* are questionable. You would, therefore, have to satisfy me on that point. Secondly, I have not accused those whom you are pleased to call puritans, I do not know with what right, of their incompetency. But I have accused them of want of faith in their own mission. And even now, taking for granted for the sake of argument that the *Swarajists*' methods are questionable, what has that got to do with the purity of the puritans? Need I be impure, if the whole world around me is impure or is not that the time for testing the strength of my purity? I may only add that the puritans have not understood the implication of their claim. If they want to make good their claim, they should not grumble, they should not find fault with anybody in the world, for less with their erstwhile co-workers, but they should silently and surely set their faces against obstacles and they should shine the brightest when the obstacles are the greatest.

Q. Is not the present attitude of the *Swarajists* worse their open hostility?

A. If the *Swarajists* are really apathetic to *charkha*, I grant that it would be for better to be openly hostile than to be secretly apathetic.

Q. If the *Swarajists* are really apathetic, is not a separate organization of *charkha* and *khaddar* advisable?

A. Yes, certainly.

Q. If that is so, is it premature to think of a separate all-India non-co-operation organization?

A. I think it is premature for the present moment. We must finish this year of grace before pronouncing judgment or taking a decided step.

Q. Many orthodox non-co-operators feel embarrassed to work together with the *Swarajists*. Can you suggest any other remedy?

A. A good non-co-operator ought not to feel embarrassed in working with the *Swarajists*. For what is the meaning of working with the *Swarajists*? For except to work *charkha* together with him if you have not got to work together with him in the Councils ? I suggest a good non-co-operator will work even with the Viceroy, if the Viceroy will kindly sit down to the *charkha*.

Q. But Mahatmaji, you should not ignore facts, they are there.

A. I suggest then they are not non-co-operators because they have not understood the secret of non-co-operation. You non-co-operate with measures, not with men.

Q. We appreciate your view, but the fact is that we feel embarrassed. They are obstructing us.

A. I have not seen any statement to corroborate the charge that they are obstructing. If they are not spinning, that is not obstruction. They will obstruct you, when you go to the villages, ask the masses to spin and they say spinning is no good. That is obstruction. But I have not known that that charge can be levelled against a single *Swarajist*.

Q. Do you not know that the scheme suggested by them for the reconstruction of the villages does not contain any scheme of *charkha* ?

A. I can simply say that it was the *Swarajists* who organised the exhibition of *khaddar* at Faridpur and it was a pure *charkha* exhibition. Deshbandhu Das has laid stress in his presidential address on the constructive programme in the Congress, without which he held that they could achieve nothing. I may further add that I know the family of at least one *Swarajist* which is devoted to spinning as much as you or I can possibly be.

Q. Your reference to the Faridpur Conference reminds me of another objectionable method of the *Swarajists*. They invited you to kill the Non-co-operation Movement in Bengal, but they have been disappointed.

A. You are too suspicious, too diffident.

Q. But man proposes, God disposes. Mr. Desai wrote to me from Delhi that Mahatmaji would not visit Bengal very soon. But when you accepted the invitation of the Faridpur Conference, they did not think you would visit Bengal. But they were simply non-plussed when you accepted our invitation. It was to us a heavenly blessing. Do you not know that they did not want you to visit Bengal.

A. I think you are hyper-suspicious.

Q. Well, it is my mental attitude.

A. You are hopelessly wrong, because my tour has been jointly arranged by the *Swarajists* and non-*Swarajists*. It is the *Swarajists* who are taking me to Chittagong and Noakhali, because Chittagong and Noakhali were not on Satish Babu's tour programme.

Q. Did you not notice that the orthdox non-co-operators were conspicuous by their absence at Faridpur ?

A. I do not know. Probably they were. If so, it was their fault.

Q. Can you ascribe any reason for it?

A. I cannot, except this that if they were absent, it was their fault.

Q. I suggest the reason is that that was the only way to save their life. .

A. I think it is a libel.

Q. Do you feel that this unnatural combination of those having faith in constructive work and those having no faith in Council obstruction is creating a political scepticism in the mass-mind?

A. Mass-mind responds to work and nothing but work. Immediately there is solid work, self-sacrifice, the mass-mind sees it instinctively. Otherwise, the mass-mind goes to sleep like Kumbhakarna.[2] It does not listen at all.

Q. Do you think any political education is necessary for educating the masses?

A. Yes, that is *charkha*.

Q. If that is so, who should do it?

A. Of course, those who have kept awake a living faith in it. They should become the instructors of the masses.

Q. Do they need any organization for it?

A. I am now coming from Calcutta, seeing two young men doing their work perfectly, effectively and systematically without any monetary or other aid. They need no organization. That is the beauty of the *charkha*.

Q. Is any change of heart possible in the hearts of our rulers who boast of tiger qualities?

A. Change of heart is possible, otherwise non-co-operation is of no use. Let there be first a change of heart among the non-co-operators, then there will be a change of heart in the rulers. I have no doubt in my mind about it.

Q. I only refer you to a case in the animal world. Do you think real friendship possible between a tiger and a sheep?

A. No, but that analogy cannot be carried to the human platform because man is man, whether he believes in spinning or in Council obstruction, whether he believes in the cult of the tyrant and the slave or in the brotherhood of man.

1. *Amrita Bazar Patrika*, 14 May 1925.
2. Brother of Ravana in the Ramayana who slept for half the year at a stretch.

DUTY OF SATYAGRAHIS

Calcutta

25 June 1925

We have been asked what is the duty of satyagrahis in view of the recent judgment of the District Court of Hooghly, appointing a Receiver for all the properties including the Temple at Tarakeshwar and purporting to belong to the Mohunt.

In our opinion, it is impossible for satyagrahis to resist the possession by the Receiver when he comes to take it, nor is there any meaning in resisting his possession. The satyagraha was offered against the Mohunt or rather his methods. He is not in possession and the Court's order does not put him in possession. On the contrary, the judgment makes it clear that the Mohunt could not succeed, though he tried in gaining whole or partial possession.

The object of satyagraha was to get rid of abuses in connection with the temple and to secure public entry to the Lakshmi Narain Temple. There is no question under the Court's order of any reversion to the old abuse or prohibition to temple entry. It is a matter of no moment to satyagrahis who has possession so long as the Temple management is pure and it is not the Mohunt who has the management.

The satyagrahis' duty will, therefore, be to hand [over], on demand, the possession to the Receiver. It will be time to reconsider the position when and if abuses creep in. It does not matter who become trustees of the Temple so long as there is a public trust properly managed. If the plaintiffs collude with the Mohunt, it will be again a matter for consideration as to what the satyagrahis should do.

The foregoing was finally approved by Deshbandhu on 8th June at Darjeeling and it was to be published over our joint signatures, if it was considered necessary. I understand that the publication of the statement is necessary. I have therefore no hesitation in permitting its publication as our joint statement. I have seen nothing since to alter my opinion.

1. *Amrita Bazar Patrika*, 9 July 1925.

DEFEATED AND HUMBLED[1]

The foregoing was written on Monday the 30th June. I wrote it, but I was not satisfied nor am I satisfied now with the performance. On reading it I feel I have not done justice to the meeting or myself. Great as the informal meeting was, the one that preceded it, and that stung me to the quick, was not less great. I do not know that I have made it clear that no speaker had any malice in him. What preyed upon my mind was the fact of unconscious irresponsibility and disregard of the Congress creed or policy of non-violence.

The informal meeting was a heart-searcher. It purified the atmosphere. The whole of Tuesday I passed in discussing with co-workers my position. My innermost wish was and still is to retire from the Congress and confine my activity merely to Hindu-Muslim unity, *khaddar* and untouchability. They would not listen. I had no right, they said, to retire at a critical period in the history of the nation. My withdrawal would not smooth matters. It would cause depression and remove from Congress meetings an active restraining influence. I must actively work the programme of which I was the author, so long as the majority favoured it. The programme had a far greater majority than the voting at the AICC would indicate. I must travel in the country and see things for myself. My second proposal was for all who fully accepted the Congress creed to retire in favour of the *Swarajists*. As the argument against it developed, I rejected it myself as thoughtless. It was the last thing the *Swarajists* wanted. I felt that it would be doing violence to them to expect them to do the impossible. I know that they would not entertain even the first proposal. I offered it to them at Juhu and renewed it in Ahmedabad. I have therefore reluctantly decided to drink the bitter cup and continue to be in the Congress organization and shoulder the responsibility for working it until the Congress puts me in an actual numerical minority.

I may not choose short cuts. I must plod. I must pocket my pride and wait till I am driven out.

I must seemingly become a party-man and show that I can still work as a no-party man. I must strive for a majority at the next Congress and endeavour, so far as it is possible, to act impartially. It is not beyond the capacity of a satyagrahi.

The conditions are incredibly simple. The striving to be in a majority consists in solid work.

1. Over and above the spinning for half an hour, every spare minute should be given to it.

2. Extra spinning can be dispensed with in order to do *khaddar* propaganda.

3. We may swell the electoral roll by getting as many Congress members as possible.

4. There should be no manipulation of papers.

5. There should be no manoeuvring for securing votes.

6. There should be no criticism of the opposite party, as distinguished from policy.

7. There should be no undue pressure exercised on the voters.

But the parties are said to have resorted in the past to unscrupulous practices in the matter of election of delegates and members of the subordinate organizations. The best way of avoiding corruption is to be indifferent to the result after having adopted all honest measures for influencing voters.

The No-change programme must be what it means. The proceedings of the Committee have but confirmed the view that the two methods cannot be worked in the same organization. The *Swarajist* method cultivates British opinion and looks to the British Parliament for *swaraj.* The No-change method looks to the people for it. The two methods represent two opposite mentalities. This is not to say that one is wrong if the other is right. Each may be right in its own place. But for one organization to work both is to weaken both and therefore to damage the national cause. Whilst one school claims to give it exclusively by working among the people and evoking its organizing and administrative capacity. One teaches to look up to a Government for popular progress, the other tries to show that even the most ideal government plays among a self-governing people the least important part in national growth. One teaches the people that the constructive programme alone cannot achieve *swaraj*, the other teaches the people that it and it alone can achieve it.

Unfortunately, I was unable to convince the *Swarajists* of this obvious truth. And I saw constitutional difficulty in the way of securing a homogengeous organization. We must now, therefore, do the next best thing. We must silently work up the constructive programme without regard to what will happen in December, in the full belief that whether the Congress rejects or accepts the programme, for us there is no other. I would ask those newspapers that call themselves No-change papers not to criticize the *Swarajists* in any shape or form. I am convinced that newspapers play a very small part in shaping the policy or programme of the masses. They do not know newspapers. The No-changers have to reach and represent those who have had no political education whatsoever.

1. *Young India*, 3 July 1925.

GANDHI PRAISES SWARAJ PARTY[1]

Calcutta,
19 July 1925

Dear Panditji,

During these few days I have been taxing myself what special exclusive contribution I can make to the memory of Deshbandhu and the situation created by Lord Birkenhead's speech, and I have come to the conclusion that I should absolve the *Swaraj* Party from all obligations under the Pact of last year. The result of this act is that the Congress need no longer be a predominantly spinning association. I recognize, that, under the situation created by the speech, the authority and the influence of the Swaraj Party need to be increased. I would fail in my duty if I neglected a single step with my power to increase the strength of the Party. This can be done if the Congress becomes a predominantly political body. Under the Pact, the Congress activity is restrained to the constructive programme mentioned therein. I recognize that this restriction should not continue under the altered circumstances that face the country. Not only do I, therefore, personally absolve you from the restriction, but I propose to ask the forthcoming meeting of the AICC to do likewise and place the whole machinery of the Congress at your disposal so as to enable you to bring before the body such political resolutions as you may consider necessary in the interest of the country. In fact, I would have you regard me at your disposal in all such matters in which I can conscientiously serve you and the Swaraj Party.

Yours sincerely,
M.K. Gandhi

1. *Young India*, 23 July 1925.

CHAPTER 4

ROLE OF C. R. DAS

THE BENGAL PACT[1]

One of the significant steps – a bold and statesmanlike act – C.R. Das did was to conclude Hindu-Muslim Pact known as 'The Bengal Pact'. The working of his mind for taking such a step was to unite the two communities on the basis of equality and justice. It gave representation to Muslims on the population basis in the Bengal Council with separate electorates, even in places where they formed the majority, subject to such adjustments as might be thought necessary by the All India Hindu-Muslim Pact. Similar representation would be given to Muslims in local bodies in the proportion of 60 to 40 in every district. In government posts, 55 per cent would go to Muslims. Music would be stopped before mosques while taking out processions. There was to be no interference with cow-killing by Muslims for religious sacrifices. No legislation or enactment relating to cow-killing for food would be taken up in the Council. Cow-killing was to be carried out in such a manner as not to wound the feelings of the Hindus. Every year, representative committees were to be formed in every sub-division of which half the members should be Muslims and the other half Hindus; such committees, choosing their President from among themselves, would have the power to prevent or attribute upon any dispute between Hindus and Muslims in accordance with the provision stated in the Pact.[2]

The Bengal Pact strengthened the position of Das who won the Council elections held in November 1923 with a clear majority. The *Statesman* declared thus : "In every kind of

Bengali constituency the *Swarajists* have triumphed. Even the Mohammedan electorate which was considered to be a safe asset for government, has been sent asunder, and 19 sympathisers with Mr. C.R. Das have been elected as against 20 of a contrary opinion." In the Hindu constituencies, the *Swarajists* captured 36 out of a total of 47 seats; in the landholders' constituencies 3 out of 5; and 4 out of 5 special seats belonging to Anglo-Indians and Indian trade and commerce also went to them.[3]

The Pact was severely criticised by a large vocal section of the Hindus who opined that Das had played into the hands of Muslims and surrendered the Hindu interests. At this, Das, greatly agitated and excited, opined, "You may delete the Bengal Pact from the resolution but you cannot delete Bengal from the Indian National Congress. Bengal demands her right of having her suggestion considered by the National Assembly. What right has anybody to say that Bengal has to be deprived of her right ? Bengal will not be deleted in this inceremonious fashion. I cannot understand the argument of those who cry 'delete the Bengal Pact'.

"Is Bengal an untouchable ? Will you deny Bengal the right of suggestion on such a vital question ? If you do, Bengal can take care of itself. You can't refuse Bengal the right to make a suggestion.[4]"

C.R. Das in his speech delivered at the session of the Bengal Provincial Conference held in Sirajganj in June 1924, clarified certain doubts raised in connection with the Hindu-Muslim Pact. "It has been argued by the opposers of the Pact that there is no necessity for it, that the Pact it passed which retard the progress of *Swaraj*. . . Does not a promise they make a pledge they have taken remind them of the great thing, for the attainment of which such a promise is made ? ... I for one will not have fathered such a Pact, which is but a mere instrument and which leaves aside the consideration that they are men first. I only call upon Hindus and Mahomedans alike to sacrifice a little bit of each other's small and petty interests for the cause of Indian *Swaraj* which is to the interest of both the communities.

"So long as Hindus and Mahomedans do not unite, *Swaraj* will be an impossibility, and will always remain a theme of impracticable fancy...To think that the two communities will merge their respective individuality and make up a new community is inconceivable...That alone will bring real unity. . . . Life is certainly greater than dogma and logic, and I want you to be men—whole men—who will obey none but the will of God, and the Pact is necessary for the growth of that high ideal of manhood and Indian nationality among the two communities. Whether you call the Pact a covenant or an instrument, it is necessary for the establishment of Indian *Swaraj*, for the attainment of which I am prepared to shed every drop of my blood. . . I have full faith in Bengal and believe that she will yet rise to the height of the occasion and accept the Pact. It is the will of God. *Swaraj* is coming and you must be ready to welcome it by your sacrifiee and suffering. Let this Bengal Provincial Conference sitting at Sirajganj lay the foundation of Hindu-Muslim unity and establish India's freedom."[5]

1. See Proceedings of Congress Session at Cocanada, 1923.
2. *Ibid*.
3. *The Statesman*, 1 December 1923.
4. *Ibid*.
5. See the English version of his speech delivered at the Session of the Bengal Provincial Conference held in Sirajganj in June 1924, in *Deshbandhu Chitta Ranjan : Brief Survey of Life and Works, Provincial Conference Speeches, Congress Speeches,* Calcutta, 1927, pp. 269 ff.

C.R. DAS LEADS THE PARTY[1]

In Bengal, Das had a clear walkover. The prominent leader of the stature of Surendranath Banerjea at whose feet Das had learnt his initial lessons of politics as a college student and who was allied to him by the marriage of his daughter, was defeated by B.C. Roy, quite a new-comer to politics. His own cousin, S.R. Das, the Advocate-General of Bengal, was defeated by Satkaripati Roy. Besides Nilratan Sarkar, the famous medical practitioner, was defeated by Bijoy Krishna Bose. But above all, the Swarajist Party achieved an absolute majority and C.R. Das was asked to form the ministry by the Bengal Governor, Lord Lytton.

In a letter to the Governor dated 16 December 1923, Das explained thus, "I placed before our party the position as explained by Your Excellency and they have just declined to accept Your Execllency's kind offer. The members of this party are pledge-bound to do everything in their power by using the legal right granted under the Reforms Act to put an end to the system of Dyarchy. This duty they cannot discharge if they accept office. The party is aware that it is possible to offer obstruction from within by accepting office, but they do not consider it honest to accept office which is under the existing system Your Excellency's gift and then turn it into an instrument of obstruction. The awakened consciousness of the people of this country demands a change in the present system of Government and until that is done or unless there is some change in the general administration indicating a chage of heart, the people of the country cannot offer willing cooperation. Under the circumstances, I regret I cannot undertake responsibility regarding the transferred departments. My party, however, wishes to place on record its appreciation of the spirit of constitutionalism which actuated you in making the offer which we feel bound not to accept."[2]

1. P.C. Roy Choudhury, *C.R. Das and His Times*, Mysore, 1979, pp. 123-24.
2. *Ibid*.

CONCEPT OF SWARAJ[1]

In an All-India Students' Conference held at Cocanada on 30 December 1923, C.R. Das who chaired the proceedings, discussed in detail the definition of *Swaraj*, import of Gandhi's message, violence and autocracy, ideal of nationalism and the need for non-cooperation. According to him, "*Swaraj* is not independence. *Swaraj* is something higher than independence. . . . It may be that you cannot get *Swaraj* without securing independence, but independence is not *Swaraj*. You want independence to enable you to develop *Swaraj*.

Today I make my position perfectly clear. *Swadhinata*'[2] which today we understand to be liberty has got to be understood, *Swadhinata* is not liberty, it is not freedom. It is same thing as *Swaraj*—dependence on the self, that is to say, yourself—your national self. It is your genius, is your temperament, is the one variety upon which you stand, and the goal of the Indian is to develop that temperament, to develop the genius, to stand in the light of that genius, to represent itself in all its glory, that is, not to confuse with the vulgar ideal of independence. Always remember that the very step which leads to independence is also the step which leads to *Swaraj*. Independence without the ideal of *Swaraj* is nothing. It is not worth the trouble.

The ideal of non-violence is a great achievement of Mahatma. The proof of the validity of this liberty will be offered to the whole world. The history of revolutions will take a new turn, that is revolution through which we are passing at the present day.

"It is impossible to live without Non-cooperation. An individual cannot grow without Non-cooperation and cannot cooperate with humanity unless in the first place he gets rid of what is violent and things which drag him down, which prevent him from growing . . . This system of Government must be removed. . . To purify yourself you must take your hands off from the machinery. You have to suffer, without suffering no nation grows, no individual grows. . . The ideal requires and demands that not one student should remain in the Government institutions today. Those that remain shall admit that they are there because of their weakness. Let all the students take part in the glory of the battle.

The ideal of non-co-operation calls upon students to leave Government Educational Institutions. I know of students in Bengal who have been turned out of their houses by their parents because they left Government schools and colleges. Shame to those parents who have turned out their children and shame on myself that I could not prevent it although I saw it with my own eyes. . . . If you have not got the courage to non-cooperate, assist those who non-cooperated. . . . You can go to villages and educate the people, teach them in the management of villages, and above all, teach them how to spin and weave. In this silent way you can help India to achieve *Swaraj*.[2]

1. *The Leader*, 1 January 1924.
2. *Ibid.*

C.R. DAS CLARIFIES AIM OF HIS PARTY

Thus the motive of the *Swarajists* was to see that the anti-national measures could not be adopted there.[1] Das clarified the aim of his party in unequivocal terms in the Bengal Legislative Council in 1925 : "...It has been said that our cry is destroy, destroy. . . Why do we want to destroy it, because we want to construct a system which can be worked with success and will enable us to do good to the masses. Can you lay your hands on your breast and say that you can do anything for the masses under this system."[2] However, he gave cogent reasons for this kind of destruction of the councils or putting serious obstructions in their day-to-day official proceedings. "I want to destroy because this rotten structure is occupying the place where a beautiful mansion may be erected. . . . We want to destroy in order that we may be able to build up."[3]

1. See *India in 1924-25*, p. 296.
2. P.C. Ray, *Life and Times of C.R. Das*, p. 201.
3. *Ibid.*

VIEWS ON EDUCATION[1]

C.R. Das stated in the Council, "Spend one crore for technical education in Bengal, spend one crore for primary education, spend 30 lakhs for special Mohammedan educational institutions, spend 30 lakhs for those who are called the depressed classes—I do not believe that they are depressed classes—they are oppressed classes—oppressed by the Government and the higher classes alike; spend one crore for the development of cottage industries, spend one core for weeding out malaria and Kala-Azar and spend 40 lakhs for the development of agriculture—you can do all this with five crores without any special efforts, if you borrow it at 6 per cent..."

1. *The Bengal Legislative Council Proceedings*, 1924, Vol. XIV, p. 179.

C.R. DAS SPELLS OUT HOME RULE AND SWARAJ[1]

In the Benganl Provincial Conference held at Faridpur on 2 May 1925, C.R. Das opined in his Presidential address thus:

Again and again has India asked, which way lies Salvation? In the dim past, it was the obstinate questioning of the individual soul,—weary of shadows and seeking for Reality. In the living present, it is the tortured cry of the soul of India.

Let me put this question to you again so that we may obtain a clear vision as to what it is that we must accomplish.

As with the individual, so with the Nation, the questions to find out the meaning of deliverance from bondage and, let me add, sin. It is a sin of those who forge the fetters of bondage. It is also as of those who allow the fetters to be forged.

Many items have been presented—Self-Government, Home-Rule, Independence, and Swaraj—but these are all names unless the full implications are vividly realized and in the process of such realization must come a consideration of the method of attaining the object in view.

There are those who declare in favour of peaceful and legitimate methods. There are others who claim that, without the use of force or violence, *Swaraj* is impossible of attainment.

I desire to offer only a few suggestions to help you in deciding these momentous questions. Let the Bengal Provincial Conference declare in no uncertain voice what is the national ideal of freedom, and what is the method it calls upon the country to adopt for the fulfilment of that very ideal.

"Independence, to my mind, is a narrower ideal than that of *Swaraj*. It implies, it is true, the negative of dependence; but by itself it gives us no positive ideal. I do not for a moment suggest that independence is not consistent with *Swaraj*. But what is necessary is not mere independence, but the establishment of *Swaraj*. India may be independent tomorrow in the sense that the British people may leave us to our destiny, but that will not necessarily give us what I understand by *Swaraj.* As I pointed out in my Presidential address at Gaya, India presents an interesting but a complicated problem of consolidating the many apparently conflicting elements which go to make up the Indian people. The work of consolidation is a long process may even be a weary process; but without this, no *Swaraj* is possible. Herein lies the great wisdom of Mahatma Gandhi's constructive programme—with that progromme I entirely agree and I cannot but too strongly urge upon my countrymen to give it not merely an intellectual assent, but practical support by working it out to the fullest extent.

Independence, in the second place, does not give you that idea of order which in the essence of *Swaraj.* The work of consolidation which I have mentioned means the establishment of that order. But let it be clearly understood that what is sought to be established must be consistent with the genius, the temperament and the traditions of the Indian people. To my mind *Swaraj* implies, firstly, that we must have the freedom of working out the consolidation of the diverse elements of the Indian people; secondly, we must proceed with this work on national lines, not going back two thousand years ago, but going forward in the light and in the spirit of our national genius and temperament. For instance, when I speak of order I mean a thing which is totally different from the idea of discipline which obtains in Europe. In Europe, the foundation of society and Government is discipline; and the spirit of discipline upon which everything rests is entirely military; and discipline, which had made England what she is today, is also of the same military type. It is not for me to decry European civilization. That is their way and they must fulfil themselves. But our way is not their way and we must also fulfil ourselves. Thirdly, in the work before us, we must not be obstructed by any foreign power.

What then have we to fix upon the matter of ideal is what I call *Swaraj,* and not mere independence, which may be the negation of *Swaraj.* When we are asked as to what is our national idea of freedom, the only answer which is to give is *Swaraj.* I do not like either Home Rule or Self-Government. Possibly they come within what I have described as *Swaraj.*

But my culture, somehow or other, is antagonistic to the word 'rule'—be it Home Rule or Foreign Rule. My objection to the word Self-Government is exactly the same. If it is defined as government by self and for self, my objection may be met; but, in that case, *Swaraj* includes all those elements.

"Then comes the question as to whether this ideal is to be realized within the Empire or outside it? The answer which the Congress has always given is 'within the Empire, if the Empire will recognize our rights' and 'outside the Empire', if it does not. We must have opportunity to live our life,—opportunity for self-realization, self-development and self-fulfilment. The question is of living our life. If the Empire furnishes sufficient scope for the growth and development of our notional life, the Empire idea is to be preferred. If, on the contrary, the Empire, like the Car of Jagannath, crushes our life in the sweep of its imperialistic march, there will be justification for the idea of the establishment of Swaraj outside the Empire.

Indeed, the Empire idea gives us a vivid sense of many advantages. Dominion Status today is in no sense servitude. It is essentially an alliance by consent of those who form part of the Empire for material advantages in the real spirit of cooperation. Free alliance necessarily carries with it the right of separation. Before the war, a separatist tendency was growing up in several parts of the Empire, but after the war it is generally believed that it is only as a great confederation, that the Empire or its component parts can live. It is realized that under modern conditions no nation can live in isolation, and the Dominion Status, while it affords; complete protection to each constituent composing the great Commonwealth of Nations called the British Empire, secures to each the right to realize itself, develop itself and fulfil itself, and, therefore, it expressed and implies all the elements of *Swaraj* which I have mentioned.

To me, the idea is specially attractive, becausc of its deep spritiual significance. I believe in world-peace, in the ultimate federation of the world. I think that the great Commonwealth of Nations called the British Empire—a federation of diverse races, each with its distinct life, distinct civilization, its distinct mental outlook—if properly led by wise statesmen at the helm, is bound to make lasting contributions to the great problem—

the problem of knitting the world into the greatest federation the mind can conceive, the federation of the human race. For the development of the idea involves apparent sacrifice on the part of the constituent nations, and it certainly involves 'the giving up for good the Empire idea with its ugly attribute of domination. I think it is for the good of India, for good of the world, that India should strive for freedom within the Commonwealth, and so serve the cause of humanity.

I now come to the question of method. In my judgment, the method is always a part of the ideal. So that, when we are considering the question of method, we cannot forget the larger aspect of the object we have in view.

Viewed in this light, the method of violence is hardly in keeping with our life and culture. I am not suggesting for a moment that the History of India shows no wars, nor the application of violence. Every superficial student of our history knows that it is not so. But sometimes things are forced upon our life which a critical student of our history must know how to separate from the real bent of our genius. Violence is not a part of our being, as it is of Europe. That violence in Europe is checked by a system of law, which in the ultimate resort, is also based on physical force. The Indian people has always been in the habit of following traditions and customs and thus keeping itself free from violent methods. Our village organizations were a marvel of non-violent activities. Our institutions have always grown naturally like the unfolding of a flower. Strifes there have been of the intellect; cravings there have been of the soul; disputes and quarrels have always arisen but only to be settled by peaceful arbitration. Anything contrary or antagonistic to this temperament, is a method which is not, only immoral from the highest stand-point, but is bound to fail. I have no hesitation in proclaiming my conviction that our freedom will never be won by revolutionary violence. In the next place, apart from the special psychology of the Indian mind, how is it possible, by offering such violence, as it is possible for a subject race to offer, to contend against the highly organized government violence of persent day? It is no use quoting the incidents of the French and other revolutions. Those were days when the people fought with spikes and often won. Is it conceivable that at the present moment we can overthrow any organized Government of the modern type by such method? I venture to think that any such armed revolution would be impossible even in England today.

In the next place, the application of violence cuts at the root of that consolidation, without which, as I have said, the attainment of *Swaraj* is impossible. Violence is sure to be followed by more violence on the part of the Government, and repression may be so violent, that its only effect on the Indian people would be to check their enthusiasm for *Swaraj.* I ask those young men who are addicted to revolutionary methods; do they think that the people will side with them? When life and property is threatened, the inevitable result is, that the people who suffer or who think they may suffer, recoil from such activities. This method, therefore, is impractical. Far be it from me to say one word against the honesty of purpose or the ardour of patriotism which these young men are capable of showing. But, as I said, the method is unsuited to our temperament; therefore, the application of it is, to quote the words of Mahatma Gandhi, 'waste of time and energy'. I appeal to the young men of Bengal who may even in their heart of hearts think in favour of violent methods, to desist from such thought, and, I appeal to the Bengal Provincial Conference to declare clearly and unequivocally, that in its opinion freedom cannot be achieved by such methods.

But if I am against the application of such methods, I feel bound to point out that it is the violence of the Government which has to a great extent belied the revolutionary movement in Bengal. I believe it is Professor Dicey who points out that for the last thirty years there has been a singular decline among modern Englishmen in their respect or reverence for law and order, and he shows that result is directly traceable to modern legislation, which has had the effect of diminishing the authority of the law courts, and thereby imperilling the rule of law. In other words violence always begets violence and if the Government stifling legitimate activities, it cannot but bring into existence, what Dicey calls, 'a zeal for lawlessness' in the subject. The history of India and particularly of Bengal, supports the observation of Professor Dicey.

The new Ordinance Act is a misguided attempt to perpetrate violence upon the people. The whole of India has with one voice condemned it, and I cannot trust myself to express my feeling about it in fitting terms, as I desire to speak with all restraint. I shall content myself by saying that I unhesitatingly condemn it, and I have given the only answer which it is possible for any Indian to give to the recent speech of Lord Birkenhead inviting me to cooperate with the Government in its repressive policy.

You will remember that Lord Birkenhead said that the Ordinance has not hurt anybody but the criminals. May I point out that His Lordship here is begging the whole question? We deny that the men imprisoned under the Ordinance are criminals, and the only way to decide as to whether they are criminals or not is to hold an open trial and proceed, not on secret information, but on actual evidence which might be tested in open court. The insecurity to which eminent writers of constitutional history in England have referred is the insecurity to the public by the attempt of the executive to arrogate to itself the position of a court of law.

I will not weary you by dealing with each particular case which has been brought forward by the Government as a justification for the policy of repression... I must also point out that it is difficult to believe in the statement put forward in support of the repressive measures by the Government.

It follows conclusively that the discretionary power which the Government in this country enjoys of promulgating illegal laws is capable of being abused. Indeed, it must be so from the very nature of things. The history of the world shows that bureauratic governments have always tried to consolidate their power through the process of 'Law and Order' which is an excellent phrase, but which means, in countries where the rule of law does not prevail, the exercise by persons in authority of wide arbitrary or discretionary powers of constraint.

Repression is a process in the consolidation of arbitrary powers—and I condemn the violence of the Government for repression in the most violent form of violence—just as I condemn violence as a method of winning political liberty. I must warn the Government that the policy of repression is a short-sighted policy. It may strengthen its hands for the time being, but I am sure Lord Birkenhead realizes that, as an instrument of Government, it is bound to fail.

I have so far dealt with the question of method in order to show that violence is both immoral and inexpedient,—immoral, because it is not keeping with our life and cultute, inexpedient, because it is inconceivable that at the present day we can overthrow any organized Government by bombs and revolvers. Then the question arises what method should we pursue in order to win *swaraj*? We have been gravely told that *Swaraj* is within our grasp if only we co-operate with the Government in working the present Reform Act. With regard to the argument, my position is perfcctly clear, and I should like to restate it, so that there may be no controversy about it. If I were satisfied that the present Act has transferred any real responsibility to the people,—that there is opportunity for self-realization, self-development and self-fulfilment under the Act, I would unhesitatingly cooperate with the Government and begin the constructive work within the Council Chamber. But I am not willing to sacrifice the substance for the shadow. I will not detain you today with any argument tending to show that the Reform Act has not transferred any responsibility to the people. I have dealt with the question exhaustively in my address at Ahmedabad Congress, and if further arguments are necessary they will be found in the evidence given before the Muddiman Committee by men whose moderation cannot be questioned by the Government. The basis of the present Act is distrust of the Ministers; and there can be no talk of cooperation in an atmosphere of distrust. At the same time, I must make clear my position—and I hope of the Bengal Provincial Conference—that, provided some real responsibility is transferred to the people, there is no reason why we should not cooperate with the Government. But to make such cooperation real and effective, two things are necessary. First, there should be real change of heart in rulers; secondly, *Swaraj* in the fullest sense must be guaranteed to us at once, to come automatically in the near future. I have always maintained that we should make large sacrifices in order to have the opportunity to begin our constructive work at once, and I think you will realize that a few years are nothing in the history of a nation, provided the foundation of *Swaraj* is laid at once, and there is a real change of heart both in the rulers and in subject. You will tell me that "change of heart" is a fine phrase, and that some practical demonstration should be given of that change. I agree. But the demonstration must necessarily depend on the atmosphere created by any proposed settlement. An atmosphere of trust may be easily felt and in any matter of peaceful settlement a great deal more depends on the spirit behind the terms than the actual terms themselves. It is impossible to lay down the exact terms of any such settlement at the present moment; but if a change of heart takes place and negotiations are carried on by both sides in the spirit of peace, harmony and mutual trust, such terms are capable of precise definition.

A few suggestions may, however, be made, having regard to what is nearest to the hearts of the people of Bengal.

In the first place, the Government should divest itself of its wide discretionary powers of constraint, and follow it up by proclaiming a general amnesty of all political prisoners. In the next place, the Government should guarantee to us the fullest recognition of our right to the establisment of *Swaraj* within the commonwealth, in the near future, and in the meantime, till *Swaraj* comes a sure and sufficient foundation must necessarily be a matter of negotiation and settlement—settlement not only between the Government and the people as a whole, but also between the different communities, not excluding the European and Indian communities, as I said in my presidential speech at Gaya.

I must also add that we, on our part, should be in a position to give some sort of undertaking that we shall not by word, deed or gesture, encourage the revolutionary propaganda, and that we shall make every effort to put an end to such a movement. This undertaking is not needed, for the Bengal Provincial Conference has never identified itself with the revolutionary propaganda. I believe that, with a change of heart on the part of the Government, there is bound to be produced a change in the mental outlook of the revolutionary movement and it will be a thing of the past, and the very power and energy which is now directed against the Government will be devoted to the real service of the people.

If, however, our offer of a settlement should not meet with any response, we must go on with our national work on the lines which we have pursued for the last two years so that it may become impossible for the Government to carry on the administration of the country, except by the exercise of its exceptional powers. There are some who shrink from this step, who point out with perfect logic that we have no right to refuse supplies unless we are prepared to go to the country and advise the subject not to pay the taxes. My answer is that I want to create the atmosphere for national civil disobedience, which must be the last weapon in the hands of the people striving for freedom. I have no use for historical precedent; but if reference is to be made to English history in our present struggle, I may point out that refusal to pay taxes in England in the time of the Stuarts came many years after the determination of the Parliament to refuse supplies. The atmosphere for civil disobedience is created by compelling the Government to raise money by the exercise of its exceptional powers; and when the time comes we shall not hesitate to advise our countrymen not to pay taxes which are sought to be raised by the exercise of the exceptional powers vested in the Government.

I hope that time will never come—indeed I see signs of a real change of heart everywhere—but let us face the fact that it may be necessary for us to have recourse to civil disobedience if all hope of reconciliation fails. But let us also face the fact that civil disobedience requires a high stage of organization, an infinite capacity for sacrifice, and a real desire to subordinate personal and communal interest to the common interest of the nation; and I can see little hope of India ever being ready for civil disobedience and until she is prepared to work Mahatma Gandhi's constructive programme to the fullest extent. To end, however, must be kept in view, for freedom must be won.

But, as I have said, I see signs of reconciliation everywhere. The world is tired of conflicts, and I think I see a real desire for construction, for consolidation. I believe that India has a great part to play in the history of the world. She has a message to deliver, and anxious to deliver it in the Council Chamber of that great commonwealth of nations, of which I have spoken. Will British statesmen rise to the occasion ? To whom I say : you can have peace today on terms that are honourable both to you and to us. To the British community in India, I say : you have come with traditions of freedom, and you cannot refuse to cooperate with us in our national struggle, provided we recognise your right to be heard in the final settlement. To the people of Bengal I say : you have made great sacrifices for daring to win political freedom, and on you has fallen the brunt of official wrath. The time is not yet for putting aside your political weapons. Fight hard, but fight clean; and when the time for settlement comes, as it is bound to come, enter the press conference, not in a spirit of arrogance, but with becoming humility, so that it may be said of you that you were greater in your achievement than in adversity.

Nationalism is merely a process in self-realisation, self-development and self-fulfilment. It is not an end in itself. The growth and development of nationalism is necessary, so that humanity may realize itself, develop itself and fulfil itself; and I beseech you when you discuss the terms of settlement : do not forget the larger claim of humanity in your pride of nationalism. For myself, I have a clear vision as to what I seek. I seek a federation of the states of India—each free to follow, as it must follow, the culture and the tradition, of its own people; each bound to each in the common service of all : a great federation within a greater federation, the federation of free nations, whose freedom is the measure of their service to man, and whose unity the hope of peace among the peoples of the earth."

1. Prithwis Chandra Ray, *Life and Times of C.R. Das,* Madras, 1929, pp. 247-56.

GANDHI'S REMINISCENCES OF BENGAL[1]

4 May 1925

I am writing these reminscences on Monday after returning from Faridpur. I write sitting on the covered terrace of the mansion formerly belonging to Deshbandhu Das. I have been in Bengal for four days but have still not recovered from the shock I felt when I first entered this mansion. I knew that the Deshbandhu had made over this building for public purposes. He had debts, I knew, but I also knew that he would clear them by practising for less than a year and keep the mansion. But he did not at all want to practise, or, rather he wanted to plead the cause of his country without demanding fees. He decided, therefore, to give away this palatial building and made over its control to trustees. He wanted, however, that whenever I travelled I should stay while in Calcutta in that old building. And so I am lodged here.

But it is one thing to know a thing and quite another to see it with one's own eyes. My heart wept when I entered the house, and my eyes were moist with tears. In the absence of its former master, and no more his property, the mansion seemed to me like a jail. I felt miserable in it, and I have still not got out of that feeling.

I know that this is ignorant attachment. By giving up his ownership of the house, Deshbandhu has in fact lightened his burden. What use had the Dases for a building in which they would lose their way? If they want, they can turn a hut into a royal palace. For both of them it was a willing sacrifice. Why feel sad about it? Well, this is being philosophical. If I did not have this gift I would feel impelled to start building a palace for myself straightway.

It is easy to escape the consequence of the *atman*[2] dwelling in a physical body? Do others in the world act as Das did? People in the world would welcome a palace if they can have it, whereas this man gave away one. All honour to him! The tears in my eyes spring from love. The shock I felt was also the result of love. But is there no selfishness in this? If I had no bond at all with Deshbandu, if I had not known his reigning like a king in this building, I would have felt no shock. I have seen many palaces whose owners departed from this world itself, leaving palaces behind them, but I shed no tears when entering them. These tears, therefore, spring from selfishness too. Chittaranjan Das has lost nothing by giving away the palatial bungalow. His services are the richer for this sacrifice.

The Bengalis are mad folk. If Das was mad, so is Prafulla Chandra Ray. He dances on the dais when addressing an audience. No one would believe that he is a learned man; he thumps his hands and stamps his feet. Whenever he likes he introduces English words and phrases in his Bengali. When speaking, he forgets himself. He is then totally absorbed in the flow of his thoughts and does not bother to know whether others laugh at him or what they thing about him. We do not understand his greatness until we hear him speak, with our eyes fixed on his face. I remember that when I was staying with Gokhale in Calcutta and Acharya Ray was his neighbour, the three of us went to the station one day. I had my third-class ticket with me, and they two had come to see me off. Anyone coming to see a third-class passenger off must be a beggar, people believe. But Gokhale's chubby face, his silken turban and silk-bordered *dhoti* were enough for the station master. But who would let this skeleton of a young bachelor, wearing a soiled long shirt and as lean as a beggar, go in without a ticket? So far as I remember, he cheerfully stayed out. Criticizing my obstinacy when he saw me literally squeezed in my seat in the compartment, Gokhale went away and rejoined his comrade. Why does Acharya Ray reign supreme over the hearts of innumerable students? Because he is also a man of self-sacrifice. And now he has gone *khadi*-crazy. He did not feel the slightest embarrassment in asking a Bengali woman officer of the Education Department : "What good can you do unless you wear *khadi*?" If he did not say this, would anyone buy *khadi* manufactured by his beggars of Khulna?

The same night we left for Faridpur. Shri Shankerlal had given Satish Babu a rather alarming account of my health. There was nothing, therefore, he would not do to make me comfortable. He, too, belonged to the mad folks' league. He had looked into the minutest of details. In order that I might rest my back while sitting, a wooden support was kept ready wherever I sat. I could accept it because it was a simple and inexpensive thing. But when we reached the station, there was a first-class compartment for my companions and me. The Faridpur Reception Committee had also a hand in this arrangement. Only a few days ago a correspondent had asked me in a letter published in *Young India* whether I was a poor man or rich. It seemed as if Bengal had answered that question. I asked them if a second-class compartment was not good enough for my comfort, and why Bengal had arranged a first-class compartment for me. I was told in reply that they had paid for a second-class compartment and secured a first-class one. How could that reply satisfy me? According to my principle, we should not avail ourselves of a thing of which we do not approve even if it is offered gratis. If there should be any one so foolish or mad as to offer me, free, a diamond necklace to wear, should I wear it? Are my companions, too, who serve me as secretaries and may even clean the lavatory, as weak as I so that for them also a first-class compartment should be provided at second-class fare? Moreover, this could not have been managed without the Railway people obliging. Should such personal favours be accepted? I saw in this arrangement the madness or excess of love.

I must find a solution to this problem. God's will be done. But, then, this madness is not confined to one class of people. We started for Faridpur at night and I had thought that I would get plenty of rest on the way and would be able to make up fully for the lost hours of sleep. But that was not to be. I had great difficulty in getting sleep, thanks to cries of "*alo, alo*"[3] and other noises. The train also stopped at almost every station. At every station there were crowds and people insisted on having *darshan*[4]. But I had resolved never to give *darshan* during night-time So I kept lying down. But that did not help. My companions, too, tried hard to explain the position to the people, but the more they explained the more did the crowds got excited. There were louder and still louder shouts of "*Vandemataram, Mahatma Gandhi ki jai*[5], *alo, alo*". *Alo* means light. The train lights had been switched off. The people wanted them to be switched on so that they could at least see me sleeping. This was the state of affairs at almost every station up to Faridpur. All the time I kept earnestly praying to God to save me from such love! When we arrived at Faridpur, there was a huge crowd, of course, but the arrangements on the whole were good. Babu Surendra Biswas, the chairman of the Reception Committee, had instructed the people in advance not to shout or rush towards me. The car, moreover, was kept right at the spot where I was to alight, so that we entered the city without harassment.

Exhibition

Before being taken to the place where I was to stay, I had to declare an exhibition open. They had accepted for it varieties of seeds and other such things supplied by the Government Agriculture Department, but the main sections related to *khadi*. Biswas Babu had decided not to permit the display of any specimen of cloth not manufactured from handspun yarn, wool or silk. This helped the *khadi* section very much; it became the centre of interest and the visitors had no chance to compare it with mill-cloth. There were, among the varieties of *khadi*, a great many specimens of fine cloth too. There was also a large quantity of fine yarn. There were even two persons sitting on a chair and spinning, neither of whom had to turn aside for winding the yarn. The yarn was being wound as it was spun. No doubt that type of the spinning-wheel did not produce more yarn at a faster rate, but there was one operation less to attend to and, as the wheel was being turned by foot, both hands remained free.

Looms had been received as exhibits from the Government factory at Serampur, and these also were accepted on condition that only hand-spun yarn must be used for both warp and woof. It was learnt on inquiry that students were now taught hand-spinning too in that factory. There were many *fataka* looms, too, on which they used only hand-spun yarn as warp. Even jute and wool were spun by hand in this section.

The processes relating to the tanning and dyeing of hides were also being demonstrated in the exhibition.

There were spinning competitions, and since many men and women had taken part in them the two sections were kept separate. Almost all of them drew fine yarn. All this created the impression on my mind that, if Bengal took up this work enthusiastically, it would come to occupy the first place in regard to *khadi*. I found very few people in Bengal who insisted on not wearing *khadi*. There is plenty of artistic sense, and much skill in spinning too. Many middle-class women spin fine yarn and with sincere devotion. The wife of the chairman of the Reception Committee, in whose house I was put up, has spun a large quantity for her family. She grows the *dev* variety of cotton on her small farm and spins it uncarded. This good lady made slivers for me with her own hands. They were very good indeed. She picks cotton from the plants as she needs it and arranges it properly to turn it into slivers. In a matter of minutes a whole heap of slivers is ready. A good many *Swarajists* in Bengal seem to have taken up spinning. Biswas Babu himself is a *Swarajist*. The chairman of one of the [Congress] committees in Calcutta is also a *Swarajist*. He had sent to me at a public meeting yarn spun by him. We saw many men in Faridpur clad exclusively in *khadi*. There was a separate meeting for women. At this meeting, too, one saw a relatively larger number of women, larger than in similar meetings in Gujarat, dressed in *khadi*. I observed that the Bengali women did not have pleats in their saris, and, therefore, did not require any great length in their saris. But this is not the explanation of there being a large number of women in *khadi* at the meeting. We can only say that women in this part are more intelligent. It is true, of course, that a number of men and women had put on *khadi* specially for this occasion.

I have given here only the impression produced on me in Faridpur. As my present tour is connected solely with the *khadi* movement, I have still many more experiences in store for me. The reader will know afterwards what the sum total of those experiences comes to. As there is no entrance fee for the exhibition, thousands of people have taken advantage of it. On the next day, before I left Faridpur, prizes were awarded to persons who had demonstrated the different processes relating to *khadi*. The recipients of medals and prizes probably included equal numbers of men and of women. Among those who received medals there were Muslims. There were graded medals and prizes for the best carders, best sliver-makers, best spinners and best weavers.

At the Conference[6]

I found Deshbandhu's physical condition to be very bad. His voice has lost its strength. There is extreme weakness. In fact, he has not recovered well enough to be fit to undertake such exertions. Just now, the doctors have advised him to go to Darjeeling or some place in Europe to recuperate his strength. But he intends to do this only as a last resort.

A *khadi* marquee was specially erected for the Conference. It displayed the utmost simplicity. Seating arrangements were made on the ground. Not a chair was to be seen. The work of erecting the marquee was entrusted only to a tent-maker. He said he made it exclusively of pure *khadi*, but all of us have serious doubts whether the cloth used was really *khadi*. I am trying to ascertain the truth. The important thing, however, is that the organizers' intention was to have a *khadi* marquee and they believed that the one which was erected was of *khadi*.

Deshbandhu's speech was short and interesting. Every sentence breathed the spirit of non-violence. He stated clearly in his speech that India's salvation could come only through a non-violent struggle. If anyone asked me to put my signature to it, I would hardly find it necessary to alter a word or phrase.

It was but natural that the resolutions should be in tune with such a speech. There was, therefore, a good deal of heat in the Subjects Committee. Matters reached a stage when Deshbandhu felt it necessary to offer to resign, but ultimately his influence carried the day and the important resolutions of the Conference were passed without unpleasantness.

Anjuman Meeting

Muslim friends had arranged a separate meeting[7] to which we both were invited. Accordingly, Deshbandhu, his wife Basantidevi and I went to it. There is some estrangement [between Hindus and Muslims] in Faridpur. I advised that the matter should be settled through arbitration and suggested that the Muslims should participate in the Conference. As a result, about a hundred of them attended on Sunday evening.

1. *Navajivan*, 10 May 1925.
2. Soul.
3. Sound on telephone.
4. Glimpses.
5. Victory.
6. Bengal Provincial Agricultural Conference.
7. Held on 3 May 1925.

GANDHI'S TRIBUTE TO C.R. DAS[1]

(24 June 1925)

In the course of an interview which he granted to a representative of *The Statesman* in Calcutta he said :

I shall remain here as long as I feel that I am required, or as long as the trusted lieutenants of Mr. Das want me. I have placed myself unreservedly at their disposal.

I have already suggested that Memorial services should be held throughout India on July 1. I am hoping that people representing every variety of opinion will attend in every important centre in India and I am likely to remain here at least up to that date.

Asked for his opinion regarding the future, Mr. Gandhi said :

It is very difficult to say as a man of the world what the future will be but as a man of faith I can say that the virtues which I was privileged to see in the late Mr. Das will be an asset, resulting in nothing but good. How it will work out I do not know.

Referring to suggestion which he had previously made that the death of Mr. Das should be marked by a union of parties, Mr. Gandhi said :

If the union can be brought about, not mechanical, but real, it would be for that united party to formulate its demand. It is no use myself personally saying what it whould be, but I can say this that, whatever I may wish, I shall not stand in the way of what the majority may wish.

"What is your definition of *swaraj* ?" Mr. Gandhi was asked.

My definition of *swaraj* is the will for the time being of the people of India, as expressed through their representatives. There cannot be any hard and fast definition of *swaraj*, as you have, for instance, of a straight line in geometry. It has a varying value according to the variation in the temperament of the people dominated by various circumstances. Therefore, the immediate definition of *swaraj* is "Dominion Home Rule".

Mr. Gandhi was asked whether he would advise the abandonment of obstructive tactics with particular reference to Bengal.

"If there is an expressed desire for a Ministry when the Bengal Council next meets, would you advise the Council as a whole to oppose it ?" Gandhiji replied with a smile :

I would prefer not to answer that question. I would like Bengal not to be despondent, not to lose faith, because that would be betrayal of the great leader who has passed away. I khow that he believed often, when there was absolutely no valid reason for belief, and yet his belief was justified by events. No good cause has ever prospered by taking a despondent view.

Bengal has great imagination and it has got great powers of endurance, as I have discovered during my tour. I would ask them to and to this an inexhaustible faith and all will be well.

Incidentally, Mr. Gandhi said that he regarded it as a privilege to be by the side of Mrs. Das at this juncture. She was bearing her grief nobly.

He also paid a tribute to the young men who helped him in the crowd at Mr. Das's funeral.

I might certainly have been crushed to atoms, were it not for their strong arms. This was particularly the case at the burning-ghat.

1. *The Searchlight*, 24 June 1925.

GANDHI'S SPEECH AT CONDOLENCE MEETING

26 June 1925

Mahatma Gandhi then said that the Gujarati community simply did their duty in framing the resolution and nothing more. The 18th day of June was a day when it was an occasion to show mourning at the death of Deshbandhu and he believed most of them present in the meeting had attended the funeral procession of Deshbandhu. He said he had already appealed for raising of a fund of at least ten lacs of rupees to commemorate the memory of Deshbandhu on the lines laid down by him in the document which might be called the will of Deshbandhu. He was at present absorbed in the task and when Seth Anandji Hari Das and other friends approached him requesting him to preside over the function, he had distinctly given them to understand that he expected a response from the Gujarati community to his appeal in a befitting manner. He enquired if they had made any collection to contribute their quota, but was disappointed to see that no such previous arrangement was made. He was a practical man and he did not like to waste a single minute he had at his disposal to raise the fund, and he hoped in the meeting he had come to receive the quota of the Gujarati community to Deshbandhu Memorial Fund. In conclusion he said that it was always his habit to create rivalry not in bad things but in good things between the different provinces. He was not sure which province would be the first to unfurl the standard of Swaraj when Swaraj was established. But he felt sure that province which would perform its duty in its real sense towards the whole country would have the good fortune. It was Gujaratis who had responded splendidly when he made an appeal for Tilak Swaraj Fund of one crore of rupees and he was glad his appeal this evening to the Gujaratis of Calcutta would not go in vain. He knew the very great depression in trade at present; he, however, had to ask for at least ten lacs of rupees from the Gujarati community and he hoped that the deficit would be made up within the next three or four days left for collection.[2]

1. *Amrita Bazar Patrika*, 27 June 1925 (The meeting was held at the Alfred Theatre).

2. After the speech was over, a collection for the Deshbandhu Memorial Fund was made. The cash and promises to pay amounted to Rs. 7,000/-.

APPEAL FOR DESHBANDHU MEMORIAL SERVICE[1]

I hope that the public will bear in mind the 1st of July. Those who are organizing the Deshbandhu Memorial Service in Calcutta have come to the conclusion that it is necessary to have three meetings—one, a mass meeting in the Maidan, north of Victoria Memorial, another exclusively for ladies at Mirzapur Park, and the third at the Town Hall, where admission would be by tickets. As the functions all over India on the 1st of July are designed to be of a non-party character and as many who did not share Deshbandhu's political opinions have signified their intention of being present at the Memorial Service and of showing their respect for his memory, it has been thought advisable, apart from the mass meeting, to hold the meeting at the Town Hall, which can be attended by people belonging to different parties and where suitable speeches can be made. The difficulty that faces the organizers is to choose names for sending tickets of admission to the Town Hall. There is, I understand, accommodation in the Town Hall only for 1,200 people. A certain number of seats will necessarily have to be reserved. For the balance, applications should be made to Sj. N.C. Sen at 98, Beltola Road, Bhawanipore. They will be received up to Sunday next. And if the number exceeds the accommodation available, lots will be drawn for deciding upon the names of those who should receive admission cards. I know the prejudice that exists against regulating attendance at such public meetings. But I hope that the public will realize the difficulty of the organizers who are anxious to have a representative gathering at the Town Hall. It will not be possible to have many or any speeches at the mass meeting. And yet, it will be a pity if those who wish to express their sentiments are not provided with a platform. This can be had at the Town Hall.

I hope, therefore that the public will heartily co-operate with the organizers in making the Town Hall function a success. Maharajadhiraj of Burdwan has kindly consented to preside at the Town Hall meeting.

1. *Amrita Bazar Patrika*, 27 June 1925.

GANDHI'S APPEAL FOR MEMORIAL

All-India Memorial

I have been asked to inaugurate an all-India Deshbandhu memorial as I have, in consultation with the Bengal friends, inaugurated an all-Bengal memorial. I can assure the reader that the matter has not escaped my attention at all. I have been conferring with the friends who are by me. But we have not yet evolved a formula. For the all-Bengal memorial there was no difficulty in arriving at the conclusion. Deshbandhu's trust-deed was there at the pole-star. But the all-India memorial is not quite so easy a matter. The delay is unavoidable. Probably, by the time this is in print, a conclusion will have been reached. For the present, I must ask everybody to accept my assurance that there will be no unnecessary delay in making the announcement. That there should be an all-India memorial I have not a shadow of a doubt. The universal testimony of grief received from every nook and corner of India is the most eloquent proof of Deshbandhu's universal popularity.

From 'A Revolutionary'

Shrimati Basanti Devi has handed me an anonymous letter received by her from a 'revolutionary', from which I take the following :

Tears roll down and blur my sight in my attempt to write to you at this moment. I tried to go for a visit to 148, but could not sum up my courage to stand before you. The sight is heart-rending.

In the death of Deshbandhu Das a great man has fallen—perhaps the greatest the country has produced. There is none to fill up the gap. I am one of those who came to know him not when he gave up his extensive practice at the Bar and its princely income, but long before that when out of his seclusion—as it were—he came out to defend Sreejut Aurobindo Ghose in the Alipore Bomb Case, and from that time came to love him, came to have the highest regard and admiration for and devotion to him. He, too, always had a very soft and warm corner for us in his heart though he has not seen eye to eye with us in politics. For I am one of those who were, in the Partition days, wrongly called Anarchists and who are now very wrongly called the "Revolutionaries". He knew we were much misunderstood and misrepresented and much maligned because of our love of freedom for our common Motherland. To everyone of us he always extended a brother's hand, always trying to guide us in the right path. We sadly miss him today. We are overwhelmed with grief today at his death, for we know there is no man in the country which we can turn to in our hour of sore need.

> Leaders will come and leaders will go; but Deshbandhu will never come. He was the hope and inspiration of the people. He was the idol of the nation. His help and guidance were always, as it were, at our disposal and our services, nay our very lives, he knew, were at his command. And here I need only assure you, my dear sister, that our service—nay our lives—are, and shall ever continue to be, at your command.

The portion omitted is a reassurance of sympathy. This letter is an unsolicited testimonial of Deshbandhu's views on revolutionary activities. The reason for his hold on young Bengal is to be sought in his fatherly care of them in spite of their faults. He loved them not because he liked their methods but because he wished to wean them from their ways. Will those who did not listen to him whilst he was alive listen to the voice of his spirit which says to them 'not through violence lies the way to India's freedom'? Will they trust to his riper judgment rather than their own ?

1. *Young India*, 2 July 1925.

DESHBANDHU MEMORIAL FUND[1]

Friends have pressed it upon me that, in the interest of the Memorial Fund that is being collected, it is necessary for me not to leave Calcutta at the present moment for the projected tour. Whilst I recognize the usefulness of my presence, after comparing notes with Satcowri Babu, I have come to the conclusion that the tour already advertised ought not to be abandoned. After all, the collections that are pouring in come from thousands of grateful hearts. Personally I have never entertained the slightest doubt the response of Bengal.

We are not an ungrateful nation, and Bengal is not (to) be surpassed by any province in gratefulness. Given the proper cause, Bengal is capable of rising to the highest height. And what cause can be more proper and sacred, more insistent, than a memorial in honour of Deshbandhu? I do not, therefore, regard my presence in Calcutta as essential for ensuring the continuous flow, and shall carry out the tour in the full confidence that the subscriptions will continue with unabated perseverance, until the whole of the sum of ten lakhs is made up. I see that at the time of writing this note, the total collections amount to over Rs. 2,40,000, of which over Rs. 61,000 being today's collection, has to be still delivered to the treasurer. If anything like the present rate of progress continues — and there is no reason why it ought not to—we shall reach ten lakhs by the middle of this month. That we were not able to collect the whole sum by the end of June means no reflection on Bengal. It was possible, but only just possible, to complete the collection in the eight days that were available. It presupposed a perfect organization or ability and willingness on the part of a few to find the whole sum. I can almost say that, wherever I have gone, found the will to pay, but owing to the great depression in trade, the ability to pay large sums has been lacking. And it must be frankly confessed that nowhere in India are we sufficiently organized to reach the names for small collections amongst them in a short time. It is a magnificent tribute to Deshbandhu's memory that, with the very imperfect organization that the Committee have been able to bring into being, small sums are pouring in such a manner as to keep at least six workers at work, receiving monies from early morning to 10 o'clock at night and even later, not to mention a number of clerks that Sir Rajendra Nath has put on the work of receiving subscriptions and copying the very long lists, containing the names of subscribers, of annas, pice and even half pice, Whilst, therefore, I shall undertake to finish the balance of the Bengal tour without any misgivings, I wishl to notify it to the friends who have invited me to different places mentioned in the tour programme, that my principa work in the tour will be to deliver the living message of the late patriot and to collect subscriptions for the memorial. I trust that they will not spend much money on reception arrangements. I suggest that all decoration will be carefully eschewed and the collections made for reception be saved to the utmost extent possible and be devoted to the Memorial Fund, as is already being done in North Calcutta. I would like here gratefully to mention the fact that telegraphic and postal money orders are pouring in from all parts of Bengal and all other parts of India where Bengalis are domiciled.

I may add that those who are at present receiving monies at 148, Russa Road, will continue to do so in my temporary absence which will begin from part of next Saturday to Wednesday following. I expect to return to Calcutta on Thursday week, the 9th instant, leaving for Serajganj and other places the same day and returning again Sunday morning, the 12th instant.

1. *Amrita Bazar Patrika*, 2 July 1925.

DESHBANDHU'S LAST JOURNEY[1]

The scriptures say that, as a man abandons an old house and goes to live in a new one, so the *atman* dwelling in a body abandons it when it grows old, builds another and lives in that. As one does not feel happy when leaving one's old house, because of long association with it, likewise the soul is not happy when leaving the body because of the association, even if the legs are swollen and look like pillars the body is emaciated into a mere skeleton and the man struggles for breath. But one forgets the old house when the new one is ready and the soul, too, when it has a new home to dwell in, retains no memory of all of the old—such is the mystery of death and birth. If this is so, what cause do we have for fear or grief? It is more correct to think of death as the last journey then as mere extinction.

If we wish Deshbandhu's soul to have peace in its last journey, there is only one thing we can do, and that is to develop in ourselves as many of his virtues as we can. Some of them we certainly can. All of us cannot command English like his or be lawyers of his calibre or do the work he did in legislatures, but we can all have his patriotism and cultivate generosity like his. We may not be able to give as much money as he did, but anyone who gives to the best of his means will have given enough. A copper coin given by a widow counts far more than the thousands a Maharja may give from the crores in his possession. After he had started wearing *khadi*, Deshbandhu never used any other cloth for his dress either at home or in public. Shall we not start wearing *khadi*? Deshbandhu never demanded fine *khadi*. He preferred coarse *khadi*. He tried to learn spinning. Will those who have not started spinning do so?

All-India Memorial

At present, money is being collected for a memorial to him in Bengal. But will it be right not to have an all-India memorial? Since all of us are busy here with the collection for Bengal, I have not been able to consult friends. But I have been thinking about the matter in my own mind. As for the kind of memorial it should be, I have Deshbandhu's trust-deed with me. This is not written down, as the written will for the memorial in Bengal, but it is as good as a written testament. I shall say no more about it in this issue; my appeal will have come out before the next issue.

The reader should get ready to loosen his purse strings. Since people will be asked to contribute only as much as their means permit, no one need get nervous. Deshbandhu gave money not out of fear but of his own free will; he enjoyed giving. If he threw up a practice worth millions, it was with no painful effort of will; he did so because he found it unbearable to continue it. Let no one, therefore, feel nervous at my suggestion. With the progressive awakening in the country, every time there is a calamity, people will have to part with some share of their earnings; they should be ready to do so willingly. That is not love which merely sheds tears and does no more. Profession without action, is no love; it is but empty words. Love gives, and acts, without talking. One who loves his father does not go about, like a band, praising the father's virtues; he preserves his legacy, improves upon it and adds to it. A father's best property consists in his virtues, which the son cultivates in himself and so brings credit both to the father and to himself. In the same way, we who are Deshbandhu's heirs must contribute that we can to enhance what he has left behind.

Gujaratis in Calcutta

There is a special bond of regard between the Gujaratis and me. I have a way of saying harsh things, and the country has put up with it. It is to the Gujaratis, however, that I say the harshest things. They do not misunderstand me, but take my words in the right spirit, regard them as the salutary doses of a *vaid*[2] and love me all the more for them. I had this experience with the Gujaratis in Calutta last week. They had called a meeting to express condolence on the death of Deshbandhu.[3] I was invited to attend and preside over it. The organizers had also promised me that they would make a collection. I was therefore, forced to say a few harsh things. We do well in holding a condolence meeting; but there should be only one, not too many. There had been one on the day on which Deshbandhu died, and again on July 1 there will be meetings in the whole country. There can be, therefore, only one reason for holding a meeting in between, confined to a particular community and that reason must be to start some constructive activity, namely to collect contributions for the fund. Some activity of this kind is the best thing which Gujaratis, Marwaris and other outsiders living in Bengal can take up. This is what I said in my speech. It did not make the Gujaratis angry; on the contrary, they understood my point and there was a shower of rupees from the galleries in the theatre in which the meeting was held, and a sum of more than Rs. 6,000 was collected on the spot. If anyone offered less than he should, there was no dearth of persons to rebuke him. I have been told that there are still many persons who have not given as much as they can. If it is so, I should like such persons to make good the deficiency. In this Note, however, my aim is to thank my Gujarati brothers in Calcutta.

1. *Navajivan*, 5 July 1925.
2. Physician practising Ayurvedic system of medicine.
3. The meeting was held at Alfred Theatre on 26 June 1925.

GANDHI'S APPEAL FOR MEMORIAL[1]

148, Russa Road,
Calcutta,
22 July, 1925

I hope that the All-India Deshbandhu Memorial appeal will not in any way disturb the all-Bengal Deshbandhu collection. The all-India collection will last a considerable period, seeing that Bengal will have paid a heavy sum for the all-Bengal Memorial. The collection in Bengal for the All-India Memorial need not be made for three months or a longer period if necessary. The attention of Bengal should not be diverted from the all-Bengal collection. It must be a point of honour with every Bengali and everyone domiciled in Bengal to make the Bengal collection a full success. Over five lakhs have now been already paid. Though the Balance, I take it, is assured, it is likely to take longer than the first five lakhs unless the workers will concentrate their effort on quickness in collection.

Sjt. Manilal Kothari has shown what can be done in the direction by specialists. In view of his success in inducing some of those who have already paid to double and even to quadruple their subscriptions, there is perhaps a possibility of some of the others, who have already subscribed, paying a second and substantial instalment. But, apart from this possibility, there are schools and colleges left untouched. Will the Principals of these institutions or the students themselves move, as I was told at the beginning of the month that they would, as soon as these institutions were open after the vacation ? There are all the Bengal merchants and traders in the busy centres of Calcutta mostly untouched. I could see, when I was taken to some of these shops, that it was possible to collect, if not the whole sum, at least a large part of it from these merchants. Again, all the districts have not yet sent in their returns, nor have the Bengalis from the other provinces, except in some cases. Will all these friends respond in good time ?

I would like to plead a little for myself. I had hoped to be able to leave Bengal by the end of the month. I ask for the assistance of those who revere the memory of Deshbandhu and who are able themselves to subscribe and induce others to do so in finishing the collection as early as possible.

M.K. Gandhi

1. *Forward*, 23 July 1925.

CHAPTER 5

ROLE OF MOTILAL NEHRU

MOTILAL NEHRU'S VIEWS ON SWARAJ PARTY

A circular letter to members of AICC & PCCs[1]

To

All Members of the All India Congress Committee and of the Provincial Congress Committees of the various Provinces.

Dear Sir,

The compromise of the 28th February last between the two wings of the Congress ceases to have effect from today. There has been carried on an intensive propaganda in the interval by the No-Change Party to complete their preparations for Civil Disobedience according to their own conception. Leading members of that party have travelled far and near and carried the campaign to the furthermost limits of India and Burma. They have set in example of unceasing, unremitting toil which members of the Swarajya Party will do well to follow. I have nothing but admiration for their single minded devotion to what they conceived to be their duty, and I hope it will not be taken amiss when I say that I am sincerely sorry that they have not met with the success they deserved. What we, who do not agree with them, were waiting to see was how the mechanical process of collecting money and registering volunteers would create the requisite mental and spiritual atmosphere needed for Civil Disobedience of the right sort. Unfortunately the day we were looking forward to has not arrived. Our friends have failed to get the men aad money they counted upon and the unique experiment has not been tried for want of this great endeavour to achieve its aim has been, it is impossible to suppress a feeling of keener disappointment at the thought of what might have been, if only the time, energy and money spent had been employed in a united effort to prepare the country to capture the Councils. Can there be any reasonable doubt that all the Councils in the country would to-day have been at the feet of the Congress to be dealt with, as the Congress pleased ? Has not the result of the recent Municipal elections in the U.P. achieved by a minimum of joint effort a lesson of its own to teach ?

Turning to the work of the Swarajya Party during this period we find that prominent members have given their time and attention whole-heartedly to the general Congress work studiously keeping the Party entirely in the background. Mr. C.R. Das and I have spent most of the time in the Punjab and Hakim Ajmal Khan has, despite his failing health, not only rendered valuable services to the Aligarh National University, but has never failed to answer the call for the Punjab in its hour of need. The compromise only suspended Council propaganda and reserved to both parties, full "liberty to work the remaining items of their respective programme in the interval without interfering with each other". It was however felt that nothing should be done to embarrass the other party in the work they had laid out for themselves, and all party propaganda was severely eschewed. This had the unfortunate effect of cooling down the enthusiasm of our organizers, the great majority of whom failed to carry out the very specific instructions given to them to establish provincial and district committees and complete the necessary spade work before the 30th April.

I regret to have to say that so far from doing any practical good to other party the compromise of the 28th February has materially prejudiced both. The idea has taken root among Congressmen and the general public, that some similar or more permanent arrangement between the two parties will soon be effected. The terms of likely compromises have from time to time been discussed among both responsible and irresponsible people, the effect of which in my opinion has been disastrous to the whole movement. The expectation of an early coalition in the minds of the workers and the public has induced habits of sloth and given rise to an inclination to wait and see how things will take their final shape. As I have said elsewhere the constant talk of compromise has relieved the people of the necessity of thinking for themselves. They have left all the thinking to the leaders and are occupying themselves with the innocent pastime of breaking each others heads.

The fact that a basis for a fresh understanding between the parties was arrived at in Delhi, the other day has already been announced in the press and is public property. It is my duty, involving in my opinion no breach of confidence, to relieve the public mind of the suspense caused by that announcement. Mr. Rajagopalachari has now wired from Ahmedabad to Mr. C.R. Das that the proposed understanding was unacceptable to Mr. Vallabhbhai Patel and Seth Jamnalal Bajaj, and the compromise has failed.

There are however certain Congressmen who are still building hopes of an amicable settlement on the meeting of the All India Committee notified for the 25th May at Bombay. I earnestly beseech them to waste no more time in the pursuit of a phantasm. It is now abundantly clear that the only possible compromise between the two parties must permit entry into the Councils either by the withdrawal or suspension of the boycott. The alternative offered at Gaya has been tried and has failed. I can conceive of no arrangement acceptable to the Swarajya Party which ignores this obvious fact, and can confidently assert that whatever happens the Party will not desist from contesting the forthcoming elections. This being so what is the clear duty of every member of the Party ? I go further and ask what is the clear duty of every true Congress man ? Is this the time to wait and look on while the moderates and hangers-on of the Bureaucracy are putting forth strenuous efforts to give the country another three years of Government by mock parliaments ?

I have no desire to enter into a discussion of the merits and demerits of capturing the Councils. The question has been discussed threadbare and we have now seen the failure of the only possible alternative suggested. It will however not be out of place here to give you the impression I gathered in the

Punjab. I have no doubt in my own mind that the Punjab Council is to a very great extent responsible for the communal differences which have arisen in that Province. You have only to glance through the reports of the interpellations and debates to see how that Council has day after day and month after month been busily feeding the fire of communal disputes for the last three years. Are you going to let the flame envelop the other Provinces as well by leaving them to the tender mercies of the existing type of the Councillor for another term ? Indications are not wanting that several districts in the U.P. have already been more or less affected by the happenings in the Punjab. I should have thought that collective individual Civil Disobedience was quite out of the question at a time when the whole of a large Provinces was rent with communal disputes culminating in bloodshed. Chauri Chaura was but a sudden outburst of mob frenzy in a small out of the way village. The causes of the Punjab trouble lie deep and are showing themselves in a sustained and determined hostility between two great communities numbering millions.

I am addressing this letter to all members of the All India Committee and of the Provincial Committees of the various Provinces as I take them to be the selected representatives of the Congress in the country. I divide them into the following groups :

1. Those who have already joined the Swarajya Party.
2. Those who were ready to join the Party but were kept back by the compromise of the 28th February last.
3. Those who did not believe in the Gaya resolution on Civil Disobedience but were desirous of giving the majority who supported it a fair chance of carrying it out.
4. Those who were against dividing the Congress under any circumstances quite apart from their own personal inclinations.
5. Those who did believe in the Gaya resolution but have now seen that it would not work.
6. The waverers.
7. The diehards or those who will not countenance any change in the original N.C.O. programme whatever the circumstances may be and however much the public may be disinclined to follow it.

I have nothing to say to the last group as it is impossible to expect them to see things as I do. To the other groups I have a word to say.

I put it to those in the first three and the sixth groups whether it is not past high time to be up and doing ? Have you not by this time seen enough to dispel all your doubts and misgivings ? Our friends are evidently anxious to keep their word and bring about some sort of Civil Disobedience as soon as possible. You have seen the Jubbulpore incident in connection with the National flag and are no doubt aware of a similar venture being contemplated at Nagpur. I confess I do not appreciate either the appropriateness or the unity of these undertakings. The net result will in my opinion be the temporary loss of the valuable services of some of the most ardent workers. Another idea has struck some of our friends in the South. They are going to disobey the Finance Act imposing the enhanced salt fax, but it is not stated how it is to be done. To an ordinary man of affairs, it seems that the tax not being a direct one the only way to withhold it is either to engage in the illicit manufacture of salt on the extensive sea-board of India or else to smuggle it into our bazars. Do you take any of these proposals seriously ? If not what else do you expect in the way of immediate Civil Disobedience ? I have not heard or read of any other suggestion and the anxious enquiries I have made on the subject have only met with evasive answers from the leading exponents of the doctrine.

Those of you whom I have classed in groups 4 or 5 will pardon me if I say that I do not understand your position. You think that the prestige of the Congress will suffer by a division among its ranks. But the division is there already and will not be removed by your backing the wrong party. And may I ask in all seriousness whether the prestige of the Congress is likely to be enhanced by the sort of civil disobedience I have just referred to ? Some of you are very nervous about the results of the Council elections if they are not run by and in the name of the Congress. You instance the success of the Municipal elections in the U.P. as showing the great weight which the name of the Congress carries with the multitude and draw from it the illogical inference that the name of the Swarajya Party will not carry any weight if the elections are opposed in the name of the Congress. Need I remind you that the converse of every proposition is not true, and that the influence of the Swarajya Party with the masses has not yet been tried ? I cannot conceive how people who had the bitter taste of the last Council Government can for a moment hesitate to throw in their lot with the party which approaches them with the election cry "mend or end the Councils". Can you imagine for a moment that the U.P. agriculturists will be persuaded by the siren voice of the moderate or the sombre access of the no-changers to grant a fresh lease of life to a Council which, by passing the Tenancy Act, has delivered him to the tender mercies of the Talukdar and the Zamindar ? If you can, allow me to say that you do not know what is passing in his mind. Take it from me who have been listening to his grievances during the last two years that he is a highly practical person and is no longer to be led away from hard facts by any inducement. Besides, are we not as much of the Congress as the no-changers ? Assuming without admitting that we will not succeed in taking a very large number of voters to the polls can you doubt that at least ten times the number which attended at the last election will gladly support us. I assure you that your nervousness is wholly unjustified and beseech you to save the Congress even at this eleventh hour. Allow another month to pass by and you will again be in the grip of the very Councils which have faithfully carried out the behests of the bureaucracy and helplessly looked on while autocracy ruled the land.

I have addressed this letter to you all as I believe that the real diehards are but few, and the great bulk of the Gaya majority is composed of the other groups I have mentioned. Do not continue to delude yourselves with the hope of a common understanding either at the next meeting of the All India Committee or at any other time in the near future. As at present advised Mr. Das, Hakim Ajmal Khan and I do not intend going to Bombay for the All India Congress Committee meeting. We do not think our joining this meeting will serve any useful purpose. I beg of you to throw off the spell, think for yourselves and come to a final decision without running further risks.

May I expect to hear from you on the subject at an early date ?

Yours Sincerely,
Motilal Nehru

Anand Bhawan
Allahabad
May 1st, 1923

1. *M.R Jayakar Papers.*

VIEWS ON DOMINION STATUS[1]

On the issue of Dominion Status for India, Motilal Nehru opined, "... There may be anarchy, if the present system of administration is continued and if our voice is not heard, or if the remedies—supposed remedies—which are not being adopted are continued to be adopted. You may talk of revolutionary crime. But what is that, Sir, except an outward symptom of the real disease. Treat that disease and not the symptom. . . . We have tried to obtain justice by means of so-called constitutional and proper ways, but we have miserably failed. The one lesson that we have learnt is that we have to depend upon ourselves."

On 5 February 1924, a resolution was moved urging the early revision of the Government of India Act of 1919 in order to secure for India full self-governing Dominion Status. The reply of the government was the off-repeated statement about India's unfitness for responsible government, let alone self-government of the Dominion Status type. The main issues which weighed with the government were the apprehensions of the Indian states, the interests of the British capitalists, the prospects of the British services; civil and military, the requirements of defence. Above all Malcolm Hailey, Home member of the Government of India declared that "there are the minority communities, for the conception of full responsible government with Dominion Status meant entrusting the interests of minorities in the hands of a majority."[2]

On 18 February, the Assembly by 76 votes against 48 adopted Motilal Nehru's amendment which ran as follows : "This Assembly recommends to the Governor-General-in-Council to take steps to establish full Responsible Government in India and for the said purpose : (a) to summon at an early date a representative Round Table Conference to recommend with due regard to the protection of the rights and interests of important minorities the scheme of a constitution for India, and (b) after dissolving the Central Legislature to place the said scheme for approval and submit the same to the British Parliament to be embodied in a statute."[3]

1. *Debates, The Legislative Assembly,* Vol. IV, Part I, 1924, p. 542.
2. *Ibid.*, 8 February 1924. See the text on the demand for responsible government.
3. *Ibid.*

VIEWS ON FINANCE BILL[1]

On 17 March 1924, on a motion by Madan Mohan Malaviya, the Central Legislative Assembly had withheld leave to introduce the Finance Bill by 60 votes against 57. Motilal Nehru's telegram, dated 18 March said, "Finance Bill again introduced today with Viceroy's recommendation. Assembly refused leave without division." On this Gandhi wrote to Motilal Nehru, "I have your telegram about rejection of the Finance Bill. I rejoice because the victory gives you joy, but I cannot enthuse over it, nor am I amazed at the victory. With proper discipline and tact it was not an impossible feat, and I never doubted your very great tactfulness and persuasive eloquence, and your patience with threats, and I entirely agree with you that, if you had more time for organization and a larger backing from the country, you would have carried everything before in the Provincial as well as the Central Legislature."

1. *The Collected Works of Mahatma Gandhi,* Vol. 23, p. 270.

VIEWS ON LEE COMMISSION[1]

Speaking on the recommendations of the Lee Commission, Motilal Nehru observed forcefully in the Legislative Assembly, "The selfish motives with which we charge the British Government be elsewhere—not in the motives of the services but in the motives which be behind the maintenance of the services. The selfish reason, however, is the maintenance of the grip over India for all time to come. That is the selfish reason. It is not that ten, twenty or a hundred young men from England should come out here every year and be provided for. No, certainly not. What we mean by selfish motives is that you are entering into our daily life day by day to such an extent that it will take—I do not know how long it will be—hundreds of years for us to shake ourselves free of you. What we want is that you should give us the right to work erect in our streets and then you can come in any numbers you like. Come as our friends, come as our neighbours, not as our rulers."[1]

1. *Debates, The Legislative Assembly*, Vol. IV, Part V, 3-16 September 1924, Simla, 1924, pp. 3160-61.

CIRCULAR FOR GUIDANCE

On 20 January 1925, Motilal Nehru issued a circular for the guidance of the leaders of Swaraj Party in U.P. to enrol new members and propagate the ideology of the party amongst the people. In my opinion it is not necessary in the U.P. to carry on an active campaign to enlist members of the Swaraj Party. All that is necessary is to consolidate the results obtained at the last elections to the Congress Committees. I have not yet had a report giving the necessary particulars as to the strength of the Swaraj Party in the *Tahsil*, District and the Provincial Committees. My instructions were that a register be opened immediately after each election showing the names of the Swarajist and non-Swarajist members of that Committee. So far as I know these instructions have not been complied with. No formal report has yet been made ever of the names of the *Swarajist* and other members elected to the All India Congress Committee from the province. I think that the time, labour and money already spent should be turned to some good purpose. With this object I now give the following instructions :

1. That Tahsil, District, Provincial and All-India

Swarajist and *non-Swarajist* members be forthwith completed and submitted to Headquarters.

2. That full accounts of all remittances made to workers to the end of December last be at once rendered.
3. That instructions be issued to the *Swarajists* in each *Tahsil*, District, and Provincial Congress Committee :

   (a) to resolve themselves into *Tahsil*, District and Provincial *Swaraj* Committees,
   (b) to carry on propaganda work among the non-*Swarajist* members of the said Committees,
   (c) to secure election of *Swarajist* members to the said Committee at bye-elections.

All this work should be honorary and can be done by the office bearers and the other prominent *Swarajists* in the various Committees. The small expenses for stationary etc. can be met by subscriptions paid by members and small donations collected from the public.

4. Registers of members should be kept up-to-date with such changes as may be made being noted from time to time and information given to the Head Office.

This is all that is necessary to maintain the integrity of the Swaraj Party in the various committees during the present years.

This will be done by newspapers and lecturing propaganda. Arrangements are being made to start a Hindu Daily at an early date. This will be followed by a Urdu Daily in due course. Lecturing propaganda will take the form of :

(a) village organisation by establishing Hindu-Muslim Unions or *Sangathans* and taking the necessary steps to raise the untouchables,
(b) taking direct charge of Kisan Sanghs and have their grievances ventilated in the Councils through *Swarajist* members,
(c) organising public meetings to support important measures of *Swarajist* members of the Assembly and the Local Council.

It will be seen that item (a) is the concern of the Congress as a whole including the Swaraj Party while its (b) and (c) have exclusive reference to the Swaraj Party.

The work detailed above required an army of workers but no specific details can be laid down before we know that assistance is to be expected from the Congress funds for (a). The work indicated in (b) and (c) will be complimentary to the work mentioned in (a). It is therefore not possible to lay down the details of (b) and (c) in anticipation of the decision of the Working Committee of the Congress. I shall take the earliest opportunity after the next meeting of the Committee to frame a scheme. Meanwhile it is requested that work indicated in the first part of this note be completed without delay. It must be understood that all paid workers engaged for that work will cease to draw their allowances from the end of January. Strictly speaking that work should have been finished by the end of December and the extension of allowances to January is a concession. It should however be borne in mind that paid workers will again be mobilized as soon as the new scheme is ready.[1]

1. *Motilal Nehru Papers.*

VIEWS ON BENGAL CRIMINAL LAW AMENDMENT ORDINANCE[1]

The resolution regarding the Bengal Criminal Law Amendment Ordinance was moved by Duraiswami Aiyangar on 28 January 1925. The resolution was that, 'This Assembly recommends to the Governor-General-in-Council that steps be taken forthwith to supersede by an Act of the Indian Legislature the Criminal Law Amendment Ordinance-I of 1924, made and promulgated by His Excellency the Governor-General for and in the province of Bengal."

Pandit Motilal Nehru stated, "Sir, the Government case is this : There is a widespread movement, a deep seated movement of a revolutionary character, which is supported by secret societies spread all over Bengal. Its object is to overthrow the British Government by murders, by other offences, and by terrorism generally. So far as the existence of a revolutionary movement is concerned, I think it may also be freely granted that it does exist. It may also be freely granted that there is some organisation which directs its operations. The question, however, Sir, is whether that movement is so deep-seated, and those organisations so widespread as to call for the exercise of extraordinary powers, and the suspension of the ordinary criminal law of the land.

"Sir, I venture to say that if you look into the history of crime in other countries, you will find many more cases of this character than have occurred in Bengal. But what is the differences ? In these countries crime is put down by the aid of ordinary law, by an honest police, by a police which know how to do their duty. Here if any prosecutions have failed, they have failed simply because the police are wholly incompetent and have miserably failed in the discharge of their duties. The only thing in all the cases I have referred to that stands to the credit of the police is the accidental discovery of the bomb factory, for which they were not responsible. The real fact is, that all these phrases, murders of approvers, murders of witnesses, intimidation of jurors, have been borrowed from the Rowlatt Committee's Report.

"I am perfectly certain that His Lordship himself, if we can imagine him taking his seat on the bench once more and having his own findings about the Bengal Ordinance placed before him, will be the very first to throw them out as wholly inadmissible and unreliable. I say that even if angels from heaven were to go into these police informers reports and to base their opinions and conclusions upon them those opinions and conclusions would be wholly unreliable because of the taint in the material, and its defective nature, and not because the materials have not been well examined.

The fact is that one kind of terrorism has been set up against another kind of terrorism. We were told by His Excellency and rightly told that no political party can continue to live with terror for a friend. Now, Sir, there is no doubt that terrorist organisations exist in this country, but the greatest and the most powerful of these organisations is the Government of India and their terrorist agencies in the provinces. It was very rightly observed by His Excellency that the parasite kills the host. I say, Sir, that that observation applies to terrorism both of political parties and of the Government, and the parasite will kill the host in either case. Neither can continue to have terror for a friend."

"Charles Innes opined, Sir, the danger was a real danger and I say that the first and paramount duty of a Government confronted with a danger like that is to suppress it by all means in its power. But let me leave the Honourable Pandit and refer to the two main criticisms which have been made against this Ordinance. The honourable Pandit Motilal Nehru asked us to look at the history of crime in other countries. I would ask him, Sir, to look at the history of crime in this country and, in particular, in Bengal. Let me give Pandit Motilal Nehru some facts. Between 1906 and 1918, there were 210 revolutionary outrages in Bengal. There were 101 attempts at such outrages. Definite information was in the hands of the police of the complicity of no less than 1,033 persons in those offences. But of these only 84 persons were convicted of specified crimes in 39 prosecutions and of these 30 were tried by tribunals constituted under the Defence of India Act. Sir, is it any wonder that the Rowlaltt Committee recorded the definite finding 'by 1916 the forces of law and order working through the ordinary channels had been beaten."

T.C. Goswami stated, "You say that there are instances of anarchism; but we have here legalised and lincensed anarchism. As I have expressed myself before, if by anarchism is meant distrust of the law, violation of law, subversion of law, then this Government is a corporation of anarchists. And, Sir, I assure you that I weigh every syllable of what I say, when I tell you that I would rather be lectured on the subject of ordered progress and peaceful citizenship by brigands and assassins than by this Government; and for this reason : that brigands and assassins cannot carry on a campaign of terrorism and personal vendetta on nearly the same scale as a government committed to a policy of terrorism. You punish honest people by means of a certain well-known law in this country for trying to bring Government into hatred and contempt. I wonder if any seditious agitator can so successfully bring Government into hatred and contempt as their own high-installed officials. The whole system of administration, by Government's arbitary acts, has become, to my mind, loathsome like a foul disease; and when I am asked by people, 'How are you going to fight this Government which is so powerful? Does not the mighties monarch bow before it ? Are not plague and pestilence powerful ? In the same way is this Government powerful ? It is our misfortune to live under this Government. I must tell this Government that if they cannot rule except by Ordinances, the only honourable course for them is to lay down this heavy load of responsibility; and I hope their passports will be made and Neptune's choicest winds will fill their sails.

There is one word with which I shall close, and that is about the revolutionaries. The revolutionaries have been condemned in this House. I hate revolutionary methods, not merely because of an instinctive abhorrence of murder and bloodshed, but because the methods of revolutionaries—the French Revolution methods—are out of date and are likely to be entirely ineffectual. The old French revolutionaries believed that across a sea of blood lay the promised land. I do not personally believe that; I believe such a policy is dangerous; and if I have used caution in my language with regard to revolutionaries it is not because my words might otherwise give a handle to this Government, but because they might offer undue encouragement to those youths, who are ready to sacrifice their lives for their country, to plunge into anarchism. All honour to their primary motive. All honour to their spirit of sacrifice which leads them to dastardly acts. We must say this to them from this Assembly—and I cannot help saying that I will not have these revolutionaries condemned in this House unless this Assembly condemns the Government which has produced these anarchists."

C. Duraiswami Aiyanger gave vent to his feelings thus : "We want substantial evidence to say that there is really a political revolutionary movement in Bengal, and for that I have been searching for evidence and there has not been a single instance quited either by the Government Member or the pro-Ordinancers. Robberies and dacoities may exist. They do exist in large numbers in all the provinces. Are you going to eradicate them? When is the millennium to come, Sir ? So far as these movements are concerned, I wish Government

Members are to point out distinctly how they trace any of the robberies or dacoities to any political party or political movement. If you want to say that all these robberies and dacoities are committed by these people for financing the Swaraj Party, say so plainly and say that your Ordinance is aimed at the Swaraj Party. Don't say in one breath that it has nothing to do with political parties and in the same breath characterise robberies and dacoities as part of a political movement in this country. I am, therefore, against accepting any statement for the mere authority of the person who makes that statement. Pandit Motilal Nehru is as far away from Bengal as I am myself, and I would ask him to produce evidence that there is a revolutionary movement, and unless we are satisfied on the point, we have no right to condemn Bengal.

Sir, India knows no liberalism; India knows no conservativism; India knows no labourism. To India there is one 'ism' and that is *Bahadurism*. Sir, liberalism may be as fine as butter so long as it is in England. But when the parcel is opened at the Gate of India, it is found melted into *ghee*, and after a little travel round India, with a little mustard oil from Bengal, ground-nut oil from Madras, cocoaunt oil from the West Coast and gingerly oil from Bombay mixed in that *ghee* where is the form of that liberalism ? Where is the taste of it ? Where is the smell of it ? It is all gone. Therefore, Sir, it is no use for us to be told that this Ordinance was promulgated by a liberal politician. We want actual justice to be imported from England to India. If you are going to give us that personal freedom which is considered a sacred birthright in England, you ought to assure us and guarantee us that freedom, and if you do that, that is proof of liberalism."

1. *Debates, Legislative Assembly*, 1925, Vol. V, Part I, pp. 820 ff.

ON IDEOLOGY OF SWARAJ PARTY

Calcutta
21 July 1925

Dear Mahatmaji,

The Swaraj Party is under a deep debt of gratitude to you for your generous support on the irreparable loss it sustained by the premature death of its great leader, Deshbandhu

Chittaranjan Das. You have now redoubled that debt by the noble offer contained in your letter of the 19th July. It seems to me that the only way to repay that debt is to accept your offer in all humility and strive with your help to meet the situation created by Lord Birkenhead's speech in the spirit of the last pronouncement of Deshbandhu made at Faridpur.

Lord Birkenhead seems to have spurned the honourable co-operation offered by Deshbandhu and to have made it clear that in our struggle for freedom we have still to face many unnecessary obstacles and many ill-informed opponents. Our plain duty at this stage is, therefore, to go ahead along the line chalked out for us and prepare the country for an effective challenge to irresponsible and insolent authority. In the words of the great Faridpur speech "We shall fight; but fight clean, not forgetting that when the time for settlement comes, as it is bound to come, we have to enter the Peace Conference not in a spirit of arrogance but with becoming humility, so that it may be said of us that we were greater in our achievement than in our adversity." You have now enabled us to fulfil the meassage of Deshbandhu with the united strength of the Congress at our back. Under such auspices we need entertain no misgivings about the result which can only be what it has invariably been in all ages and countries: the ultimate triumph of right over might.

I desire to say one word about the Pact from which you have so generously absolved the Swaraj Party. As you know, both Deshbandhu and I had no desire to have the conditions of the Pact altered in the course of the year. We wanted to give it a full and fair trial and it was our wish to help personally in every way in making it a success. Ill-health and many pre-occupations prevented us both from doing as much for it as we had wished, but I entirely agree with you that a new situation has been created by recent events and under the circumstances the Congress should without loss of time adapt itself to this situation by making itself a predominantly political body. I, therefore, welcome your offer. This, however, does not mean that the Congress should give up in any way the constructive programme. All our efforts would be of little avail if they are not backed up by the organized strength of the nation.

We shall now go ahead in full confidence with our work inside the Councils and outside in the country and if the occasion demands organised action in the country I need not assure you that the *Swaraj* Party will whole-heartedly help in such activity.

Yours Sincerely,
Motilal Nehru

1. *Young India*, 23 July 1925.

SUGGESTS ACTION AGAINST TAMBE

On the 17th October in the course of a press interview, Pandit Motilal Nehru stated the following in reply to Mr. Jayakar's statement: "I can only express my regretful surprise at the statement reported to have been made by Mr. Jayakar on Mr. Tambe's action and the general policy of the Swaraj Party. I cannot conceive how a gentleman in the position of the leader of the *Swarajists* in the Bombay Council could possibly commit himself to the opinion that the difference between Mr. Tambe's acceptance of office and Mr. V.J. Patel's is merely technical. There is a most essential and substantial difference on general principles between the one man accepting an office in the absolute gift of the Government and another accepting office to which he is elected, not only by the suffrage of his own party, but in the teeth of Government opposition.

It will be remembered that Government block not only voted solidly against Mr. Patel, but made unusual efforts to secure the votes of those dependent upon it. Mr. Tambe, in office, is a creature of the Government, pure and simple. Mr. Patel in office, is as much an elected representative of his party, as he was out of office. There is no doubt one important difference between Mr. Patel in the Presidential Chair and Mr. Patel on the Opposition Bench. In the former place he is to decide impartially questions arising between his party on the one side, and the Government and other parties on the other. In the latter, it was his business to put forward the case of his own party with all the strength and ability he cold command. The difference is the same as there is between a Judge and an

Advocate, but is limited to points of order and procedure. Mr. Patel in the Chair is fully entitled to have his own opinions though he may not express them. That is a situation, which frequently arises in inter-party matters, quote independently of the Government. When a joint meeting of two more parties is held it has to be presided over by a members of one of the parties concerned, who is duly elected. In agreeing to preside, such a member is bound by the same obligations of fairness and impartiality, as Mr. Patel is in the Presidential Chair of the Assembly, but he does not thereby cease to be a member of the party to which he belongs nor is released from the undertakings he has given. Apart from these well-established general principles, the constitution of the party, while it clearly and absolutely prohibits acceptance of office in the gift of the Government equally clearly, provides that "the party may adopt one of its own members or any other elected member of the Assembly as a candidate for election to the office of the President of the Assembly. It will thus be seen that there is not the remotest analogy between the two cases. It is not true that both men have been lost to the party in the same sense. Mr. Patel will, on the expiry of the term of his office, be free from the limitations. I have mentioned above and resume his place in the party, as a fullfledged *Swarajist*, while Mr. Tambe has cut himself off completely from the Party, at the very outset, and, can never hope to return to it.

I can understand how Mr. Tambe's action can have a weakening effect on the future issues. By his action he has only shown himself up and left the Party as it was. I do not know what Mr. Jayakar is referring to, when he speaks of the 'present laxity of discipline'. There have been, and will always be, black sheep in every class. The mere defection of a member does not show any laxity of discipline. It all depends upon how the particular member is dealt with by the party and Mr. Jayakar would have done well to wait for the action which is going to be taken by the Executive Committee of the Central Council, of which he himself, is a member. It is painful to find the leader of the Party in the Bombay Council professing ignorance as to whether the party programme has succeeded or not. Mr. Jayakar's remarks about the party action like 'honourable, courageous and patriotic men' and 'honestly putting the case before the electors' are quite out of place and unwarranted. He doubts that the reception accorded to Mr. Patel in Bombay was genguine. All I can say is that I see no reason to doubt the genuineness of the reception and that, in my judgment, the public of Bombay appreciated the position more correctly than Mr. Jayakar has done. They honoured Mr. Patel, because he wrested the office of the Assembly from the unwilling hands of the Government by the vote of his own party and that of other independent and impartial members of the Assembly, and also because, having accepted the office, he discharged his duties in a manner which has exhorted the admiration of friends and foes alike. Mr. Tambe can expect no such honour, however ably he may discharge the duties of his new office."

Motilal Nehru advanced a severe comment on Tambe and the office-hunting *Swarajists*. He wrote to Seth Govind Das on 13 October 1925 "Mr. Tambe must be severely dealt with and the office-hunting propensities of the C.P. Councillors must be effectively stopped."[1]

1. *Seth Govind Das Papers*: Motilal Nehru to Govind Das, 13 October 1925.

ACTION AGAINST TAMBE

On the 8th October 1925 a government communique announced from Simla that H.M. the King-Emperor had approved of the appointment of S.B. Tambe, president of the Central Provinces Legislative Council and a member of the Swaraj Party, to be a member of the Executive Council of the Governor of the Central Provinces in succession to M.V. Joshi. This announcement gave rise to considerable political interest throughout India. Tambe was elected president of the C.P. Council by a large majority of *Swarajist* votes on the 4th March 1925. According to the *Swarajist* constitution, Tambe, as a *Swarajist* member, could not accept the post without the consent of the General Council of the Swaraj Party.

Soon after the announcement, in an interview, Tambe informed the Associated Press that he accepted the post of the Executive Councillor in his individual capacity and not as a member of the *Swaraj* Party, nor in pursuance of the policy of the *Swaraj* Party. Though he had not formally resigned the membership of the Swaraj Party, his appointment was tantamount to resignation.

On the 15th October Pandit Motilal Nehru, the president of the Swaraj Party, issued the following statement to the press on Tambe's appointment to the Executive Council of the Central Provinces:

"The reports received from the three Congress Provinces from which the members of the C.P. Legislative Council are drawn, namely, C.P. Hindustani, C.P. Marathi and Berar, show that Mr. S.B. Tambe did not resign his membership of the Provincial or of the Council Swaraj Party before accepting office as a member of the Executive Council of H.E. the Governor. He acted entirely on his own initiative and responsibility, without consulting or informing any of these bodies. I am informed that he has now tendered his resignation, but he has not yet replied to my telegram, asking him to send me such explanation as he might have to offer in justification of the step he has taken. I have called a meeting of the Executive of the All-India Swaraj Party at Nagpur on the 1st November, to deal with Mr. Tambe's resignation, and other matters connected with the C.P. Legislative Council, in consultation with the joint meeting of the Provincial Swaraj Committees of the three Congress provinces named above. The decisions arrived at will be duly announced in the press."

On the 16th October M.R. Jayakar, leader of the Swaraj Party in the Bombay Council, expressed his opinion on Tambe's action in the following statement: "I am bound to say that Mr. Tambe's acceptance of this office represents the growing weakness of the Swaraj Party, which has been manifest for some time. I do not see much distinction, except in one or two technical aspects, between Mr. V.J. Patel accepting for a salary paid out of the 'tainted' sources of Government, the presidentship of the Legislative Assembly and Mr. Tambe accepting Executive Councillorship for an equally 'tainted' salary. In both cases these two *Swarajists* have been lost to the Party. The Party is deprived of the benefit of their active co-operation in carrying on its work. These two are rendered dumb and voiceless and are in receipt of salaries paid by a Government described in the old phrasaeology as 'satanic'.

"When the Swaraj Party laid down the rule at the time of its formation that its members should not accept office, no distinction was made, so far as I remember between nominated and elected offices. The underlying principle was a double one: (1) that all important men in the party should be vigorously carrying on the work of the party amongst the people and not be trammelled by the restraints of office and (2) that the salary paid by the 'corrupting' Government should not be accepted. Now, both these reasons are as potent in Mr. Patel's case as in Mr. Tambe's. Nay, they are more so in Mr. Patel's case because of his courageous, energetic and fighting propensities. The loss of Mr. Patel to the party is far more regrettable from this point of view, than the loss of Mr. Tambe.

"Pandit Motilal's acceptance of a place on the Skeen Committee stands on a different footing. Notwithstanding that fact, he remains available to the Party, with his energy and influence, to carry on its work openly and in public. I certainly feel that the time has come when the *Swarajists* should meet and reconsider their programme. Either it has succeeded or not succeeded. If it has succeeded, strengthen it up. Make it more firm, strong and unalterable so that such lapses may become impossible. Personally, I would recall to the fighting ranks all those who have become stipendiarily dumb and mute. If, on the other hand, the programme has not succeeded, then let us be honest and true to ourselves and our country, and proclaim that in the altered circumstances of the country our opposition to the bureaucracy is out to take another form, that the time has come when all places of power, influence, and constructive responsibility ought to be taken, without hesitation, for the good of the country. Like honourable, courageous and patriotic men we should say that we shall accept these offices, with all their risks, because we feel the conviction, proud as it may seem, that we alone can save the country.

"This step involves the risk of being misunderstood, but that risk has to be run. Events will prove whether we, the *Swarajists*, remain firm and uncorrupted by the temptations of office. We must boldly take the lead, agreeing to be judged by the events. But anything is better than the present laxity. Owing to it, and the consequent indefiniteness, the *Swaraj* Party threatens, very soon, to become the laughing-stock of their supporters."

Expressing his opinion on Tambe's acceptance of office, N.C. Kelkar, the leader of the Maharashtra Swaraj Party, referring to the telegram of congratulation he sent to Tambe, said: "The telegram I sent to Mr. Tambe was a personal one. He is a friend of mine and was a friend of the late Mr. Tilak when the Maharaj Case being conducted at Aurangabad twenty-three years ago. I always considered him as a level-headed man and one always taking a common sense view of things. Therefore I thought it my duty to send him a personal telegram expressing my congratulations on his personal good fortune and also for the fact that his general merits were thus recognised. I took it for granted, when sending my telegram, that he must have sent in his resignation of his membership of the Swaraj Party before accepting offer of the Executive Councillorship.

"I see the point of the blame that is being laid on him, but technically I do not see much difference between this and Mr. Nehru's acceptance of a nominated seat on the Skeen Committee, at a time, when the Swaraj Party rules do not expressly provide for such acceptance, but I had advised Pandit Motilal to accept the post because, in my opinion, things were bound to come round to responsive cooperation. The accepting of the post of Executive Councillor is responsive cooperation for, as I wrote to Pandit Motilal when advising him to accept membership of the Skeen Committee every one now takes it for granted that there is a world of difference between a *Swarajist* accepting post like that and some one else doing it. The mentality of the *Swarajist* is recognised to be different from that of the non-*Swarajist*. I do nothing that the passing of a mere vote of censure on Mr. Tambe at the Executive Council meeting of the Swaraj Party will help matters much. The time has come when the Swaraj Party must take a broader view of things and give greater facilities for introducing a spirit of opposition inside the preserves of the Government. I am sure that, though technically at fault, Mr. Tambe may be relied upon for achieving in the Executive Council of Nagpur, what

Mr. V.J. Patel is expected to do in the Assembly as the President, and Pandit Motilal on the Skeen Committee, as member."

On the 16th October Mr. Y.K. Kale, a leading *Swarajist* member of the C.P. Legislative Council from Berar, wired: "There is absolutely no truth in the suggestions, made by certain newspapers, that the action of Mr. Tambe, in accepting the Executive Councillorship, has the normal support of the Berar *Swarajists*. Mr. Tambe has no such support, inside or outside the Council, except perhaps, of one or two of his friends, who along with him, were trying to form a ministry in C.P. All Berar *Swarajists* view Mr. Tambe's action as sacrilegious and unprecedented in the political life in India. As the silence of the Berar leaders is already being misconstrued, Mr. Kale thinks that this repudiation is necessary, prior to the party meeting which is arranged to be held at Amraoti on the 25th instant."

1. *Motilal Nehru Papers.*

VIEWS ON REFORMS INQUIRY COMMITTEE[1]

Commenting on the recommendations of the Reforms Inquiry Committee, the leader of the Swaraj Party put forward a few amendments regarding the revenues, property relationship between Governor-General-in-Council and the legislature, Secretary of State and his Council, admittance of Indians in the army, constitution of central and provincial legislatures, the principle of responsibility in the legislatures. He opined thus : '. . . We understand various systems of governments known to the civilised world or that were known to the ancient world, but this hybrid system which has been brought into being by speculative constitutionalists is a thing which is unrecognisable, and impossible to be identified with any of the past and present constitutions of the world.' On the operation of Dyarchy he stated, '. . . It must therefore be taken that the system has been universally condemned, and yet the irony of fate is that we are held bound to it. . . . The Government want to give them the Moon. We say it is unattainable. . . . It is simply this, that you have either to give us real reforms or to go back to your time-honoured methods of autocratic rule. . . The history of the so-called reforms is painful and depressing reading at present, but as it develops in the near future, it will, I am confident, furnish the brightest chapter to the chequered history of this land. The struggle for freedom once begun must sooner or later have its appointed end, and that end is no other than the achievement of the fullest freedom. It remains to be seen whether England will share the credit of that achievement by willingly giving a helping hand or suffer that achievement to be wrested from her unwilling hands. These are the only alternatives. It is for England to choose.'

Besides he opined forcefully pleading against the recommendations of the Reforms Inquiry Committee. "If there is any principle to be inferred from the recommendations, it seems to me to be the principle which governs the whole system of Government, and that is, 'Give as little as you can and make sure that in the little you give, the power and prestige of the bureaucracy is not in the least jeopardised.' But there is one question of principle which the majority have approached, though they have left it undetermined. It is the question whether dyarchy in the provinces coupled with absence of responsibility in the Central Government can under any circumstances be a sound basis of administration . . . I maintain that there was any doubt in the minds of those who invented and introduced the system or of those who would like to work it at all costs that it was wholly unworkable as such. . . . We respectfully decline not only because the attempt is vain but also because the attempt has actually been made and has miserably failed. What is then the position ? It is simply this, that you have either to give the real reforms or to go back to your time-honoured methods of autocratic rule. This is, Sir, all that, have got to say about the majority report. It must be scrapped and some new revenue found to make political life possible . . . .

"In making these suggestions we point out the principle which should be followed in framing any constitution that is likely to be agreed upon. If the principle is not first established, how is it possible to frame a constitution which would answer the requirements of the position according to the lights of the framers ? The first essential for the successful framing of a constitution is that we must agree as to what is to be the basis of that constitution . . . . Briefiy it is this—that we want responsible Government in the Central Legislature. We want the executive to be responsible to the Legislature except in certain particulars detailed here, namely, the expenditure on the military services up to a fixed limit, expenditure classed as political and foreign and payment of debts and liabilities. The reason why we do that is that it is in the nature of a proposal with a view to settlement.

". . . make us masters in our own home, but whatever else is outside the home and pertains more to your Imperial interests, you are welcome to keep. . . What progress have representative institutions made in India. . . . We say we are absolutely fit for self-government, as fit as you are yourself in your own Island. That is wbat we say. Here we are occupying that position and you tell us as you would tell school boys. Be good boys and you will be promoted to a higher form.

"Then, Sir, there is the plea for cooperation. Lord Birkenhead, His Excellency, the Viceroy and my friend the Honourable the Home Member have all said that the first condition, a very clear one, is that you must cooperate with us. I say that my first condition, as clear a condition as your own is, is that unless you show a change of heart, we are not going to cooperate. The hand of fellowship was extended to you in no grudging spirit by the late founder and chief of the Swaraj Party. You have rejected it, but I am here to say that I and my Party stand by what he said . . . ."

Another prominent member of the Swaraj Party, Jamnadas M. Mehta supported the contention of Motilal Nehru. He observed, ". . . We have been told that what Government are yearning for is cooperation. Here is an opportunity for them to get it. . . Its very fundamental condition of cooperation today is wanting. Who can cooperate ? People who are on equal terms, who can offer honourable help to each other. On what terms are Government demanding of cooperation at present. They carry a bludgeon in one hand, a sword in another and a pistol in their pocket and armed with these weapons of vetoing, certification and brute force they give us a challenge and say, 'These are our weapons, we shall use them. We shall use them whenever necessary and we demand your cooperation on these terms' . . . it requires no moment's thinking to say that no honourable man with a sense of self-respect can agree to cooperate in working a system like this which would only mean cooperation in the continuous enslavement of the country; it is clear from the speech of Pandit Motilal Nehru that the cooperation which this House and this country are willing to give is cooperation only on the terms of reciprocity and not cooperation of a one-sided kind.

Today the Government of India are insignificant in England. They are impotent abroad. They are tyrannical only at home. That is the correct description of the Government of India. Lord Curzon described it as a subordinate branch of the British administration six thousand miles away, and as regards the impotence of the Government of India to save Indians from humiliation and injustice in the Dominions and Colonies it is so notorious that even they are themselves ashamed of it. Pandit Motilal Nehru's amendment proposes to remove the thraldom to the Secretary of State in which the Government of India find themselves today.

Sir, I must now come to the Muddiman Committee Report. The Home Member is a gentleman, clear headed and sincere, and from all his speeches we can find that he has a genuine desire to come to terms with us. But what is it that this Committee does. I am reminded of a poem by Lord Tennyson, the late Poet Laureate, entitled Mand. His critics described it as '*mud*' *or* '*mad*'. With great regard to the personality of the Home Member, the Committee which is distinguished by his name was surely a muddy committee. The Committee had evidence from Ministers, Executive Councillors and men whom they delighted to honour. These people told the Committee that it was impossible to work dyarchy . . . . Give us some freedom, some breeze of freedom. . . . The Government of India are today working as a bureau; and the speech of Sir Charles Innes was the clearest indication that bureaucrats are unfit to be statesmen. Like experts, they are good as advisers, but very bad when they are masters of the situation. Sir Charles Innes' speech was a further indication that bureaucrats like *purdanashin* women have no access to the free air of nature. They live behind close doors. They do not care to know opinion from outside and they are so self-opinionated that they will not accept advice given by others. Instead of greater freedom we had the other day from Lord Birkenhead a most fire-eating speech. He rattled the sword. He told us that we were slaves who had been conquered with the sharp edge of the sword."

Alexander Muddiman intervened and stated, ". . . . Could any of the arguments suggested be valid ? Could we point to the history of these new institutions since their commencement and say : Now the time has come when without which no great reform as far as I know in connection with India has ever been carried out, we recommend these great steps to be taken."

"Sir, you have heard the speeches of the Secretary of State; you have learnt the terms on which he made his offer and it was an offer he made. He made it clear that acceleration of political progress was a matter of cooperation. He made it clear that to refuse to work what you have got is not in itself a claim for further progress—it is indeed likely to obstruct further progress. He laid down the position that the Government at home were not unsympathetic—that they did recognise that to stick to dates is not necessary, wise or desirable. He gave what my Honourable friend, if he was not speaking ironically, described as a very generous offer. Sir, I say, do not close the door by making the position more difficult. Do not give us an ultimatum, under the guise of an offer. Do not say, 'We will grant you the fee of Blackacre if you empty the sea.' Do not suggest terms of that kind. It is neither wise nor, I suggest, likely to be effective. I earnestly hope that you will believe when I say that we are not merely giving you a blank answer to what I recognise is an attempt to put down on paper what we have never seen on paper—the united amendment of both parties."

1. *Debates, The Legislative Assembly,* 1925, Vol. VI, Part II, pp. 854 ff.

DEEP INTEREST IN ASSEMBLY DEBATES[1]

Undoubtedly Motilal Nehru prepared the details of the agenda to be discussed in the Assembly like a serious and conscientious student doing his home-work to be shown the next day. His superb intellect, masterly adroitness and resonant voice put forward forceful arguments which put new life even in the dull and drab discussion on various issues. Jawaharlal Nehru mentioned in his *Autobiography* thus about Motilal Nehru's deep interest in the deliberations of the Central Assembly. "Father had taken to the work in the Assembly like a duck to water. It suited his legal and constitutional training and, unlike *Satyagraha* and its off-shoots, he knew the rules of this game."[1] George Rainy, Leader of the House, later on, paid glowing tributes to the memory of Motilal Nehru. He said, "The quickness of his intellect, his skill in debate, his adroitness as a tactician and his strength of purpose rendered him a formidable adversary in controversy."[2]

1. Jawaharlal Nehru, *An Autobiography*, p. 131.
2. See *Debates, Legislative Assembly*, February 1931.

CHAPTER 6

EFFORTS FOR UNITY

AGREEMENT AMONG LEADERS

After an exasperatingly long period of controversy and conflict the two sections of the Swaraj Party managed to come to an agreement between them. The conference was convened at the initiative of Motilal Nehru on 20 and 21 April 1924 at the Sabarmati Ashram, Ahmedabad. Attended by prominent leaders like Gandhi, Motilal Nehru, Mrs. Sarojini Naidu, Lajpat Rai, M.R. Jayakar, M.S. Aney, B.S. Moonje, D.V. Gokhale and G.A. Ogale, the discussion lasted for two days in which both the parties entered in a frank and friendly spirit. The conference adopted the following agreement :

"It is hereby agreed between the undersigned, subject to the confirmation of the All-India Congreess Committee that the response made by the Government shall, for purpose of Clauses (a) and (b) of the resolution 11-B (4) of the All-India Congress Committee, dated 6th and 7th March 1926, be considered satisfactory in the provinces if the power, responsibility and initiative necessary for the effective discharge of their duties are secured to Ministers. A sufficiency of such power, responsibility and initiative in each province shall be decided, in the first instance, by the Congress members of the Legislative Council of that province subject to confirmation by a Committee consisting of Pandit Motilal Nehru and Mr. M.R. Jayakar.

It is further agreed that the said Committee will decide all disputes about selection of candidates in the Congress Provinces of Bombay, Maharashtra, Berar and C.P. Marathi.

Lajpat Rai while supporting the stand of Jayakar and Kelkar, laid blame for the wrangle on Motilal Nehru. "...We wish the Pandit had exercised more restraint....He knows his business and may be expected to give the proper lead to his flock but we cannot help remarking that this is hardly the time to lose temper and become angry...The two wings of the Party are busy fighting each other...Messrs Jayakar and Kelkar have resigned their seats on the Party Executive. In view of Motilalji's recent utterances perhaps that was the only dignified course left to them. The Party has split over responsive cooperation."[2]

Lala Lajpat Rai resigned his membership of the Swaraj Party on 24 August 1926 on account of his differences with Motilal Nehru.[3] He explained thus : "I joined the Swaraj Party in the hope that I would be able to pull on with them, but soon after I found that I was mistaken...I would have gladly withdrawn from any kind of contest with the Swaraj Party had my sense of duty to the country allowed me to do so. I feel that such a conduct at the present juncture would be cowardly. I owe it to myself and the country to myself and the country to vindicate the principles for what I stand."[4]

After his resignation, Lajpat Rai and Pandit Madan Mohan Malaviya founded the Independent Congress Party on 12 September 1926.[5] In the elections it achieved an astounding success against the Congress in U.P. and the Punjab. Lajpat Rai was elected to the Central Assembly from two constituencies against the Congress candidates.[6]

1. *The Bombay Chronicle*, 22-24 April 1926.
2. M.R. Jayalsar, *The Story of My Life*, Vol. II, p. 593.
3. A.K. Majumdar, *Advent of Independence*, Bombay, 1963.
4. V.C. Joshi (ed.), *Lajpat Rai : Writings and Speeches*, Vol. I, p. 317.
5. *The Tribune*, 14 September 1926. (Madan Mohan Malaviya was elected as president and Lajpat Rai as secretary).
6. V.C. Joshi, *op. cit.*, p. ix.

GANDHI'S SURRENDER

On 30 August 1924, Gandhi informed Motilal Nehru, "... I made a full surrender *i.e.* as full as I am capable of making...

You will have me therefore almost on your terms. The 'almost' is necessary because there are some few things I hold dearer than life and than all the ties of the world...As a matter of fact *Swarajists* may organize themselves fully in every province without let or hindrance from the Congress. But the Congress organization everywhere should have only one programme. Thus Das may convert the Congress organization into a *Swaraj* organization and form himself and permit others to form a Congress organization...'[1]

1. *The Collected Works of Mahatma Gandhi*, Vol. 25, pp. 53-55.

AGREEMENT BETWEEN MAHATMA GANDHI, MOTILAL NEHRU AND C.R. DAS[1]

Whereas, although *Swaraj* is the goal of all the parties in India the country is divided into different groups seemingly working in opposite directions, and whereas such antagonistic activity retards the progress of the nation towards *Swarajya*;

And whereas it is desirable to bring, so far as possible, all such parties within the Congress and on a common platform, and whereas the Congress itself is divided into two opposing sections, resulting in harm to the country's cause;

And whereas it is desirable to re-unite these parties for the purpose of furthering the common cause;

And whereas, a policy of repression has been commenced in Bengal by the local Government, with the sanction of the Governor-General;

And whereas, in the opinion of the undersigned, the repression is aimed in really not at any party of violence but at the Swarajya Party in Bengal and, therefore, at constitutional and orderly activity;

And thereas, therefore, it has become a matter of immediate necessity to invite and secure the cooperation of all parties for putting forth the united strength of the nation against the policy of repression, we, the undersigned, strongly recommend the following for adoption by all parties, and eventually by the Congress at Belgaum :

The Congress should suspend the programme of non-cooperation as the national programme, except in so far as it relates to the refusal to use or wear cloth made out of India.

The Congress should further resolve that different classes of work of the Congress may be done as may be found necessary by different sections within the Congress and should resolve that spread of hand-spinning, hand-weaving and all the antecedent processes and the spread of handspun and hand-woven *khaddar* and the promotion of unity between different communities, specially between Hindus and Mahomedans, and the removal of untouchability by the Hindus from amongst them, should be carried on by all sections within the Congress, and the work in connection with the Central and Provincial Legislatures should be carried on by the Swarajya Party on behalf of the Congress and as an integral part of the Congress organisation, and for such work the Swarajya Party should make its own rules and raise and administer its own funds.

In asmuchas experience has shown that without universal spinning India cannot become self-supporting regarding her clothing requirements, and inasmuch as hand-spinning is the best and the most tangible method of establishing a visible and substantial bond between the masses and Congress men and women and in order to popularise hand-spinning and its product *khaddar*, the Congress should repeal article 7 of the Congress constitution and should substitute the following therefor :

No one shall be a member of any Congress committee or organisation who is not of the age of 18 and who does not wear hand-spun and hand-woven *khaddar* at political and Congress functions or while engaged in Congress business and does not make a contribution of 2,000 yards of evenly-spun yarn per month of his or her own spinning, or in case of illness, unwillingness or any such case, a like quantity of even-yarn spun by any other person.

1. *The Leader*, 8 November 1924.

THE AGREEMENT[1]

The following is the statement issued in Calcutta on the 5 November 1924 over the signatures of Gandhi, C.R. Das and Motilal Nehru. "The Congress should suspend the programme of non-cooperation as the national programme, except in so far as it related to the refusal to use or wear cloth made out of India. The Congress should further resolve that different classes of work of the Congress may be done as may be found necessary, by the different sections within the Congress and should resolve that the spread of hand-spinning, hand-weaving and all the antecedent progress and the spread of hand-spun and hand-woven *khaddar*, and the promotion of unity between different communities, specially between the Hindus and the Mussalmans, and the removal of untouchability by the Hindus from amongst them should be carried on by all sections within the Congress; and the work in connection with the Central and Provincial Legislatures should be carried on by the Swaraj Party on behalf of the Congress and as an integral part of the Congress organization and for such work the Swaraj Party should make its own funds.

"No one shall be member of any Congress Committee or organization who is not of the age of 18 and who does not wear hand-spun and hand-woven *khaddar* at political and Congress functions or while engaged in Congress business, and does not make a contribution of 2,000 yards of evenly spun yarn per month of his or her own spinning or in case of illness, unwillingness or any such cause a like quantity of yarn spun by any other person.

In an article entitled "The Agreement" in *Young India* he explained the implications of this agreement. "I thank God that he gave me strength to surrender to the *Swarajists* all that it was possible for me to surrender—much more than I or many friends had expected. I must acknowledge my indebtedness to the *Swarajists* for their accommodation .. The agreement puts *Swarajists* on a par with the no-changers...*Swarajists* claim to be a growing body. They have made an impression on the Government cannot be gainsaid.... They have shown determination, grit, discipline and cohesion and have not feared to carry their policy to the point of defiance. Once assumed the desirability of entering Councils and it must be admitted that they have introduced a new spirit into the Indian Legislatures.... The Congress was weakened by the session of the Liberals and the Besantites. The cleavage was inevitable because they were opposed to non-cooperation on principle. We must avoid further cleavage if it is at all possible. We must not lightly set up as principle mere matters of opinion and engage in pitched battles over them.

"The agreement is what it professes to be—a strong recommendation. I have signed it in my individual capacity.... I want it to be considered on merits. I would urge everyone to eliminate me from consideration.... Deep cherished convictions cannot and must not be set aside from any consideration whatsoever."

1. *Young India*, 13 November 1924.

RESOLUTION ON CALCUTTA AGREEMENT AT BELGAUM CONGRESS

December 26, 1924

(a) (i) The Congress hereby endorses the following agreement between Mahatma Gandhi on the one hand and Deshbandhu C.R. Das and Pandit Motilal Nehru acting on behalf of the Swaraj Party on the other.

The Agreement

(ii) The Congress hopes that the agreement will result in true unity between the two wings of the Congress and will also enable persons belonging to other political organizations to join the Congress. The Congress congratulates the *Swarajists* and others arrested under the New Ordinance or Regulation III of 1818 and is of opinion that such arrests are inevitable so long as the people of India have not the capacity for vindicating their status and liberty, and is further of opinion that such capacity can in the present circumstances of the country be developed by achieving the long-deferred exclusion of foreign cloth; and therefore as a token of the earnestness and determination of the people to achieve this national purpose, welcomes the introduction of hand-spinning as part of the franchise and appeals to every person to avail himself or herself of it and join Congress.

(iii) In view of the foregoing, the Congress expects every Indian, man and woman, to discard all foreign cloth and to use and wear hand-spun and hand-woven *khaddar* to the exclusion of all other cloth. With a view to accomplish the said purpose without delay, the Congress expects all Congress members to help the spread of hand-spinning and the antecedent processes and the manufacture and sale of *khaddar*.

(iv) The Congress appeals to the Princes and the wealthy classes of India and the members of political and other organizations not represented on the Congress, and municipalities, local bodies, panchayats and such other institutions, to extend their help to the spread of hand-spinning by personal use and otherwise and especially by giving liberal patronage to the classes of artists, still surviving and capable of working artistic designs in fine *khaddar*.

(v) The Congress appeals to the merchants engaged in the foreign cloth and yarn trade to appreciate the interests of the nation and discontinue their importation of foreign cloth and yarn and help the national cottage industry by dealing in *khaddar*.

(vi) It having come to the notice of the Congress that varieties of cloth are manufactured in mills and on other looms out of mill yarn and sold in the Indian market as *khaddar*, the Congress appeals to the mill-owners and other manufacturers concerned, to discontinue this undesirable practice and further appeals to them to encourage the revival of the ancient cottage industry of India by restricting their operations among those parts of the country that have not yet come under the Congress influence and appeals to them to discontinue the importation of foreign yarn.

(vii) The Congress appeals to the heads and leaders of all religious denominations whether Hindu, Muslim or any other to preach to their congregations the message of *khaddar* and advise them to discontinue the use of foreign cloth.

(b) The present Article VII of the Constitution to be repealed and the following to be substituted therefor :

(i) Every person not disqualified under article IV shall be

entitled to become a member of any primary organization controlled by the Provincial Congress Committee, provided that no one shall be a member of any Congress Committee or organization who does not wear hand-spun and hand-woven *khaddar* at political and Congress functions or while engaged in Congress business and does not make a contribution of 20,000 yards of evenly spun yarn per year of his or her own spinning, or in the case of illness or unwillingness or any such cause, the same quantity of yarn spun by any other person; provided also that no person shall be a member of two parallel Congress organizations at one and the same time.

(ii) The year of the membership shall be reckoned from the 1st January to the 31st December. The said subscription shall be payable in advance and may be paid in instalments of 2,000 yards per month payable in advance. Members joining in the middle of the year shall contribute the full quantity due from the beginning of the yar.

Transitory Provision

During 1925, the subscription shall be 20,000 yards only and shall be payable on or before 1st March or in instalments as aforesaid.

(iii) No person shall be entitled to vote at the election of representatives or delegates or any committee or sub-committee of any Congress organization whatsoever, or to be elected as such, or to take part in any meetings of the Congress or any Congress organization or any committee or sub-committee thereof, if he has not contributed the yarn subscription or the instalments due. Any member who has made default in the payment of subscription may have his or her rights restored by paying the subscription in respect of which the default has occurred and the instalment for the month then current.

(iv) Every Provincial Congress Committee shall send to the General Secretary, All-India Congress Committee, from month to month returns of membership and of the yarn received by it in virtue of this Article. The Provincial Congress Committee shall contribute ten per cent of the yarn subscriptions or their value to the All-India Congress Committee.

(v) Omit present Article VI (c) and Article IX (b).

Proposed by :

Deshbandhu C.R. Das (in English)

Seconded by :

Sjt. S,V. Kaujalgi (both in Kanarese and English)
Sjt. N.C. Kelkar (in English)
Sjt. S.V. Abhyankar (in English)
Pandit Motilal Nehru (in English)

Opposhd by :

Maulana Hasrat Mohani (in Urdu)
Maulana Azad Sobhani (in Urdu)
Swami Govindananda (in English)

1. *Report of the Thirty-ninth Indian National Congress*, 1924, p. 1.

TOWARDS UNITY

The All-Party Committee met to consider the questions referred to it by the Conference. It appointed a sub-committee of nearly fifty to consider the question. The sub-committee appointed a smaller committee to consider all possible *swaraj* schemes and report to the sub-committee the results of its deliberations. Dr. Besant is labouring at this smaller committee with her usual application and energy which put to shame younger men and women. But naturally the attention centred round the Hindu-Muslim problem; not that it is intrinsically more important except for individuals like me but because it blocks all progress towards *swaraj*. The sub-committee proved too formal for the task. It was necessary to avoid the reserve and the stiffness even of a committee and to be absolutely informal and to have a still smaller number of persons. This was done and a few of each community met at Hakim Saheb's house. The result has been succinctly given to the Press by Pandit Motilal Nehru. I agree that there is no cause for anxiety or disappointment. For all want a solution. Some want it at once, some regard the time not to be seasonable, some would sacrifice everything to get a solution, others would be cautious and would wait till they have secured what to them is an indispensable minimum. But all agreed that a solution of the problem was essential to *swaraj*. And as all want *swaraj*, a solution must not be beyond the reach of those who are engaged in finding it. The prospect was never so bright as when we parted to meet again on 26th February. Meanwhile everyone is to explore fresh avenues to a settlement.

The public will want to know my view of communal representation. I am opposed to it with all my heart but I would agree to anything so long as it ensures peace and is honourable to both the parties. In the absence of agreement on the plans suggested by either party I have presented a solution which might answer the purpose. But I need not discuss it at the present stage. I hope that the responsible members of both the communities will leave no stone unturned whether by means of private, quiet talks or by means of a public expression of their opinions. I hope too that newspapermen will write nothing to irritate any party but will observe discreet silence where they cannot usefully assist.

1. *Young India*, 5 February 1926.

THE AGREEMENT AND THE SPINNING FRANCHISE

A. (i) The Congress hereby endorses the following agreement entered into between Mahatma Gandhi, on the one hand, and Deshbandhu C.R. Das and Pandit Motilal Nehru, acting on behalf of the Swaraj Party, on the other.

Whereas although *Swaraj* is the goal of all the parties in India, the country is divided into different groups seemingly working in opposite directions; and whereas such antagonistic activity retards the progress of the nation towards *Swaraj*, and whereas it is desirable to bring so far as possible all such parties within the Congress and on a common platform; and whereas the Congress itself is divided into two opposing sections resulting in harm to the country's cause; and whereas it is desirable to reunite these parties for the purpose of furthering the common cause, and whereas a policy of repression has been commenced in Bengal by the local government what the sancion of the Governor-General, and whereas, in the opinion of the undersigned, this repression is aimed in reality not at any party of violence, but at the Swaraj Party in Bengal and therefore at constitutional and orderly activity; and whereas, therefore, it has become a matter of immediate necessity to invite and secure the cooperation of all parties for putting forth the united strength of the nation against the policy of repression, we the undersigned strongly recommend the following for adoption by all parties and eventually by the Congress at Belgaum.

The Congress should suspend the progamme of non-cooperation as the national progamme except in so far as it relates to the refusal to use or wear cloth made out of India.

The Congress should further resolve that different classes of work of the Congress may be done, as may be found necessary, by different sections within the Congress and should resolve that the spread of hand-spinning and hand-weaving and all the antecedent processes and the spread of hand-spun and hand-woven *khaddar* and the promotion of unity between different communities, specially between the Hindus and the Mahomedans and the removal of untouchability by the Hindus from amongst them, should be carried on by all sections within the Congress and the work in connection with the Central and Provincial Legislatures should be carried on by the Swaraj Party on behalf of the Congress and as an integral part of the Congress organisation, and for such work the Swaraj Party should make its own rules and administer its own funds.

Inasmuch as experience has shown that without universal spinning India cannot become self-supporting regarding her clothing requirements and inasmuch as hand-spinning is the best and the most tangible method of establishing a visible and substantial bond between the masses and Congressmen and in order to popularise hand-spinning and its products, the Congress should repeal article VII of the Congress constitution and should substitute the following therefor:

> "No one shall be a member of any Congress Committee or organisation who is not of the age of 18 and who does not wear hand-spun hand-woven *khaddar* at political and Congress functions or while engaged in Congress business and does not make a contribution of 2,000 yards of evenly spun yarn per month of his or her own spinning or in case

of illness, unwillingness or any such cause a like quantity of yarn spun by any person."

(ii) The Congress hopes that the agreement will result in true unity between the two wings of the Congress and will also enable persons belonging to other political organisations to join the Congress. The Congress congratulates the *Swarajists* and others arrested under the new Ordinance or Regulation III of 1818 and is of the opinion that such arrests are inevitable so long as the people of India have not the capacity for vindicating their status and liberty, and is further of the opinion, that such capacity can in the present circumstances of the country be developed by achieving the long deferred exclusion of foreign cloth; and therefore as a token of the earnestness and determination of the people to achieve this national purpose welcomes the introduction of hand-spinning in the franchise and appeals to every person to avail himself or herself of it and join the Congress.

(iii) In view of the foregoing, the Congress expects every Indian man and woman to discard all foreign cloth and to use and wear hand-spun and hand-woven *khaddar*, to the exclusion of all other cloth

With a view to accomplish the said purpose without delay, the Congress expects all Congress members to help the spread of hand-spinning and the antecedent processes and the manufacture and sale of *khaddar*.

(iv) The Congress appeals to the princes and wealthy classes and the members of political and other organisations not represented on the Congress, and municipalities, local boards, panchayats and such other institutions, to extend their help to the spread of hand-spinning and *khaddar* by personal use and otherwise, and specially by giving liberal patronage to the class of artists, still surviving, who are capable of working artistic designs in fine *khaddar*.

(v) The Congress appeals to the merchants engaged in the foreign cloth and yarn trade to appreciate the interests of the nation and discontinue further importation of foreign cloth and yarn and help the national cottage industry by dealing in *khaddar*.

(iv) It having come to the notice of the Congress that

varieties of cloth are manufactured in mills and on hand-looms out of mill yarn and solid in the Indian market as *khaddar* the Congress appeals to the mill-owners and other manufacturers concerned, to discontinue this undesirable practice and further appeals to them to encourage the revival of the ancient cottage industry of India by restricting their operations among those parts of the country that have not yet come under the Congress influence, and appeals to them to discontinue the importation of foreign yarn.

(vii) The Congress appeals to the heads and leaders of all religious denominations whether Hindu, Muslim or any other, to preach to their congregations the message of *khaddar* and advise them to discontinue the use of foreign cloth.

B. The present Article VII of the Constitution to be repealed and the following to be substituted therefor:

(i) Every person not disqualified under Article IV shall be entitled to become a member of any primary organisation controlled by the Provincial Congress Committee, provided that no one shall be a member of any Congress Committee or organisation who does not wear hand-spun and hand-woven *khaddar* at political and Congress functions or while engaged in Congress business and does not make a contribution of 24,000 yards of evenly spun yarn per year of his or her own spinning, or in case of illness, unwillingness or any such cause, the same quantity of yarn spun by any other person provided also that no person shall be a member of two parallel Congress organisations at one and the same time.

(ii) The year of the membership shall be reckoned from 1st January to 31 December. The said subscription shall be payable in advance and may be paid in instalments of 2,000 yards per month payable in advance. Members joining in the middle of the year shall contribute the full quantity due from the beginning of the year.

Transitory Provision: During 1925 the subscription shall be 20,000 yards only and shall be payable on or before 1st March or in instalments as aforesaid.

(iii) No person shall be entitled to vote at the election of representatives or delegates or any committee or sub-committee of any Congress organisation whatsoever, or to be elected as such, or to take part in any meetings of the Congress or any

Congress organisation or any committee or sub-committee thereof, if he has not contributed the yarn subscription or the instalments due.

Any member who has made default in the payment of the subscription may have his or her rights restored by paying the subscription in respect of which the default has occurred and the instalment for the month then current.

(iv) Every Provincial Congress Committee shall send to the General Secretary, All-India Congress Committee, from month to month, returns of membership and of the yarn received by it in virtue of this Article. The Provincial Congress Committee shall contribute 10 per cent of the yarn subscriptions or their value to the All-India Congress Committee.

(v) Delete Article VI(e) and Article IX(b) of the Constitution.

GLOSSARY

Ahimsa	non-violence
Bapu	father, name often given to Gandhi
Bharat	India
Charkha	spinning-wheel
Dharma	religion
Goondaism	hooliganism
Guru	teacher
Harijan	a name which Gandhi gave to an untouchable
Hartal	stoppage of work and business
Himsa	violence
Jai	victory
Jatha	numerous persons
Khadi	hand-spun and hand-woven cloth
Kisan	peasant
Lakh	1,00,000
Lathi	stick
Mahila	a woman
Mahatma	a high-souled person
Murdabad	down with
Nari	woman
Purna	full
Raj	kingdom; commonly used for British rule in India
Ryot	a peasant
Sabha	a meeting or an association

Samaj	an association
Samiti	an association
Sari	a long piece of cloth worn by Indian women
Satya	truth
Satyagraha	civil or non-violent resistance
Satyagrahi	one who practised *satyagraha*
Swaraj	self-government
Vakil	a lawyer
Zamindar	landlord
Zulum	oppression

INDEX